Judy Garland:

The Movie Roles That Might Have Been

by

Richard Irvin

Judy Garland: The Movie Roles That Might Have Been

This book is an independent work of research and commentary and is not sponsored, authorized or endorsed by, or otherwise affiliated with, any motion picture studio or production company affiliated with the films discussed herein. All uses of the name, image, and likeness of any individuals, and all copyrights and trademarks referenced in this book, are for editorial purposes and are pursuant of the Fair Use Doctrine.

The views and opinions of individuals quoted in this book do not necessarily reflect those of the author.

The promotional photographs and publicity materials reproduced herein are in the author's private collection (unless noted otherwise). These images date from the original release of the films and were released to media outlets for publicity purposes.

Published in the USA by
BearManor Media
1317 Edgewater Dr. #110
Orlando, FL 32804
www.BearManorMedia.com

Softcover Edition
ISBN-10:
ISBN-13: 979-8-88771-086-0

Printed in the United States of America

Table of Contents

Acknowledgements

The author would like to thank the following for their help with this book:

Margaret Herrick Library for copies of documents from the following collections: Gene Allen Papers, George Cukor Papers, John Huston Papers, Agnes Johnston/Frank Dazey Collection, Abe and Charlotte Levitow Papers, Turner/MGM Scripts, MPAA/PCA Records, Jean and Dusty Negulesco Collection, and Paramount Picture Scripts;

Special Collections Research Center, Syracuse University for material from the Jerome Chodorov Papers;

University of California Los Angeles for information from the Larry Gelbart Papers and the Mark Robson Papers;

Dr. Sandra Garcia-Myers, Ned Comstock, and other staff from the Cinematic Arts Library at the University of Southern California for material from the MGM Script Collection and the Arthur Freed Collection;

American Heritage Center, University of Wyoming for copies of screenplays and treatments from the Stella Unger Collection, the Aleen Leslie Collection, and the George Wells Collection;

Robert D. Farber University Archives and Special Collections, Brandeis University for material from the Arthur Laurents Collection;

Princeton University Library Special Collections for documents from the F. Scott Fitzgerald Papers;

Library of Congress, Music Division, for material from the Oscar Hammerstein Collection;

New York Public Library for copies of various stage play scripts as well as information from the Betty Comden Papers;

Yale Music Library for material from the E.Y. Harburg Collection; and

Garry Settimi for proof reading and editing the manuscript.

Preface

Judy Garland was one of, if not, the greatest popular singer of the twentieth century. She was also a superb actress, a combination of talent rarely found.

This book attempts to build on previous works describing potential projects in which Ms. Garland may have starred. A book by John Fricke, *Judy: A Legendary Career*, details the thirty-four motion pictures in which Judy appeared between 1936 and 1963. One section of the book, "The Rumor Mill," lists over one hundred movies in which Garland may have had a role. Fricke writes: "And while one can't even pretend that the following list is complete, it may well inspire further research and serve as a good foundation on which to build."[1]

This work is a contribution to such research by attempting to find evidence that Judy was indeed considered for a leading or a supporting role in the motion pictures chronicled herein. Many of the projects listed in *Judy: A Legendary Career* are fleshed out in more detail in this book including, where possible, a synopsis of the screenplays written at the time to include Judy in the project. If no documentation could be found of Garland's involvement in a film, then it is excluded from this book. This doesn't mean that such evidence is non-existent – just that this author could not find it. Also, based on research of newspaper archives, some motion picture projects not heretofore associated with Judy are included in this work.

Chapters in the book are arranged according to the stage of Judy Garland's career from child actress to mature adult. Within each chapter, movie projects are listed according to the year in which Ms. Garland was first considered for a role. The years do not necessarily reflect when the movie was made if it was produced at all. The final chapter describes the last three films in which Garland starred. Also, included is an appendix detailing potential Broadway plays for which Judy was considered.

Introduction

Judy Garland was a truly remarkable singer with a rich, warm, passionate quality to her voice. Those who worked with her best described her talent:

E. Y. Harburg, who wrote the lyrics to "Over the Rainbow:" "Judy was an unusual child, with an ability to project a song and a voice that penetrated your insides. She sang not just to your ears, but to your tear ducts. Just like a great cantor, she combined the superb voice with an understanding of the music and lyrics and this ability to sing into your soul."

Actor Gene Kelly, who starred with Judy in *For Me and My Gal*, *The Pirate*, and *Summer Stock*: "You can't define charisma, but she had it always. The amazing thing about her talent was the swiftness with which she could grasp and interpret things that would take other people (and I mean talented people) ten times as long to catch."

Actor and Senator George Murphy: "I have always said that I believe that Judy had one of the most complete and limitless talents of anyone that I have ever known in show business . . ." Murphy co-starred with Judy in *For Me and My Gal* and *Little Nellie Kelly*.

Producer Joe Pasternak: "As a singer-actress-comedienne, she was the most talented person – she could make you laugh and cry at the same time."[2] At MGM, Pasternak produced *In the Good Old Summertime, Presenting Lily Mars*, and *Summer Stock* among other movies starring Judy Garland.

Judy immortalized many songs like "Over the Rainbow," "You Made Me Love You," "Have Yourself a Merry Little Christmas," "The Man that Got Away" as well as giving new meaning to the "Battle Hymn of the Republic," which she sang on her variety show in 1963 after the death of President Kennedy.

During her relatively brief life (she passed away in 1969 shortly after her forty-seventh birthday), she was the first woman to win a Grammy Award for Album of the Year for the 1961 live recording of her concert at Carnegie Hall. Garland had two nominations by the Academy of Motion Pictures Arts and Sciences for her performance as Best Actress in a *Star Is Born* in 1954 and for her role as Best Supporting Actress in 1961's *Judgment at Nuremberg*. She had previously won a special Oscar as a juvenile performer for her role in the *Wizard of Oz* (1939). Her 1963-64 self-titled variety series on CBS was also nominated for an Emmy as Best Variety Show.

Judy Garland's life and career had many ups and downs caused by her dependency on prescriptions drugs and other health issues. She appeared in over thirty movies (mostly musicals and mostly for Metro Goldwyn Mayer) between 1936 and 1963. She was in demand for even more motion pictures. This book covers many of these other film projects in which Ms. Garland may have starred.

There are several reasons why Judy did not appear in the projects included in this work – scheduling problems, overwork leading to Judy's drug dependency and health issues, MGM's reluctance to loan her services to other film studios, interference by her managers with her career, and her later reputation as undependable.

As producer Jerry Wald remarked about Garland's reputation as not dependable on movie sets:

"She's one of those rare talents that comes along once in a producer's life. I'm not afraid of her. There are lots of personalities who come into the studio at 8 am, work 12 hours a day and nobody goes to see them. She's one of the greats, like Jolson, Crosby, or Kaye." He continued, "I don't know what she has. She hits you in the heart and the head at the same time. I'm one of her fans. I respect talent and I don't care how much trouble you have to go through to get it. Talent's always worth the price."[3]

Chapter 1:

The Child Actress Roles That Might Have Been

Judy Garland (aka Frances Gumm), along with her sisters, Mary Jane and Dorothy, initially appeared in several venues in the West and Mid-West as a singing trio. In 1935, Metro Goldwyn Mayer signed Judy to a contract at age thirteen. Arthur Freed, who produced most of Judy's musicals at MGM, recalls the Gumm sisters audition at the film studio: "Their mother played the piano for them and it was, incidentally, the worst piano playing I have ever heard. I kept wishing I could hear the little girl sing alone. So when they finished I asked for a solo, and Judy belted out 'Zing! Went the Strings of My Heart.' She was just great, in spite of the piano. I signed her to a contract right away."[4]

Judy Garland with Sophie Tucker in 1937's Broadway Melody of 1938.

The Unexpected Father – 1931

Judy Garland's first movie role might have been as "Pudge" in a film titled *The Unexpected Father* starring Slim Summerville and Zasu Pitts made by Universal in 1931 and released in 1932.

According to an interview with Cora Sue Collins, the actress who played Pudge in the motion picture, Garland, nine-years-old at the time, was originally cast in the part but, when the producers saw Cora Sue, who was four-years old, they reworked the role for a much younger child.[5]

In the movie, Jasper Jones (Summerville), strikes oil and instantly becomes wealthy. His fiancée wants to marry him right away. On his way to meet with his girlfriend and her family for lunch, he sideswipes a Mrs. Hawkins who is smuggling bootleg liquor in a baby carriage holding her stepdaughter Pudge. When police appear, Hawkins beats a hasty retreat leaving Pudge with Jones. After hearing that Pudge was mistreated by Hawkins, Jones decides to adopt her. He hires a nurse, Polly Pickerill (Pitts), to take care of the child. At the wedding ceremony, Jasper informs everyone that Pudge is his daughter and that his fortune actually belongs to her. Realizing that the fiancée will not inherit the money, the ceremony is called off. Jasper and Polly decide to marry and become Pudge's adoptive parents.

Cora Sue Collins' movie career ended in 1945 when she retired from acting at the age of eighteen. Her final appearance was in *Roughly Speaking* starring Rosalind Russell. She played the Russell character as a young girl.

Yours and Mine – 1935-36

On the *Shell Chateau Hour* hosted by Metro star, Wallace Beery, Beery introduced Judy Garland stating that she had signed a seven-year contract with MGM and that she will be featured in a new movie to be made by Sam Katz called *Yours and Mine.*[6] The proposed film appears to have started out as a project called *This Time It's Love.*

In the planned movie, Judy was to be featured with Buddy Ebsen and/or his sister Vilma Ebsen in a specialty number. A letter from Judy's father, Frank Gumm, stated that she would play opposite "Buddie Ebson" in the film.[7] However, *Film Daily* reported that Vilma Ebsen and Judy Garland had been cast in the picture.[8]

Louella Parsons wrote in her September 1935 column that English actress Jessie Matthews had been signed by Metro to star in *This Time It's Love* in which she would co-star with Robert Montgomery and Clifton Webb.[9] The script would be written by Sid Silvers and Jack McGowan with music and lyrics by Nacio Herb Brown and Arthur Freed.

After signing Matthews to a contract, MGM apparently became disenchanted with her. Lloyd Pantages indicated, "The writers of 'Broadway Melody of 1936' (Silvers and McGowan) have whipped up another little epic entitled 'Yours and Mine,' which will cost a lot of money and which they intended using for Miss Matthews' first American vehicle.[10]

Eleanor Powell replaced Matthews in the project. Ray Bolger and Reginald Gardner were also reported to be added to the cast. The supporting cast was to include Robert Montgomery, Buddy Ebsen, Sid Silvers, and Una Merkel.

From the song titles, apparently the planned picture would have been a musical about romance. Nacio Herb Brown and Arthur Freed did write at least five songs for the movie. They included "Yours and Mine" which was later used in *Broadway Melody of 1938* sung by Eleanor Powell, danced to by Powell and George Murphy and by Judy Garland and Buddy Ebsen, and "I'm Feelin' Like a Million" which was also performed in *Broadway Melody of 1938*, sang and danced to by Eleanor Powell and George Murphy as well as by Judy Garland, but the Garland number was cut from the final film.[11]

Other numbers for *Yours and Mine* included "Busy Body," "Something's Gotta Happen Soon," and "Got a Pair of New Shoes" meant for a female singer. This number was sung by a chorus and danced to by Eleanor Powell in the finale of *Broadway Melody of 1938*.

Yours and Mine was never produced.

Three Smart Girls – 1936

As Joe Pasternak tells it: "I've made many discoveries in my life. Unfortunately, Judy wasn't one of them. . . Everybody always gives me credit for discovering Deanna Durbin. Actually, it was an accident that I discovered Deanna, because I wanted Judy. My casting director called up Metro to see if Judy was available for *Three Smart Girls*. He was told that Metro had an option on both girls but they were keeping Judy and letting Deanna go."[12]

Three Smart Girls focused on three sisters – Joan (Nan Grey), Kay (Barbara Read), and Penny (Deanna Durbin) who travel from Switzerland to New York City with their housekeeper after learning that their divorced father, Judson Craig, whom they haven't seen in ten years, is going to marry gold-digger, Donna Lyons (Binnie Barnes). Through a series of misadventures, the girls succeed in having their father end his engagement to Donna and reconcile with their mother. Of the three sisters, Penny is the one with the excellent singing voice – the role for which Pasternak wanted Judy Garland.

Between the time Deanna Durbin was signed by Universal to star in *Three Smart Girls* and before filming had begun on the movie, MGM had her appear in a musical short with Judy Garland titled *Every Sunday*. The film concerned Judy and Deanna performing songs at a concert in a town park to prevent city officials from canceling performances put on by Deanna's grandfather's orchestra. In the short, Deanna performs an aria while Judy sings a pop number.

As described in subsequent chapters, MGM loved to contrast the singing style of Judy Garland with that of an operatic-type singer which, after canceling Durbin's contract, was often that of Kathryn Grayson.

Blue Blood – 1937

Reported in *The Los Angeles Times* in early 1937, "Stardom is just around the corner for Judy Garland. That's evident from the fact M. G. M. is purchasing stories with this adolescent star in mind." The item goes on to state, "First purchase is 'Blue Blood,' written by Myles Connolly, who produces pictures at Columbia. It has a boarding-school background, and is laid in the South."[13]

Variety, also noted in a brief article, "'Blue Blood,' story of life in a fashionable girls' school by Myles Connolly, producer at Columbia, has been put on the MGM production schedule. Andy (sic) Garland will have her most important part in the picture."[14] There was no subsequent mention of this project in the remaining 1937 issues of *Variety*.

The Myles Connolly screenplay for this project is apparently lost. Nonetheless, one could surmise that Judy would have played a young misfit at the school for rich girls. Her character would no doubt have been poor with her gaining admittance to the school probably because her mother worked there as a maid or a cleaning lady. Because of her terrific singing talent, Judy's character would have impressed the staff and students at the institution, and the character would probably have become the star of the school's spring pageant.

Mary Rose of Mifflin - 1937

In his April 1, 1937 column, Edward Schallert reported that Metro had purchased the book, *Mary Rose of Mifflin* as a possible starring vehicle for Judy Garland.[15] Published in 1920, the work chronicled the life of a young orphan, Mary Rose, moving to an apartment building in a large city to live with her aunt and uncle.

Both Mary Rose's mother and father had passed away. She travels from Mifflin to stay with her Aunt Kate Donovan and her husband, who is janitor at an apartment building that doesn't permit pets or children. So as not to break the apartment's rules, Kate wants Mary to pretend that she is nearly fourteen-years old. Mary is really ten. Mary Rose brings with her a cat and a canary. She asks the young man living next door to the apartment building to board her cat, but she is permitted to keep the canary called Jenny Lind with her. Kate obtains a job for her niece with tenant Mrs. Bracken washing her dishes. Mary plans to use the money she earns to pay the neighbor for taking care of her cat.

Mary Rose is mystified that, unlike in the small town where she came from, most of the tenants in the apartment building do not know one another. One tenant, Mr. Wells doesn't believe that Mary is almost fourteen and complains to her uncle.

A young boy named Jimmie Branson brings Mary's dog to her from Mifflin which also is boarded with the neighbor taking care of Mary's cat. Mary makes friends with everyone in the building except for Mr. Wells. The tenants eventually become acquainted with one another.

One day, Mary Rose places the bird cage containing Jenny Lind in the vestibule while she delivers a large package to a tenant. When she returns, the cage with the bird is gone. Everyone in the building thinks that Mr. Wells took the bird except for Mary who stops by his apartment to tell him that she doesn't believe he stole Jenny Lind.

Subsequently, Mary fails to return from school, and everyone in the building searches for her. Finally, late at night, a police officer brings Mary to the Donovan flat. She discovered that a messenger boy had taken her pet from the vestibule when delivering a package The boy thought that the bird had been abandoned. He gave the canary to his sister who has been bedridden for seven years. The following day, Mr. Wells gives Mary money to buy a new bird for the sick girl. Mr. Wells, the real owner of the apartment building, lets Mary stay with her aunt and uncle even though she is not yet a teenager.

Movie audiences of the 1930s seemed to love heartwarming stories of orphans who bring happiness to everyone they encounter. However, MGM failed to turn *Mary Rose of Mifflin* into a feature film.

Pigskin Parade Sequel – 1937

On loan-out from MGM, Judy appeared as Sairy Dodd, the sister of Amos Dodd (Stu Erwin) who becomes a star football player in *Pigskin Parade* about a small college, Texas State University, competing against Yale University in an Armistice Day football game. The movie, produced by Twentieth Century Fox, was released in 1936 and was so successful that Fox sought to produce a sequel the following year. Louella Parsons reported, "So the sequel to 'Pigskin Parade' will be "The Corn Husker,' based on an annual corn husking bee held in Indiana where the winner gets a prize of $100. Stuart Erwin, who was so well as the farmer lad in 'Pigskin Parade,' gets the lead with Judy Garland again featured with him."[16]

Fox did make a follow-up to *Pigskin Parade* called *Life Begins in College*, released in 1937. The plot involves a Native American named George Black enrolled at Lombardy College who becomes a star on the school's football team but can't compete in the final big game when it is discovered that he had played professional football. Neither Judy Garland nor Stu Erwin were in this sequel which starred the Ritz Brothers along with Joan Davis and Tony Martin.

The Sarah Bernhardt Story – 1937

Several motion picture studios wanted to film the biography of French actress Sarah Bernhardt in the mid-1930s. Actress Alice Brady urged Universal to film the biography with her in the starring role. Metro considered the film in 1937 with Luise Rainer playing Bernhardt and with Judy Garland appearing as the actress in her younger years. Bernhardt's grandson-in-law, Louis Verneuil, was put under contract by Metro to write her life story for this proposed feature. When that project failed to move forward, Warner Brothers sought to make *The Career of Sarah Bernhardt* in 1938 with Bette Davis in the lead role and George Brent also starring.

None of these efforts ever saw the light of day. Nevertheless, in 1942, Louis Verneuil published a biography of Bernhardt called, *The Fabulous Life of Sarah Bernhardt*, which may have started out as the basis for the MGM screenplay. The second chapter of the Verneuil book, "Childhood, Youth, Beginnings," gives a flavor of what may have been in the screenplay with Judy Garland playing Bernhardt during her teenage years.

Bernhardt was born in Paris on October 23, 1844, the daughter of Julie Van Hard, an unmarried dressmaker. Van Hard had fallen in love with

Edouard Bernhardt, a young law student, who supported his daughter, Sarah, until his death. Julie Van Hard subsequently became a mistress of several wealthy men in French society and had two other daughters out of wedlock.

Julie was disinterested in raising Sarah and left it up to servants and other staff to raise her. She eventually sent Sarah to boarding school. Her father later installed Sarah at a convent for her education where she remained until 1859.

Sarah then went to live with her mother in a large, luxurious apartment. During this period, she becomes friends with a neighbor, Madame Guerard who later became Sarah's private secretary and companion. Guerard's apartment was a refuge for Sarah from the large parties her mother gave for French society which Sarah disliked.

One of her mother's friends suggests that Sarah enter the theater to become an actress. She attends classes at the Conservatoire in France mostly in an effort to get away from her mother. She spends two years at the Conservatoire winning a prize for her first year of studies but not for her second year when she had a different instructor. Her stage debut was on September 1, 1862 in the tragedy of Racine. Sarah starred in other plays but without attracting much attention.

On January 15, 1863, Sarah took part in a ceremony honoring Moliere presented by the Theatre Francais. Sarah has brought her youngest sister, Regina, to the occasion. Regina inadvertently stands on the train of a pompous older actress who pushes the little girl away causing her to fall against a wall and injure her head. Sarah slaps the actress for injuring her sister. She is ordered to apologize, but, instead, tears up her contract with the Theatre Francais. Without any acting jobs, Sarah decides to enhance her beauty and explore her sexuality.

In 1864, she finds her way back into acting. After appearing in a play in which her mother says Sarah looked ridiculous, she quits and moves to Spain. However, she returns to France shortly thereafter when she finds that she is pregnant.

The father is Prince Henri de Ligne, who befriended Sarah after she had unknowingly recited a poem before Napoleon III that offended the head of France. She gives birth to a son she names Maurice on December 22, 1864 and resumes acting.

Reconciling with Prince Henri, he asks Sarah to marry him on the condition that she will give up acting. Unbeknownst to him, his relatives intervene with Sarah to prevent the marriage. Sarah returns to acting. From the end of 1866 until the end of 1922, she continues her acting career becoming a legend of the stage.

While it isn't clear why Metro decided not to produce *The Sarah Bernhardt Story,* the studio may have found it difficult to develop a script dealing with a bastard child who later gives birth to her own child out of wedlock since, during the 1930s and 1940s, having illegitimate children was considered a grievous sin.

Nonetheless, other studios in the 1940s attempted to launch a motion picture about Bernhardt. In 1946, David O. Selznick was reported to be developing a film based on the actress' life. Selznick hoped Greta Garbo would star as the legendary actress. If Garbo couldn't be enticed to take the role, the producer may have considered Valli for the part.[17]

In 1947, columnist Sheilah Graham reported that Charles Rogers wanted to make a film called *The Divine Sarah* with Tallulah Bankhead. Graham went on to write, "As I've told you before, Bette Davis contemplates doing a Bernhardt picture with Curt Bernhardt – no relation – directing. Also, a French film company is doing the life story of Bernhardt, and an English company ditto."[18] Nevertheless, no biographical film of Sarah Bernhardt evidently was ever made.

National Velvet – 1937

Even though the film did not premiere until 1944, as far back as 1937, MGM began plans to make *National Velvet.*

A 1937 newspaper article stated: "The report is out that MGM is planning to put Judy Garland in the role of Velvet in 'National Velvet. '.. Paramount bought it first for heaven-knows-whom, then RKO had it in mind for Katherine Hepburn until MGM came along and purchased it supposedly for Jean Harlow. Anyway, Judy certainly fits the age requirements for Velvet, who was a very young girl, and if she seems a surprising choice after all the glamour girls, maybe it's because we're confusing her dramatic ability with her talent for singing swing songs."[19] Elizabeth Taylor eventually won the role of Velvet Brown in this story of a young girl from Sussex, England who wins a horse in a raffle and decides to train him for the Grand National sweepstakes with the help of a young drifter played by Mickey Rooney.

Molly, Bless Her (aka Molly and Me) – 1938

The back story of *Molly, Bless Her* is that when actress Marie Dressler was very ill, her friend, MGM screenwriter and journalist, Frances Marion, wanted to write a story for her that would be easy for her to play.[20] She wrote *Molly, Bless Her* and sent it to MGM telling the studio to use it if they could for Marie. The studio returned the manuscript with a big "N.G." written across it. And so, Marion fashioned the story into a novel and published it in 1937. MGM then gave her $25,000 for the film rights. Marie Dressler died about three years before the book was published.

The planned film was to star Judy Garland playing a younger version of the main character Molly Drexel, a down-on-her luck actress who had been a big star on Broadway at one time.

The book opens with Molly, who hasn't acted in two years, trying to obtain a supporting role in a new play. Molly lives with two other actresses – Julia Fayne and Lily Pringle, who have also been out of work for some time. Across the hall from their apartment, live Clara and Musette, two other unemployed actresses.

After being rejected for the supporting role in the new play and in desperate need of money, Molly goes to an employment agency to apply for the job of housekeeper at an estate on Long Island for a widower, Mr. Graham, and his son. She lands the job after being interviewed by Graham's butler who had been a dancer and knew Molly.

Molly moves to the Graham estate where she is in charge of a staff of five consisting of a chef, his assistant, the upstairs maid and a downstairs maid, and a gardener. The butler has sworn her to secrecy about their backgrounds in show business since Mr. Graham's former wife, an actress, divorced him shortly after giving birth to their son and left Long Island with another man. Graham has never gotten over this experience and is reticent about any changes in the running of his estate.

Molly finds that the staff take advantage of Mr. Graham by doing the least amount of work possible. The staff, not liking how they are managed by the new housekeeper, quit one-by-one. Molly replaces them with her show business friends including her two roommates, the women across the hall in her apartment building, and Ronnie Burgess, a former playwright Molly knows. All are pledged to secrecy about their backgrounds, but they do maintain and indeed improve the estate to Mr. Graham's satisfaction. Molly makes the place less gloomy, and, when Graham's son returns to the estate after summer camp, she befriends the lonely boy and finds a dog for him.

Eventually, Molly has to confess to her boss that all of the staff used to be in show business. Graham orders them to leave immediately. For a period of time, the former staff land menial jobs, except for Molly, who comes down with pneumonia and is near death.

In the evenings, Ronnie Burgess begins to write a new play based on the experiences of the group working on the Graham estate. He finds a backer to produce the play called *Higher than High* and has the actresses, including Molly, who has recovered from her illness, begin rehearsals.

They perform the play in various small towns before taking it to Broadway where it is a resounding success. Molly makes a major comeback in the main role and receives critical acclaim and movie offers.

One day in New York City, Molly runs in to Mr. Graham and his son who have returned from a lengthy trip to England. She suggests that he not see the play because it does not present him in the best light, but he replies that he has already seen it three times and likes it.

Graham and his son, Jimmy, attend the play again and go backstage to meet the cast. Burgess, in attempting to come up with a good final act for the play, had the Graham character propose marriage to the Molly character, and, as the novel ends, Mr. Graham does make a marriage proposal to Molly.

Apparently, the film project would have expanded on the story of Molly's earlier life when she was auditioning as a young woman for plays, playing the piano, and singing. Portraying the younger Molly would have been Judy Garland. There is a scene in the book where Molly reveals to Mr. Graham that she has vocal and musical talents, and the two engage in an impromptu duet with Molly playing the piano. The screenplay may have also provided more details on Molly's romance with Freddie Markham, a character referenced in the book, who was Molly's first love. The two were unable to marry because Markham's wife would not grant him a divorce.

In addition to Garland, other stars that were reported as receiving roles in the project were Fanny Brice, Wallace Beery, and Sophie Tucker.[21] According to an item in *Variety*, MGM was seeking to build up Sophie Tucker to take over the Marie Dressler roles in the hearts of movie goers. The studio thought that Tucker would be ideal to star in *Molly, Bless Her.* "Soph knew only too well that the cemeteries of show biz are full of performers who were 'second' Barrymores or 'second' Bernhardts. Soph was looking for parts to build up Sophie Tucker and was quite right in believing she couldn't be made over into anything but Sophie Tucker."[22]

In 1939, Twentieth Century Fox purchased the rights to the Marion novel and intended to make a film based on it in England. World War II interrupted those plans, but a film was ultimately made called *Molly and Me* which was released in 1945. Starring Gracie Fields as Molly, the movie differed from the original novel in certain respects. Filmed in the United States but set in 1937 England, Molly Barry, a vaudeville actress needing a job, finds one in the home of John Graham. As in the novel, Molly hires her former theater acquaintances to become Graham's household staff. Graham decides to run for Parliament but is concerned about an old scandal involving his former wife running off with another man. The former Mrs. Graham resurfaces trying to extort 1000 pounds from her ex-husband. Molly resolves the threat by using her friends to convince Mrs. Graham into believing that she has participated in a murder and so she flees the country. Monty Wooley starred as John Graham.

Wonder Child – 1937-38

Originally called *B Above High C*, this project was to star twelve-year-old Suzanne Larson who later changed her name to Susanna Foster. Mary Garden, MGM's scout for vocal talent, was also to appear in the movie playing herself. Garden, known as the "Sarah Bernhardt of opera," had retired from the opera stage and worked for Metro developing new talent.

Although signed by Metro, that studio never featured Suzanne Larson in a motion picture. Larson subsequently signed a contract with Paramount in 1939 where she made *The Great Victor Herbert*. Her most famous role was in Universal's 1943 film *Phantom of the Opera*.

Presumably, the original MGM project, to be directed by Norman Krasna, would have featured Suzanne Larson as a child prodigy with an amazing vocal range singing opera-like songs.

As newspapers subsequently reported, "Orders have been issued by Metro to rewrite 'Wonder Child,' with Judy Garland in the title role."[23] At some point in its development, the title of the project was changed from *B Above High C* to *Wonder Child*. Dalton Trumbo and Arthur Sheekman wrote the screenplay with Bert Kalmar and Harry Ruby to do the music. The change in title and star no doubt meant that instead of focusing on a young girl singing soprano, the revised film would concentrate on a young singer of popular songs who was also wise beyond her years.

MGM never made this feature.

Topsy and Eva – 1938

Another movie that MGM never produced was *Topsy and Eva*. As described in newspapers at the time, "Betty Jaynes will play little Eva, and naturally Judy Garland will be Topsy. That's the prospect for the film of 'Topsy and Eva,' to be produced by Mervyn LeRoy for M.G.M. Which means that Miss Garland will practically become a LeRoy star, since she is also nominated for the role of Dorothy in 'Wizard of Oz.'"[24]

The Duncan sisters – Rosetta and Vivian, had appeared as Topsy and Eva in a stage play and silent movie. Judy was to appear in black face as Topsy with Betty Jaynes as her friend Eva. Jaynes was another child singer signed by MGM in the late 1930s. As might be expected, given Metro's concept of pairing sopranos with so-called "jazz" singers, Jaynes had an operatic type voice. Her most notable screen appearance was in *Babes in Arms*.

At the time of this project's announcement, Judy was in Pittsburgh with her mother and was interviewed about her upcoming films. In response to a question about her role as Topsy and her role in *The Wizard of Oz,* she replied that "... she was thrilled over the 'Oz' assignment. The reporter opined, "She didn't look thrilled ... She looked tired ... And her throat was bothering her just a little." The newspaperman also asked the star what her ambition to be was when she grew up. Judy's mother said that someday Judy hoped to be a great dramatic actress like Bette Davis and that Miss Davis is Judy's idol.[25]

Catherine Cushing had written *Topsy and Eva,* a musical based on the Harriet Becher Stowe book, *Uncle Tom's Cabin*, at the request of Rosetta and Vivian Duncan who toured with the show for several years.

The planned motion picture would have been based on the Catherine Cushing stage play.[26] If it had been made, the movie would have detracted from the legacy of Judy Garland since the play, written in the 1920s and set in the 1850's is, to say the least, cringeworthy in its depiction of slavery. To a modern audience, the play is grossly stereotypical.

In the Cushing play, Emily Shelby has had to sell her plantation and its slaves after her husband dies leaving the family's finances in shambles. However, Mrs. Shelby and her son, George, are permitted to live in the house for six months.

Augustine St. Clare, working through an agent, has purchased the property. St. Clare had refused to permit George to marry his ward, Mariette. All this was payback for the refusal by the guardian of Emily Shelby to allow her to marry St. Clare. Among the Shelby slaves sold to St. Clare is Uncle Tom.

Mariette still wants to marry George, but he seeks to rehabilitate the family fortune first. He travels to New Orleans with Mariette to see St. Clare.

One of the Shelby slaves being sold to St. Clare is Topsy, an impish young girl. Eva, St. Clare's young daughter, likes Topsy because she is so entertaining. Because of Topsy's behavior, Eva gets Topsy for free. To Eva, having Topsy is like receiving a new toy. Topsy is mischievous and, among other bad habits, likes to steal items from white people.

At the St. Clare house in New Orleans, Mariette is having a birthday party. Eva and Topsy want to have a party also even though it's not their birthday. Before they can have a party, Aunt Ophelia, St. Clare's sister, insists that Topsy and Eva study their lessons. Topsy begins taking stuff from Ophelia's wardrobe. The aunt attempts to punish Topsy who says that Ophelia doesn't know where to whip a black person. Topsy relates how Simon Legree, a slave trader, punished her with a cowhide whip until it broke. Topsy sings a song called "Lickins" about being paddled for causing mischief.

Eva is concerned that Ophelia will send Topsy away because of her stealing. She has the idea of sleeping with Topsy outside by a fountain thinking that they both will be safe there.

In the end, Topsy and Eva are not separated. St. Clare and George return from New Orleans to the Shelby plantation in Kentucky. St. Clare deeds the property back to Mrs. Shelby with the understanding that she will repay the small amount for which he purchased the property. St. Clare then proposes marriage to Mrs. Shelby.

MGM resurrected the idea for a musical version of *Uncle Tom's Cabin* in 1944 with Lena Horne as Topsy and Margaret O'Brien as Little Eva based on the Harriet Beecher Stowe novel.[27] However, after protests from African-American groups and others, the planned film was abandoned.

In 1952, there was an effort by Paramount Pictures to make a biopic about the Duncan Sisters who had starred as Topsy and Eva. Ginger Rogers and Betty Hutton were to play the sisters. However, this film also was never made.

Bad Little Angel (aka Looking after Sandy) – 1939

Louella Parsons reported in June 1939 concerning Judy Garland that: "Now that she has reached sweet 16, Louis Mayer has decided she's old enough to have a dramatic part, so 'Looking After Sandy,' a story by

Margaret Turnbull, has been bought for her. In this she plays a 16-year-old orphan girl who moves into a large American family and wins all their hearts." Parsons went on to write, "Anyway, it is Judy's first dramatic part and it is not a musical although she'll sing several songs."[28] Noteworthy at the time is that Judy was actually seventeen - not sixteen when the Parsons' article was written.

Judy was to star in the film with Freddie Bartholomew.

Filming for the motion picture began on August 28, 1939, but instead of Garland, Virginia Weidler played Patsy Sanderson with Gene Reynolds as her co-star, young Tommy Wilks. The title of the picture also changed to *Bad Little Angel*. The movie concerned a lonely orphan girl living in a small town in New England who, upon the advice of a dying woman – her temporary caretaker, seeks to live according to the Bible. After the death of the caretaker, Patsy is returned to the orphanage and told that she is a "jinx," since the various people that cared for her suffered misfortune. She is also told that her little dog will be sent to the pound. Not wanting to stay at the orphanage and after reading in the Bible about Egypt, Patsy, along with her small dog, decides to flee and so purchases a train ticket to Egypt, New Jersey.

In Egypt, Patsy meets Tommy Wilks who introduces her to Jim Creighton (Ian Hunter), the editor of the town paper. She is taken in by the Creighton family and becomes involved in a conflict between wealthy Mr. Marvin (Guy Kibbee), the owner of a paint factory, and Jim Creighton who plans to publish an editorial about how unsafe the factory is. Jim is informed by the owner of his paper to submit his resignation over the paint factory issue. Patsy thinks that she jinxed him. She visits Mr. Marvin to unsuccessfully plead for Creighton's job. Patsy and Jim then read a Bible passage about fighting the good fight. Patsy returns to Mr. Marvin and finds a Bible passage about forgiveness which Marvin ignores. The paint factory suddenly bursts into flames. Jim, a volunteer fireman, is injured putting out the blaze. Patsy and Tommy help rescue Jim who is critically injured. Patsy again believes that she is a jinx and begins losing her faith in God. However, Mr. Marvin admits that he has changed and persuades Patsy to pray for Jim's recovery which she does, and Jim gets better.

Despite Judy not starring in the movie, she still had a connection to it. Terry, who had appeared as Toto in *The Wizard of Oz*, also had a role in this film as Patsy's dog.

Valedictory – 1939

Based on a short story by MacKinlay Kantor, MGM considered making a film starring Judy, Freddie Bartholomew, and Lionel Barrymore.

Edwin Schallert reported that Metro wanted to follow-up *Goodbye Mr. Chips* with a story about an American school to be called *Valedictory*. A janitor instead of a professor would be the main character in the project. Schallert went on to write: "Lionel Barrymore is probable for the role, while Freddie Bartholomew and Judy Garland are equally wanted for the cast."[29]

The short story focused on seventy-six-year old Tyler Morley who has worked as a janitor in the Shelldrake school district for over twenty years. He is retiring at the end of the school year. His final duty as janitor is to set up the school's gymnasium for the graduation of the class of 1922. During the preparations, Ty reflects on the students he has known.

Morley had fought in the Civil War on the Union side and is often asked by history teachers at the school to answer students' questions about the conflict.

One of the students that he recalls was named Rowena Snow who is now the class valedictorian. She would sneak off into an unfinished part of the school's basement to eat her lunch since all she had to eat were some baking-powder biscuits. She lived with an aunt who was very poor. Mr. Morley would share his lunch with Rowena so she had more to eat, and he got a local charity to assist the aunt. Rowena, a very smart student, has received a scholarship to attend Iowa University after graduation

Morley also remembers Porter Fosselman who contracted polio when he was in middle school and now walks with a crutch. Porter is good at science. Morley befriended him when a girl he had asked to a party refused to go with him.

Morley recalls the time he found two students at night in the school about to make love because they thought they would eventually marry. He told them about the consequences of having sex so early in their lives

The janitor had hoped that Rowena may have mentioned him in her valedictory address when thanking parents and teachers. However, she did not. After the graduation ceremony, Morley gives his keys to the school to his replacement and goes home. There he finds a small package on the dinner table. Opening it, he discovers a watch with the inscription: To Tyler Morley, From His Friends. Class of 1922. S.H.S. "Blessed Be the Ty."

While Lionel Barrymore would have played Tyler Morley, apparently Garland would have appeared as Rowena Snow and Freddie Bartholomew as Porter Fosselman. The film, however, was never made.

Susan and God – 1939

"Rating more and more attention as an actress at M.G.M. – and she's quite versatile, too – Judy Garland is now all but determined as the daughter in 'Susan and God,' which will star Greer Garson as the mother," so announced Edwin Schallert in his column in *The Los Angeles Times.*[30] Supposedly the role of the daughter was to be enhanced in the movie version of the Broadway play.

Garland did not play the daughter in the film released in 1940. Actress Rita Quigley landed the role of Blossom. Instead of Greer Garson, Joan Crawford appeared as Susan Trexel, an upper-class woman self-obsessed with her own importance. Married to Barrie Trexel (Frederic March), her behavior has driven her husband to drink.

When she returns from a European vacation having found God, she begins to spread her new- found religion to all of her friends. Her daughter is a slightly introverted teenager having been shuttled between boarding schools and summer camps most of her life. She wants her mother and father to become a real family. Barrie convinces his wife to spend an entire summer with Blossom and him trying to, among other things, have the three become a more stable family.

Rita Quigley, who played Blossom, quit acting in the late 1940s to marry and start a family.

The Youngest Profession – 1940

Judy was announced as the star of this feature about young autograph seekers based on a book by Lillian Day. As a columnist reported, "For years fans have been an important part of the careers of screen stars. Now the fans will be glorified on the screen. Judy Garland will star as a young girl who idolizes movie folk and collects autographs in a story called 'The Youngest Profession.'"[31] Nevertheless, when the film began production in 1942, Virginia Weidler had the starring role. The film, released in 1943, included cameos featuring several MGM stars.

The movie opens with high school student Joan Lyons (Weidler) receiving a letter from Lana Turner thanking her for her fan letter. When the local paper reports that Greer Garson is coming to town, Joan and her friends want to meet the star. After missing her at the train station, Joan has her dad (Edward Arnold), a lawyer, give her $2 to make phone calls to locate Garson. Joan and her friend Patsy Drew (Jean Porter) go to Garson's hotel hoping to obtain her autograph. They see her in the hotel's lobby and are invited to Greer Garson's suite for tea and cakes. While there, Walter Pidgeon stops by, and the two obtain his autograph as well.

Later that night, Joan and her boyfriend, Skylar, attend a movie starring Hedy Lamar and William Powell despite the fact that Joan's father told her not to go out as punishment for her coming home late for dinner after meeting Garson and Pidgeon. The next day, Joan's father declares that his daughter will receive no more allowance for the month for her misbehavior.

Joan holds a meeting of her club of autograph seekers, called Guiding Stars Ltd, to admit a new member whose father has a mimeograph machine so the club can start publishing a star-focused newspaper. Each club member is required to obtain four autographs a month to remain in the club. One of the members mentions seeing Judy Garland returning from a government bond tour. When the girls hear that Robert Taylor is in town, they want to seek his autograph.

Taylor just happens to be staying in an apartment across the hall from the Lyons' flat. He stops in the Lyons' apartment at the request of Mr. Lyons in order to free up the telephone that the girls are using to attempt to locate the actor. As all the girls look for their autograph books, Taylor leaves.

Miss Thayer (Ann Ayers), Mr. Lyons' secretary, comes by the apartment to pick up an overnight bag for her boss' business trip. Miss Featherstone (Agnes Moorehead), the Lyons' long-time governess, jumps to the conclusion that Mr. Lyons and Miss Thayer are running away together. She informs Joan of her suspicions and spreads the rumor to others.

Joan thinks of enlisting a man to pretend he is in love with Mrs. Lyons (Marta Linden) in order to make Mr. Lyons jealous. At a museum, Joan and Patsy see Mr. Hercules (John Carroll), a body builder, and they think that he would be perfect for the role. To obtain money to hire him, Joan sells her beloved autograph book to another club member for $25.

After her dad returns from his business trip, he and his wife attend a Red Cross ball. Joan and Skylar bring Hercules to the ball where he poses as a diplomat to woe Mrs. Lyons. He asks Edith Lyons to dance. Mr. Lyons argues with Hercules who then punches him. Hercules divulges that he was hired by Joan to make Lyons envious. Joan disappears. The Lyons fire Miss Featherstone for spreading the rumor about a supposed affair between Mr. Lyons and his secretary. Joan's parents eventually find her volunteering for the Salvation Army where she was atoning for her sins. They bring a sleepy Joan back to their apartment, riding up in an elevator also occupied by William Powell, who is totally ignored by the family. Mr. Lyons buys back Joan's autograph book and gives it to her.

The original story line for *The Youngest Profession,* the one in which Judy may have starred, was different in many ways from the film. Jane Lyons – not June Lyons, is celebrating her birthday. Her father, Dr. Lyons, to be portrayed by Walter Pidgeon, is away on business. He is a scientist, not a lawyer, who writes books and appears on the radio. Dr. Lyons, a widower, forgets his daughter's birthday and has to be reminded of it by Sarah, the housekeeper.

Jane and her friends are still into autograph seeking. She receives a letter from Eleanor Powell congratulating her on her birthday. At school, Jane has to fib about what birthday present her dad gave her. She says she received a white lupin evening coat from him. When her teacher offers her the editorship of the school magazine, Jane declines saying how busy she is with her *Fan Dust* magazine and starting a service called "The Star Guiding Service."

After school, Jane attends a fan meeting at a friend's house where the group discusses how to meet Spencer Tracy who is arriving in town the next day. They plan to welcome him with a harmonica serenade since fan magazines reported that the actor has taken up the harmonica.

During Jane's birthday party that evening, her dad returns from his trip and presents his daughter with a set of the works of Robert Browning. She is disappointed that she didn't receive the coat she wanted but tells her friends that the coat is still in the dress shop.

After the party, Jane gives her dad her report card to sign. He is surprised to see that she has been absent from school for nine days. He puts two and two together and asks his daughter if she is still occupied with the foolishness of hunting down film stars. She attempts to convince him of the seriousness of her hobby and reminds him that her own mother was also stage struck.

As with Judy Garland, Virginia Weidler died at the relatively young age of forty one in July 1968, a year before Judy's death in 1969. Having had rheumatic fever, she passed away from a heart ailment. Her final appearance was on an episode of *Hollywood Theatre Time* in 1951 titled "Hollywood Club for Girls."

Strange Things Can Happen in Brooklyn – 1940

On December 14, 1940, *The New York Times* reported that MGM was negotiating for rights to a short story by Daniel Fuchs called "Strange Things Can Happen in Brooklyn" as a vehicle for Judy Garland.[32] In addition to novels and short stories, Fuchs wrote several screenplays including *The Big Shot* with Humphrey Bogart, *Panic in the Streets, Criss Cross*, and *Love Me or Leave Me*, which won an Academy Award.

Joe Juley is a cab driver and bachelor in Brooklyn to whom fellow cabbies always go for help.[33] A cabbie asks Juley for help with a blonde he found in his cab who is broke. Juley thinks that she is just trying to obtain money from the cabbies. The blonde says that she has a good job waiting for her, but her money has run out. She needs some cash to keep going. Juley responds that she will receive no money from the taxi drivers but that they will buy her food at the diner where the drivers hang out.

When the counterman brings her roast beef, mashed potatoes, vegetables, and bread, Juley is troubled that the blonde isn't eating like a beggar. She is friendly and doesn't forget her manners.

She needs a place to stay for a few days. Juley asks that one of his colleague's volunteers to take her to his place to stay. However, the cabbies, who are married, say that their wives would object. They suggest that Juley take her to his place since he will be working the night shift.

Chuncery, a driver whose wife has left him, says that she can stay at his home while he works the night shift, and so the blonde is taken there. But then Chuncery is informed that his wife wants to reconcile with him. She has gone back to their home, and Chuncery knows that his wife will throw a fit if she finds the blonde at the house.

His fellow taxi drivers persuade Juley to take the girl to his place. He arranges for her to have the place to herself after 6:00 pm when he goes to work but she must leave his flat by 7:00 am. One night he drops in on her, and they discuss her past. The blonde says that her father used to own timber land in Canada and is fairly well off and that he has asked her to quit acting. She makes coffee for Juley and says that she admires him because his fellow workers always ask him for help.

Juley replies that the only reason the guys come to him is because he is single. He tells her that he doesn't trust anyone and that he will never have his heart broken with disappointment. Juley then goes back to work and stops at the diner.

He sees Chuncery who says that his wife is now paying attention to his needs ever since she returned to him and saw the blonde there. His wife figures that if the blonde saw something in him, then maybe he has something.

When Juley enters the diner, the guys say that he is acting more human and that it must be the effect the blonde is having on him. Juley thinks that his co-workers are crazy. After that, Juley stays away from his apartment while the blonde is residing there.

On her last night at Juley's place, he stops in to see the blonde. He confronts her by saying that her name is not Valerie La Tour but is Emmy Dahbach from Scranton, Pennsylvania. She had moved to New York City to perform imitations on an amateur hour and got some nutty idea that she wanted to be a movie star. Chuncery's wife had found out about Emmy by following her when she went back to her rooming house to retrieve her suitcase.

The blonde confesses that she did make up stories about her father and being an actress because they made her feel better. The stories made her believe that she could be something in the world – not just a girl by herself. Emmy declares that she will never see Joe Juley again.

Juley doesn't really want Emmy to leave. He realizes that she is the most beautiful thing that has ever happened to him and that he has chased her away.

Later, Juley and Chuncery listen to the amateur hour on the taxi's radio. They hear Emmy do her impersonations of Greta Garbo, Ronald Coleman, and Bette Davis quoting lines from movie roles they played. People phone in to the radio show to vote for the performers they like the most. In the initial round, Emmy comes in second. In the next round, Emmy comes in first.

Juley tells Chuncery to leave his cab. He wants to be left alone to drive around Prospect Park, and finally Juley drives back to his place. He finds Emmy standing at the kitchen door. She says that she is going away but wanted to thank him first. She found out after the broadcast, when she went back to the diner to get her suitcase, that Juley had gone to all the garages and made the drivers find people to phone in votes for her.

She says that she is returning to Scranton. Juley begins saying that he is just a dumb hacker with no brains who doesn't know better. He tells Emmy that he wants her to stay with him and not return to Scranton.

Why MGM failed to develop the story into a motion picture is not known. Given Garland's age at the time (she was eighteen-years old), the studio may have considered making the Emmy character younger with Juley being more of a father figure to her. Also, with Garland in the proposed film, Emmy's talent no doubt would have been singing instead of doing impressions.

The Corporal's Cousin Kate – 1941

Little is known about the story line of this potential project for Judy Garland and George Murphy. The only information that seems to exist relating to the project is a blurb in Edwin Schallert's column on February 21, 1941 stating, "George Murphy and Judy Garland may be seen in a training camp story, because Norman Taurog, director, has recommended purchase of 'The Corporal's Cousin Kate' by Joseph Wallaby to M.G.M."[34] Obviously, Judy would have played Kate with Murphy as the corporal. The story appears to be the highpoint of Joseph Wallaby's writing career since no information could be found concerning him.

Very Warm for May – 1941

This Broadway musical with songs by Jerome Kern and Oscar Hammerstein was to be a vehicle for Judy starring along with Ray McDonald and Marta Eggerth. Arthur Freed abandoned the idea of turning the play into a movie because he felt that the story line was contrived and unworkable. A play script dated July 22, 1941 by Oscar Hammerstein and sent to MGM starts with the introduction of the Graham family – daughter May who yearns to leave school and be an actress, son Johnny who is already a successful Broadway actor, writer, and producer, and father William, a former vaudevillian. The family lives in Great Neck Long Island. May has been missing from the house. Johnny finds her with a group of actors.[35]

Johnny reviews May's report card. She is doing well in dramatic literature, but less well in the sciences. She will flunk out of school if she does not attend summer school. Nevertheless, May wants to spend the summer performing in a barn theater. Johnny insists that she go to school. He doesn't like summer stock because a girl, Liz Spofford, that he likes, broke up with him to appear in a play presented at her mother's barn.

Johnny is going fishing in Maine and asks his friend Kenny to look after May in his absence.

After her brother leaves, May is planning to run away again to act in summer theater. She dashes out with her suitcase and takes the family's speed boat to the Spofford property in Connecticut.

At the property, actors and actresses are rehearsing an original operetta by Ogdon Quiler who is there with Jethro Hancock, a writer for a Connecticut newspaper previewing the work. Liz Spofford is the star of the operetta which takes place in a Connecticut garden over a period of 200 years. Liz and Ogdon play the lovers. Other actors appear as an old musket, a brook, a picket fence, and a willow tree.

Kenny enters the theater barn looking for May. He wanders around while rehearsals are taking place.

Since the two lovers are too shy to express their love directly, Ogdon has singers playing the lovers' "heart voices." Ogdon plays Adam; Liz, Hester. Liz's mother, Winnie, interrupts the rehearsal with refreshments for everyone. Subsequently, a young boy auditions for the production by playing his accordion.

Kenny leaves, and the actors find May hiding in a wishing well prop. She claims she loves Ogdon's play. So that she isn't sent away, she makes up a story related in a song "May Tells All." She goes on to say that she ran away with a man who turned out to be a bigamist. When Ogdon questions the story, she admits it is a lie.

Winnie claims that the real story about why May doesn't want to go back to her family is that she is pregnant. May responds that Mrs. Spofford is correct. The Spofford's agree that May can stay with them during the summer.

Johnny Graham stops by on his way to Maine hoping to see the rehearsal. Sonny tells Johnny about the operetta. From what he hears, Johnny doesn't think that Ogdon is very talented.

Johnny asks Liz to go with him to see all the new Broadway shows in the fall, but she says she is dating Ogdon. Johnny and Liz begin to dance with Johnny singing "Music in My Heart." Liz and others join in.

Ogdon enters and glares vindictively at the two of them.

Winnie and Sonny invite Johnny to stay for a few days. Although Sonny really wants Johnny to help fix the operetta, Johnny leaves. May comes out of hiding confessing that she is not really pregnant. She divulges why she ran away. Winnie says that May can stay as long as she wants.

A month passes. The players are still rehearsing the operetta with the opening a day away. May has become friendly with Raymond who wrote most of the score for the play. During the month, May has also deepened her relationship with Sonny.

Raymond is jealous when he learns May sang a song he wrote to Sonny. After Raymond and Sonny exit, Winnie advises May that she is asking for it when she plays two guys at the same time.

Ogdon is quarreling with the head of the carpenters' union over the installation of scenery for the operetta. He is staging a scene "The Strange Case of Adam Standish" spotlighting the human brain featuring a ballet with him narrating.

Later, Sonny advises May that he is going away but might stay if May marries him.

Winnie asks Ogdon to audition a chamber music ensemble to be added to his play. During the audition, Johnny and Kenny return to the Spofford's. He hasn't gone fishing in Maine. Instead, he has been touring barn theaters looking for May and finally finds her at the Spofford's.

Liz asks Johnny to stay for the night's dress rehearsal hoping he can help with the production.

Johnny decides to stay for the rehearsal. At 3:30 am, the players have yet to finish the first act. Ogdon becomes frustrated that his "little play" is caught in the arguments among carpenters, electricians, dressmakers, and others over how to stage the various scenes. Johnny takes charge hoping to present the play so everyone can understand it.

Meanwhile, Sonny asks May to elope with him, but she won't go since Johnny is allowing her a role in the operetta. The show goes on with Johnny's changes.

In the end, Winnie concludes the play saying: "Everything's going lovely now, but hell might break loose again any minute. This would be a good time to ring down the curtain, before they get in any more trouble . . ."

If Arthur Freed felt that the foregoing story line was contrived, one wonders what his opinion would have been about the original plot for *Very Warm for May* that was featured in the play's tryouts before hitting Broadway.

In the initial story, May's father, William Jarman is in debt to a gambler, Barney Matson, who wants May to help him kidnap a wealthy boy who is infatuated with her. May runs away to avoid cooperating with Matson. Jarman is held hostage until he agrees to introduce Matson to wealthy Winnie Spofford, with whom he was once in love. Winnie has two grown offspring – Sonny and Liz, one of whom Matson seeks to kidnap and hold for ransom.

By coincidence, May hides out at the Spofford barn in Connecticut which has been converted to a summer theater for a play being directed by Ogdon Quiler. May falls in love with Sonny. May's father along with Barney Matson arrive. In another coincidence, Ogdon Quiler is also under obligation to Matson and must obey when the gangster sends him on an errand. Sonny accompanies Ogdon.

May believes that Sonny has been kidnapped and reports this to the authorities. Johnny Graham takes over the direction of the play and turns it into a swing musical. Sonny returns and admits he kidnapped Ogdon in order to allow Johnny to improve the play. May gives FBI agents information about Matson's gang, and they discover drugs in Barney's car which leads to the arrest of the crooks. May and her father are saved, and she can pursue her romance with Sonny.

The story line was subsequently reworked to that indicated above in the July 22, 1941 play script.

Presumably if the movie version of *Very Warm for May* had been made, Garland would have had the role of May Graham, Ray McDonald would have appeared as her brother, and Marta Eggerth would have played Liz.

Jerome Kern and Oscar Hammerstein wrote two new songs for the planned movie – "Contrary Mary" and "Good Girl."

Jack Cummings, another producer at Metro, eventually made a version of *Very Warm for May* called *Broadway Rhythm* which featured the song "All the Things You Are" with the other Jerome Kern/ Oscar Hammerstein numbers played on the piano. The 1944 release starred George Murphy, Gloria DeHaven, Ginny Simms, and Charles Winninger. The three family characters – a successful Broadway producer/writer named Johnnie Demmings (Murphy), his younger sister Patsy (DeHaven) who yearns to be in show business, and their father Sam (Winninger), a former vaudevillian who doesn't like retirement, are about the only ones that remain from the original show. Also, in *Broadway Rhythm* is a Hollywood actress named Helen Hoyt (Simms) who seeks to star in Johnnie's next Broadway show.

When Patsy arrives to see Johnnie in mid-week, he wonders why she is not in school. He wants Patsy to complete her education instead of performing on the stage. Johnnie hires Helen for his new show after seeing her impersonate a Brazilian songstress. But Helen doesn't like the script of the new show thinking it is too high-brow. Sam, who misses show business, persuades Helen to listen to a reading of one of Johnnie's old plays which Johnnie never produced. Sam thinks that, if presented now, it would be a hit. Helen and Sam decide to produce the show on their own in a barn in Connecticut.

At night, Johnnie drops by Helen's hotel suite, sees *Very Warm for May* sheet music on her piano and sings a medley of the songs while playing the piano. Helen sings "All the Things You Are." Johnnie begins falling in love with Helen. When he learns that Sam and Helen are producing his old show, *Let Me Dream*, he attempts to talk them out of the project but with no success.

Patsy graduates from high school and announces that she too will appear in *Let Me Dream*. After Helen lies to Johnnie saying that the leading man in the show has broken his leg, Johnnie takes over the lead role. Naturally, the show is a success with Johnnie planning to take it to Broadway.

Chapter 2:

The Movie Roles That Might Have Been with Mickey Rooney

Judy Garland's first picture with Mickey Rooney was *Thoroughbreds Don't' Cry* – the first of ten films starring the pair. Released in 1937, *Thoroughbreds Don't Cry* also starred Sophie Tucker. Described in this chapter are other projects that could have starred Judy and Mickey.

Judy Garland with Mickey Rooney.

The Captured Shadow – 1938

F. Scott Fitzgerald published a short story titled "The Captured Shadow" in the December 29, 1928 edition of the *Saturday Evening Post* about a budding teenage playwright named Basil Duke Lee. *The Captured Shadow* was Fitzgerald's first stage success when he was a high school student. The writer proposed that Mickey Rooney and Judy Garland, among others, star in the movie adaptation of this work.[36]

Excited after attending a play with his friend Ripley, Basil decides to complete a play he has been writing, *The Captured Shadow*, a farce in three acts, and have his friends act in it. The lead female character in the work is Leilia Van Baker and the main male role is that of a gentleman burglar, the "Shadow." The play is to be performed at the Martindale School for the benefit of the Baby Welfare.

Basil elicits sixteen-year-old Evelyn Beebe to play the Baker character and Hubert Blair for the "Shadow." Basil himself has a small part in the play, but his major task is that of director. Basil has the most problems with Hubert being unwilling to learn his lines and being late for rehearsals. Eventually, Hubert proclaims that he doesn't want to be in the play and never did prompting Basil to find a new leading man. He decides to give the part to a boy, Mayall De Bee, who has acted in plays at another high school. And then another disaster strikes. Evelyn tells Basil that her family is traveling to the East next week and she'll have to drop out of the production.

Basil sees Evelyn's nine-year-old brother Ham who says that he is going to play with Teddy Barnfield, Basil's next door neighbor who has the mumps. Instead of informing Ham that Teddy has the contagious disease and not to interact with him, Basil keeps his mouth shut thinking that if her brother comes down with the mumps, Evelyn's family trip will have to be postponed and she can continue as the leading lady.

The curtain finally rises on the play. In the first big scene, Mayall, in full evening dress as the burglar, opens a window and climbs over the sill. Evelyn as Leilia enters the room and sees the thief who tells her that he is a friend of her brother's. She has been reading about the burglar and replies that she hopes the "Shadow" will not break in to her house this evening as the family jewels are all in the living room safe. Leilia offers him some food since he is hungry and then a policeman arrives noting that the Shadow has been seen climbing in the window and stating that no one is to leave the house.

The second act is very similar to the third act. Mayall begins speaking his third-act lines in the second act confusing everyone. Ordering the curtain to be lowered, Basil informs the audience of the mistake. The play resumes with the correct dialogue. In the end, the Shadow hugs Leilia confessing that he is a burglar and "a captured Shadow at that," and the play ends with great applause.

Walking home with his mother, Basil says he was satisfied with the performances but divulges that he feels sort of sad. He states that he is sad about a little boy – little Ham but that his mother would not understand.

"The Captured Shadow" was somewhat autobiographical since Fitzgerald, when fifteen-years-old, had written a play, *The Girl from Lazy J.*, which was produced by a local theater organization in his home town of St. Paul, Minnesota. He also, while still in his teen years, wrote a play called *The Captured Shadow*. The title not only refers to the arrest of a debonair thief but also to the depressed feeling writers may have when they stop at nothing to get their work produced even, in this case, purposely causing a little boy to contract the mumps.

In a letter dated October 26, 1938 that Fitzgerald wrote to Edwin Knopf of MGM, the writer outlined the story line for a film version of *The Captured Shadow.* The letter states in part, "My idea is based on the fact that you have three adolescent stars (Rooney – Garland – Bartholomew) under contract – and that the woes and triumphs of adolescence have absorbed me more than any author except (Booth) Tarkington."[37]

Fitzgerald points out that the screenplay he has in mind will not be based exclusively on *The Captured Shadow* but also on his short stories, "He Thinks He's Wonderful" and "The Perfect Life."

He summarized the story line of the proposed film as follows:

> A bright sensitive boy of fifteen or sixteen (Freddie Bartholomew) has written a play. He needs someone with acting talent to play the lead (Mickey Rooney) – some person over twenty-one to watch over and chaperon the enterprise (Virginia Bruce) – and

the presence in the show of a rich little girl (Judy Garland) in order to secure some modest backing. How he manages by intensity of purpose, intrigue and good luck to get the help of all three and bring off the play is the substance of the picture.

The sub-plot and love interest concerns the Virginia Bruce character. When Freddie approaches her for help, she has just had a tragic love affair. The young and tremendously earnest boy makes a great appeal to her and she undertakes it as a distraction – finally coming to take a real interest in it. In the course of it, she wins back her lost love.[38]

In a general outline for the proposed motion picture, Fitzgerald adds some details about the characters and the play Freddie wants to produce.[39] Freddie goes to a private school while Mickey attends a public high school and works in the summer delivering groceries for his father's store. Mickey is very choosy about the girls he wants in the play. He doesn't think that Judy, a sissified girl from a wealthy family, is worthy of consideration for a part in the production. The play Freddie has written is a gangster drama.

Nonetheless, no film version of "The Captured Shadow" was ever made.

High School – 1938-39

In a September 26, 1938 column, Louella Parsons indicated that Judy Garland along with other juvenile actors on the MGM lot like Mickey Rooney, Freddie Bartholomew, and Gene Reynolds would be featured in a film to be called *High School* with a screenplay written by Katherine Brush.[40] While no such script could be found, there is an outline of a project titled *High School* done by Agnes Christine Johnston dated August 6, 1938 at the Margaret Herrick Library. Johnston wrote the screenplays for several *Andy Hardy* films including *Out West with the Hardy's*, *Life Begins for Andy Hardy*, and *Andy Hardy's Double Life*.

The never-produced film was to focus on the relationship between best friends, Mary and Barbara.[41] Barbara is beautiful and popular, while Mary is plain but athletic. They enter high school together where Barbara is instantly popular; Mary is not. Mary is attracted to Ronnie, but Ronnie likes Barbara. A boy named Joe is interested in Mary but only as a friend.

Ronnie and Joe invite Barbara and Mary on a double date. The friendship between Joe and Mary might develop into something more were it not for Joe sensing Mary's love for Ronnie. Barbara attempts to persuade another guy to take out Mary. Mary accepts the date, but the guy tends to ignore her with both him and Ronnie paying more attention to Barbara.

At a dance, Barbara has Ronnie ask Mary to be his partner at an Ice Carnival Exhibition. At the exhibition, Mary hopes that Ronnie will ask her to be his queen, but she is hurt when he doesn't.

Mary breaks off her friendship with Barbara. Ronnie, however, is able to have the two reconcile.

At graduation, Ronnie and Barbara and Mary and Joe celebrate together. After the celebration, Barbara confides to Mary that she and Ronnie are going to marry. Mary is shocked at the announcement and says that she is off to college.

With Barbara married, Joe now feels that he has a chance with Mary. He believes that it is up to him to make Mary love him. Finally, he convinces her to marry him.

In order to complete her college major sooner, for their honeymoon, Mary and Joe take a "field trip" to New Mexico to study cliff dwellings for her class in archaeology. As a young architect, Joe can study the building methods of Native Americans on the trip. As Joe and Mary depart, Ronnie remarks, "Look at 'em. Tickled to death because they've got themselves married – They don't know what they're in for!" While Mary and Joe enjoy their trip, Mary still secretly loves Ronnie.

Barbara and Ronnie seem to have the perfect marriage. They attend numerous parties, but under the surface, their married life is not as happy as it appears.

Returning from their honeymoon. Mary and Joe fix up an old mill as their home. On Saturday nights, many friends drop in. Barbara and

Ronnie hold a party for an important business connection of Ronnie's, but the business connection, after talking with Mary at the affair, wants to go to her place to see the relics that she and Joe have brought back from their honeymoon. Barbara becomes jealous of Joe and Mary's lifestyle while Ronnie admires it.

Ronnie and Barbara quarrel. Meanwhile, Mary announces that she is going to have a baby. Barbara says that she is going on a little "marriage vacation" to visit her family by herself. Joe suggests that Ronnie stay with them during Barbara's absence.

While watching Mary with the baby, Ronnie realizes that he loves Mary. Barbara returns and sees that her husband is more restless than ever. She tells Mary that Ronnie ". . . loves your home. . . He loves the baby. . . He loves Joe. He loves you –" Ronnie comes in and admits it.

Mary feels that it is up to her to reconcile Barbara and Ronnie. During a drive, Mary persuades Ronnie to return to his wife. Mary is tempted to confess her love for Ronnie but resists temptation. She goes back to Joe and realizes that she really loves him.

Presumably, if the film had been made, Judy would have appeared as Mary, and perhaps Mickey Rooney would have portrayed Joe.

Dear Old Broadway – 1939-1940

Louella Parsons reported the following in her November 13, 1939 column:

> Mickey Rooney and Judy Garland are going to have to learn a lot of new imitations. After the way they delighted the customers doing Mr. and Mrs. F.D.R. in Babes in Arms and Mickey's knockout caricatures of Gable and Barrymore, the exhibitors are clamoring for more the same. They're going to get their wish, for their boss, L.B. Mayer, himself suggested the idea that will star them in "Dear Old Broadway." It will be in a reminiscent mood with Mickey and Judy taking off the great and near great who ever wrote history on the Great White Way.[42]

A few months later on March 16, 1940, John Monks and Fred Finklehoffe wrote a synopsis for the proposed film. It opens in 1941 with the premiere of a musical comedy. A girl on stage dressed in a present day costume is doing a number with a boy attired in an outfit from 1914. After the musical, "Nifty" Miles and Robert Murdock are outside the stage door. The female star of the performance comes out with her mother. "Nifty" tries to persuade Robert to talk to the girl's mother, but he replies, "It's all been said, Nifty, and a lot better, a long, long time ago."[43]

The story flashes back to New York City in 1914 to the home of Wall Street tycoon Hamilton Wyndham married to a former star of the theater. They have two daughters – Terry and her younger sister Alice, sixteen. Also living with the Wyndham's is Mrs. Wyndham's brother, a former actor. Terry has just informed her family that she wants to seek a professional career and not simply marry and live the social life of a wealthy man's daughter. The father blames his brother-in-law, Brutus Anthony, for giving Terry the idea of pursuing a career. To calm the situation, Mrs. Wyndham gives her brother three tickets to the theater for himself and his two nieces.

Brutus sees two friends of his, "Nifty" and Robert, at the theater who want to be introduced to the Wyndham daughters. After the play, the daughters desire to go to a prominent actors' restaurant where Brutus introduces Terry and Alice to Nifty and Bob. Nifty is a budding singer, dancer, author, and composer. Bob is an aspiring singer-dancer.

The following Sunday afternoon, Terry and Alice are out for a walk in the park with their two cousins where they encounter Nifty and Bob. The guys take the sisters to their boarding house for Sunday dinner where the girls meet the other residents. Nifty and Bob have just gotten their first job in several months – a split week in Atlantic City.

Later, the sisters take Nifty and Bob to meet their father introducing them as two young men from Harvard. Mr. Wyndham is impressed until his brother-in-law reveals that they are really actors. Mr. Wyndham exiles the girls to Atlantic City where Bob and Nifty are appearing. The father is not pleased when he eventually discovers them there.

Mrs. Wyndham suggests to him that one of the reasons the girls have no interest in their own social set is because their father never gives them a chance to meet young men of their own social standing. The father grants permission for a birthday party for Terry. But the party will be held the same night as an amateur contest at a New York theater.

Brutus tells his brother-in-law that he wants to take the girls to a big concert. Mr. Wyndham agrees even though it is the same night as the birthday party. After they dress for the concert, they are greeted by the customary "surprise" when they go downstairs to depart. Meanwhile, Bob and Nifty are awaiting the girls' appearance at the amateur night. Alice and Terry finally manage to leave the house and rush to the theater. They do the number that they had planned and captivate the audience.

The following day, Terry confronts her father after he learns from the newspaper about her participation in the amateur contest. She wants to embark on a stage career and leaves home. Terry marries Bob.

They both rehearse for an upcoming production. During rehearsals, Bob is dismissed from the cast and realizes that he is not a great dancer and probably never will be. Terry says that she no longer has any interest in show business and suggests that they both pursue something else. Bob, however, wants her to continue to follow her dreams.

Terry is a success on opening night. As the final curtain descends, Bob and Nifty leave the theater and walk out of her life, feeling that it would interfere with her success if they stayed.

Apparently, the idea relayed in the Parsons' column of Judy Garland and Mickey Rooney impersonating Broadway greats may have been part of the rehearsal and performance of the musical.

While *Dear Old Broadway* was never produced, Fred Finklehoffe, who co-authored the treatment, did include a "Ghost Theater" segment in the screenplay for the 1941 Garland/Rooney motion picture, *Babes on Broadway*. This sequence had Garland impersonating actress, comedienne, and singer, Fay Templeton, performing "Mary's a Grand Old Name." Judy also did an impression of Broadway entertainer Blanche Ring doing "I've Got Rings on My Fingers," and of Sarah Bernhardt performing "La Marseillaise."

There They Grow – 1940

Director Norman Taurog, who helmed several MGM films starring juvenile actors, such as *The Adventures of Tom Sawyer* and *The Men of Boys Town*, had the idea of making a movie about child actors who grow up and then lose their show business careers. The concept was to have actors and actresses like Judy Garland, Mickey Rooney, Jackie Cooper, and Shirley Temple appear in the feature with the juveniles getting together and making a great musical, proving that there is really no awkward age for a film star.

Taurog's concept was never developed into a screenplay, let alone a feature film. One of the biggest difficulties with such a project may have been in convincing juvenile actors that, as they aged, their star power would no doubt diminish.

Good News – 1940-41

Good News, a musical for Mickey Rooney and Judy Garland, was reported on a list of movies promised by the major film studios in 1940.[44]

In July 1941, Devery Freeman and Roger Edens developed a treatment for a film adaptation of the Broadway show *Good News* about the goings on at Tait College. In the treatment, there is no mention of Mickey Rooney. Possibly, he was up for the role of the star football player for which Ray McDonald was subsequently considered.

In the treatment, a motion picture studio selects Tait College to film a movie called *Campus Queen*. Dean Baylor, the president of the school, and the Board of Trustees accept the production company's offer to film location scenes at the college. The movie company sends director Gilbert West, writer Tobey Coots, and starlet Enid Adams to the school.

Meanwhile, Coach Martin is under pressure at Tait to win an upcoming football game against the school's archrival, Colton College. The star player on the team is Pinky Wright (Ray McDonald) who is Connie Martin's (Judy Garland) boyfriend. Connie is the coach's daughter.

Pinky's friend on the football team is Smythe who works at the local ice cream parlor and is dating Letty Loring. Pinky's father was in vaudeville, and Pinky has developed a talent as a dancer.

The entire school turns out to greet the arrival of the movie company with many students hoping for parts in the film.

Pinky sneaks into Connie's dorm room to see her unaware that Enid Adams is now occupying that room. Upon seeing Enid, Pinky beats a hasty retreat. Later, at a dance, to which Pinky has brought Connie, Enid begins flirting with Pinky and complements him on his dancing. Connie is left alone. Pinky ends up giving his varsity sweater to Enid although he had promised it to Connie. He has to borrow Smythe's sweater to give to Connie.

Pinky begins neglecting football hoping for a role in the movie and is suspended from the football team for a game against Gridley College. Subsequently, Coach Martin suspends the entire first string team from that game.

Connie attempts to play peacemaker between the team and her father. She asks her boyfriend to visit her father and request that he reinstate the team. Nonetheless, Pinky would rather take a role in the movie that Enid has said he can get.

Tobey Coots learns that the boys won't play football and decides to help get them back on the team. He suggests that Connie and the other girls on campus not date any of the football team until the team asks the Coach to be reinstated. All the girls begin snubbing their boyfriends.

Pinky advises his teammates to not allow the girls to intimidate them. The girls throw a party for themselves without any boys. Nevertheless, some of the boys dress up as girls to crash the party. The boys are quickly discovered and bedlam breaks out. When the Dean comes to investigate, the boys quickly depart.

Connie runs to the boys' dorm to warn Pinky that the Dean spotted him and is on his way over. The trellis she is standing on up against the dorm breaks. Connie falls and is taken to the hospital with a possible concussion. Pinky and Coach Martin visit Connie in the hospital where Pinky asks the coach to reinstate the team.

At the big game with Colton, the Tait team, particularly Pinky, performs poorly in the first half. Tobey goes to the locker room at halftime to tell Pinky that there might be a spot for Connie and him in the film and that the director needs some shots of spectacular touchdown runs from the Tait-Colton game. The Tait team begins scoring in the second half and wins the game. Coach Martin has his contract renewed, and the director finishes his film.

Roger Edens made some notes on the Devery Freeman treatment indicating that besides Judy Garland and Ray McDonald, Marjorie Main and Virginia O'Brien would also be featured in the planned film. He referred to the Pinky Wright character as Tom Marlowe and noted at least three songs to be included – "Good News" sung by Judy Garland; "The Best Things in Life," also performed by Judy; and "Movies Gonna Let You," sung by O'Brien and McDonald. Both "Good News" and "The Best Things in Life Are Free" were from the original 1927 Broadway production of *Good News* as well as from the 1930 film. "Our Love" was set as the title song for the movie with Busby Berkeley directing.

Concerning this attempt at a Judy Garland version of *Good News*, Louis B. Mayer told Arthur Freed, "Arthur, I've had second thoughts about *Good News*. I don't think we should go with it right now. Don't ask me why – I really don't know – it's just a hunch. Instead, I'd like you to go with *Strike Up the Band* – it sounds so patriotic."[45]

In the early 1940s, Arthur Freed resurrected the idea of making *Good News* with Judy Garland. In a letter to Jack McGowan, Freed wrote:

> I think you know what I have in mind for Good News. It is to make it a fast collegiate musical, based on the original story. Of course, this should be a very free basis and I'm sure that you'll depart from the original substantially in your treatment. Judy Garland, of course, will be the lead and any other parts you will write we can cast with good people. I think the spirit of the piece should be comedy. Offhand, the songs we should retain from the old piece are "Good News," "The Best Things in Life Are Free," and "Just Imagine." We should get a new song in place of "Varsity

Drag" that is more modern, along the lines of "The Conga" we did in *Strike Up the Band*.[46]

McGowan replied: "I was able to give some thought to *Good News*. I read the original Broadway book and believe I have found a plan that will give Judy a much better opportunity than the original sappy part of the girl. I am figuring on (Charles) Winninger also for a hoky part. He is not her father nor any relation."[47]

Other than the foregoing, no additional details about what Jack McGowan had in mind for *Good News* could be found. Nonetheless, a treatment written by James H. Hill in 1942 took a different slant to sports at Tait College. On the first day of college registration, Gloria Dade arrives on campus. She is one of the school's greatest swimmers and will be on the college swim team as well as participating in its water carnival. She will be joining the Kappa Gamma sorority where Lil is the cook and all-around gopher for the sorority.

Tom Marlowe, the editor of the school newspaper and manager of the water carnival, is also enrolled and Gloria considers him her fiancé. Lil, the cook, has paid tuition for a girl named Connie to enroll as a freshman at the school. Lil had given Connie's father, a former swim coach, the money for Connie to attend the school. The young girl lands a job in the kitchen of the sorority.

Connie is very attractive and demonstrates her swimming prowess. Tom wants to meet her and have her join the water carnival. He finally encounters Connie in science class after she causes an explosion making her look bedraggled and black-faced.

Johnny Weissmuller, Olympic swimmer and star of several *Tarzan* movies, is coming to the school to sign the winners of the big swim meet for an aquacade film. Nervous at the swim meet try-out, Connie fails to make the team.

The sorority is holding a reception for Weissmuller. Gloria suggests that he attend a masquerade ball and swim with someone there which she assumes will be her. Seeing Connie at the ball, she and Tom begin to get to know one another.

When Connie doesn't have a sarong or cape for the ball, Lil secretly purchases an outfit for her. At the event, after introducing Johnny Weissmuller, the spotlight falls on Connie wearing a mask looking resplendent in her attire. She joins Weissmuller in a waltz in the water. At midnight, everyone takes off their masks, but Connie slips away. Gloria is waiting for her and announces that she is engaged to Tom Marlowe (which is not true) and that Connie should drop out of school immediately.

Connie is on her way to the train station when Lil catches up with her. She has second thoughts about leaving and tells Lil that she will never give up again and that she intends to beat Gloria in the next swim meet test.

With coaching from Weissmuller, Connie trains for the meet. Her father comes to observe her performance. The winner of the girls' 100 meter free style will become queen of Tait's water carnival and have a featured role swimming opposite Johnny Weissmuller. Connie moves ahead of Gloria in the swimming competition and finishes first. Tom greets her explaining that he was never engaged to Gloria. Tom and Connie are then named king and queen of the school's water carnival.

All of the above ideas for *Good News* were dropped except for the names of the leading characters when a 1947 version was made starring Peter Lawford and June Allyson. Lawford played football star Tommy Marlowe who wants to date a new coed at the school, Pat McClellan (Patricia Marshall). She resists his advances and is more interested in studying French. Tommy enlists the help of part-time school librarian Connie Lane (June Allyson) in studying French and eventually falls in love with her.

Charles Walters, who directed *Good News*, would later direct the movies *Easter Parade* and *Summer Stock*, both starring Judy Garland.

Funny Face – 1940

Both Mickey Rooney and Judy Garland were to star in this initial effort to bring the Broadway musical play, *Funny Face*, to the screen.[48]

Fred Thompson and Paul Gerard Smith wrote the book for the 1927 Broadway musical with music and lyrics by George and Ira Gershwin. The play starred Fred Astaire and his sister Adele. The Fred Astaire character, Jimmy Reeves, has guardianship over his foster parents' three biological daughters: Dora, June, and Frankie. The latter played by Adele Astaire. Dora and June are throwing a party for Jimmy's birthday. The guests include Dora's boyfriend, Dugsie Gibbs. Frankie has written scandalous lies about Jimmy in her diary. He confiscates the book and places it in an envelope within a safe. She tries to play up to Jimmy to have him return the diary.

When that doesn't work, Frankie persuades Peter Thurston, an aviator and sportsman, to break into the safe to retrieve her diary. Meanwhile, Jimmy places Dora's bracelets in an envelope in the same safe.

Two thieves, Chester and Herbert, break into the safe and steal the envelope containing the diary. Peter and Dugsie end up taking the envelope with the bracelets.

Pursued by the thieves who really intended to steal the bracelets and by the police, Frankie, Peter, and Dugsie take flight to an inn in New Jersey. Peter and Frankie begin falling in love, while Dora plots to blackmail him into marrying her. Frankie seeks to thwart Dora's plans by falsely announcing that she has already married Peter. The police recover the bracelets from Peter.

Later, Jimmy confronts Frankie who explains that she is not really married to Peter but only engaged to him. Dugsie and Dora reunite. Jimmy drops charges against Chester and Herbert upon recovering the diary and allows Frankie to marry Peter.

If Metro had adapted the play as written, Mickey would have no doubt appeared as Jimmy Reeves and Judy as Frankie. Nevertheless, this version of *Funny Face* was never produced. The same title with a completely different plot was used by MGM for the 1957 movie, *Funny Face*, starring Audrey Hepburn and Fred Astaire.

Lady Be Good – 1940

The on-again, off-again love affair between two songwriters – Dixie Donegan (Ann Sothern) and Eddie Crane (Robert Young), was the theme of *Lady Be Good*, another MGM musical. Eddie Crane is struggling with the lyrics to music he has written when his girlfriend Dixie provides the words and the song becomes a great success. After the two marry, Dixie finds that Eddie is spending more time with wealthy New York society, than composing. They divorce, but realize that they still must work together to continue their successful songwriting. Eventually, they marry a second time. Dixie seeks to begin writing songs for a new project, but Eddie wants to go on a honeymoon first. After they agree to a separation, Eddie starts working on a symphony under the aegis of a wealthy benefactor. Dixie files for divorce a second time. When Eddie arrives in court too late to object to this divorce, he proposes to Dixie again not realizing that the judge has refused to grant the divorce.

"Metro has bought 'Lady Be Good,' an old Broadway musical, for Rooney and Garland," as was reported by Monroe Lathrop on October 13, 1940.[49] The "old Broadway musical" debuted in 1924. Written by Guy Bolton and Fred Thompson with music and lyrics by George and Ira Gershwin, the Broadway version of *Lady Be Good* was another musical that starred Fred Astaire and his sister Adele.

The plot of the musical was dramatically different than the film version described above. A down-on-their luck brother and sister dance team, Dick and Susie Trevor, crash a garden party put on by wealthy Jo Vanderwater who has designs on Dick. However, Dick is attracted to Shirley Vernon, but because he is penniless, he is afraid to pursue her. Susie finds herself falling for a guy named Jack Robinson, a charming hobo. When Jack's uncle dies, he inherits a fortune. A lawyer offers Susie $50,000 to pretend that she is Jack's widow to obtain the money from the Robinson estate. Eventually, Dick proposes marriage to Shirley. Jack Robinson finally learns he has inherited money and is surprised that Susie is claiming his fortune as his widow. He declares his love for her and both couples become man and wife.

If MGM had stayed with the original version of *Lady Be Good*, then no doubt Mickey and Judy would have starred in the movie version as the brother and sister dance team.

No, No Nanette – 1940

Metro wanted the rights to *No, No Nanette* as another vehicle for Mickey and Judy with the latter as Nanette. The studio engaged in a bidding war with RKO for the musical comedy which started as a Broadway play and then a 1930 film. RKO won the rights for $200,000 and made the movie starring Anna Neagle.

The story line of the original 1925 Broadway musical focused on Bible publisher, Jimmy Smith, whose business has made him a millionaire. Nonetheless, Jimmy's wife Sue is very frugal with her husband's wealth. Sue concentrates on raising her and Jimmy's ward, Nanette.

Jimmy is a soft touch for women in distress. He provides money to three different women to help them while seeking only a platonic relationship with each. However, he realizes how bad his relationships with the women could look if Sue became aware of them. Jimmy asks his lawyer, Billy, to help him untangle his associations with the women. The two make plans to meet all three girls in Atlantic City, New Jersey to break off any further contact with the females.

Coincidentally, Nanette decides to visit Atlantic City to have some fun before settling down with Tom Trainor, her intended. As fate would have it, Nanette runs into Tom; Sue and Billy's wife, Lucille, encounter Jimmy and Billy along with the three females Jimmy has supported. Chaos ensues, but everything works out in the end.

The most famous songs from the musical were "Tea for Two" and "I Want to Be Happy."

The 1930 film based on the musical had basically the same characters but their relationships with each other were different. Tom has written a musical for his intended, Nanette, and is attempting to find a backer for the show. Nanette persuades Jimmy Smith, a former friend of her father's and a millionaire Bible publisher to finance the musical. Smith has given money to support two chorus girls, but their manager, Billy Early, has not given them the funds. Billy's suspicious wife, Lucille, notifies Jimmy's wife, Sue. Jimmy goes to Atlantic City to see Tom's show followed by Billy Early and the wives. Again, chaos ensues, but the men claim they are amateur talent scouts and are forgiven when Tom's show is a success.

The 1940 version of *No, No Nanette* produced by RKO was also different from the preceding iterations. Jimmy is still a wealthy Bible publisher with a tight-fisted wife. He has problems with three women. Sonya from Syracuse is demanding money that Jimmy promised her for her acting career. Jimmy's niece, Nanette, asks Jimmy's old friend, producer Bill Trainor, to put Sonya in his new show. In the process, Bill falls in love with Nanette.

Jimmy has to deal next with Kitty from Kansas for whom he has promised an artistic career. Nanette asks artist Tom Gillespie to teach Kitty about art. As with Bill Trainor, Tom also falls in love with Nanette. Betty from Bridgeport subsequently appears and demands $5000. To raise the money, Nanette sells the portrait Tom had painted of her to a cigarette company which disappoints him.

Nanette decides to go out with Bill Trainor who persuades her to meet him at the airport so that they can elope to Nevada. In the meantime, Jimmy's wife Sue, who has found out about the three women whom her husband is helping, boards the plane to Nevada seeking a divorce from him. Jimmy, who decides to fly to the Virgin Islands, books passage on the same flight. As the plane is flying to Nevada, Jimmy and Sue reconcile, and Nanette discovers that Bill has brought Tom aboard to marry her.

One might wonder how MGM would have adapted the play if it had been successful in purchasing the rights to *No, No Nanette* for Judy and Mickey. One thing for certain, the songs "Tea for Two" and "I Want to be Happy" would have been included in Metro's version.

Panama Hattie – 1941

A note in newspapers in March 1941 indicated that Metro was attempting to sign actor Jack Oakie for their big musical, *Panama Hattie*, which had starred Ethel Merman in the Broadway version. The report also indicated that the film would star Ann Sothern, Mickey Rooney, and Judy Garland.[50]

While Ann Sothern played Panama Hattie in the film, Jack Oakie, Mickey Rooney, and Judy Garland did not appear.

The movie, released in 1942 and produced by Arthur Freed, concerned Panama Hattie, a singer at Phil's Place in Panama, who is in love with Dick Bulliard (Dan Dailey), a sergeant in the Army who comes from a wealthy family. He had been married before and has a young daughter, Geraldine (Jackie Horner) who comes to Panama to visit him and meet Hattie for the first time.

Red Skelton, Rags Ragland, and Ben Blue played three sailors, friends of Hattie, who try to help her.

When Hattie meets Gerry, the young girl thinks that the singer looks funny with her many pieces of costume jewelry, a big feather in her hat, and a parasol. Upset, Hattie begins drinking while commiserating with Red, Rags, and Rowdy (Ben Blue).

The following day, Dick apologizes to Hattie and introduces her to Leila (Marsha Hunt), the admiral's daughter, who has her eyes on the Sergeant. Like Gerry, Leila also insults Hattie's wardrobe.

Hattie tries to make up with Gerry who takes a pair of scissors to snip bows off Hattie's latest attire to make it look more conservative. Gerry also shows Hattie how to walk like a lady. The two then begin a friendship.

Leila discourages Hattie from thinking that Dick will marry her saying that Hattie and Dick come from two different backgrounds. Hattie is poor; Dick is wealthy. Hattie decides to leave Panama. Even though Red, Rags, and Rowdy attempt to dissuade her, she won't change her mind. When Dick finds out that Hattie is leaving, he convinces her that he really loves her. Hattie marries him and stays in Panama.

MGM may have considered Mickey Rooney for one of the three sailor roles played in the film by Skelton, Ragland, and Blue. What role Judy Garland may have had in the film is not entirely clear. It's fairly certain that Ann Sothern, who was thirty-two at the time, would have appeared as Panama Hattie. Judy perhaps would have played Geraldine, the daughter of the Dan Dailey character. Judy was in her late teens in

1941, and producers may have envisioned making the Geraldine character a teenager instead of, as in the final movie, a youngster.

Babes in Hollywood – 1941-42

The Los Angeles Times in 1934 reported that the Gumm sisters – Mary Jane, Frances, and Dorothy "Jimmie" Gumm, would appear in a two-reel picture called *Babes in Hollywood.*[51] While that project never saw the light of day, in 1941, Sid Silvers and Frances Swan drafted a treatment for a Mickey Rooney/Judy Garland movie to be called *Babes in Hollywood.*

Eddie Grady (Rooney) decides to leave his home town of Galesburg, Illinois and travel to Hollywood to make it in the movies. His Uncle Dan gives him a letter of introduction to W.T. Dixon, the head of MGM. On the bus, he meets Kate Brown (Garland) and her little cousin Peanuts (Dickie Hall). Kate is bringing her cousin to Hollywood to live with her and her father, David. Despite living in Hollywood, Kate is not interested in movies like Eddie is.

Kate's father, a former silent movie actor, runs a boarding house where Eddie can stay until he makes it big in the film industry. Among the boarders are Chick Dale (Ray MacDonald), a stand-in at Metro, Veronica Pond (Virginia Weidler), a would-be actress, and Louie Stern, a third assistant director at the studio. Kate and her dad live in a guest house on the rather rundown estate. In addition to owning the boarding house, David Brown is also a night watchman at MGM.

Kate and Eddie visit the film factory where Eddie is confident that he will become a successful actor. He presents his letter of introduction at W.T. Dixon's office. Dixon thinks the letter is from MGM's important distributor in the Mid-West and gives Eddie the chance for a job at the studio.

That night, at the boarding house, Eddie throws a lavish party thinking that he will soon be a movie star. He assures Kate that his initial success won't change him and that she will always be his leading lady as they kiss.

The following day, Eddie returns to MGM thinking he will start as an actor in a film but finds that his job offer is for that of an office boy.

Disappointed, Eddie attempts to see Dixon again to, at least, ask him for a loan to pay for the party he threw. He breaks into a Board of Directors meeting. After Dixon allows him to plead his case to the Board, it agrees to advance him the money. That night, Eddie informs Kate that he is not an actor but a mere errand boy.

Three months pass with Eddie still being an office boy. He takes Kate to lunch at the studio commissary where they overhear discussion of the need for a stand-in for a young actress, Minna Courtney (Betty Wells). Kate lands the job. On the set of the movie, to make her co-star jealous, Minna asks Eddie to a party at her home.

Eddie receives a telegram that his mother will soon be arriving in Hollywood to witness the success that he has been relating to her in his letters.

Eddie invites Kate to attend the party at Minna's house so that the two can do the number they have been rehearsing for the studio executives and directors in attendance. Kate and Eddie have to bring Kate's little cousin, Peanuts, to the party with them. Peanuts ends up stealing the show and is put under contract with Metro.

Eddie is upset that he has missed a great opportunity. Knowing that his mother will arrive soon, he worries that she will find that he is nothing but a big liar. He decides to fix up the old boarding house to make it look like his estate with some of the boarders playing his servants. Kate threatens to tell his mother the truth but relents when she hears Mrs. Grady, upon seeing the house, say "This is just what I needed."

Louie Stern had "borrowed" a car from MGM to transport Mrs. Grady to the boarding house. The next day at the studio, Kate and Louie have to explain to Mr. Dixon why they took his personal automobile. Kate makes an impassioned plea to Dixon on behalf of Eddie. Eddie is summoned to Mr. Dixon's office with his mother. Dixon and his staff put on a show pretending that Eddie is a big star. The show even includes Eddie performing a number with Kate in front of the cameras. After the performance, the crew applauds wildly. Louie, who directed the scene, gives away the fact that it was all make believe. Eddie's mother learns the truth about her son, but she says she knew it all along.

W.T. Dixon sees the film of Eddie and Kate's performance and thinks that the pair would be ideal for a new feature he is making called *Babes in Hollywood*.

According to columnist Dorothy Kilgallen, "M-G-M is considering dropping plans for 'Babes in Hollywood' with Judy Garland and Mickey Rooney. The script calls for a couple of kids of high school age – but with Judy a young matron and Mickey a Coast Casanova, the studio is wondering if it won't seem a little silly."[52]

Jumbo – 1940's

In 1943, MGM purchased the screen rights to this 1935 musical for $100,000. Legendary Billy Rose produced the project with music and lyrics by Richard Rodgers and Lorenz Hart. The Hippodrome in New York was turned into a circus tent with acrobats, animal acts, and other carnival-type acts performing during the show with Jumbo, a large elephant, as the main attraction. The thin storyline concerned a financially-struggling circus with the daughter of its owner falling in love with the son of the owner's main competitor.

Initially, Arthur Freed wanted to star Garland and Rooney in the film adaptation with Wallace Beery and Frank Morgan. According to the October 11, 1943 issue of *The New York Times*, the picture was to be made after Mickey Rooney finished filming *National Velvet*. Subsequently, Freed considered Garland along with Frank Sinatra and Red Skelton for the leads in the film.

A November 10, 1943 article in *Variety* reported that Aleen Leslie was hired by MGM to adapt *Jumbo* for the big screen in the first attempt for a Garland/Rooney vehicle. Presumably, Judy would have appeared as the daughter of the financially strapped circus owner with Mickey as her love interest. Beery and Morgan would have played the competing owners. Jimmy Durante, in a role he created in the Broadway play, would appear as a circus worker.

Aleen Leslie took at least two different approaches to the script for *Jumbo*. The first approach, set in the year 1892, began with a Sheriff's

Sale of all the animals and fixtures of John Considine's circus. Brains Bowers (to be played by Jimmy Durante) was Considine's right hand man. Considine has a two-year-old daughter named Kitty whom he tries to protect from seeing the animals being auctioned off.

Matt Mulligan Sr., owner of Mulligan's Medicine Show and Considine's competitor, comes to the auction to bid on Jumbo. His son, Matt Jr., four-years-old, begins to play with Kitty Considine. After successfully placing the winning bid for Jumbo, Mulligan Sr. leaves with his son with whom Kitty has grown fond. Threatening Mulligan, Considine says that Jumbo won't perform for him; the elephant will only do his act for Considine.

Flash forward sixteen years to 1908 with John Considine rebuilding his circus. Kitty, now eighteen, is one of the star attractions riding horses and singing. Still fighting Mulligan's show, the Considine Circus has been "jumping the dates" of the Mulligan circus by arriving in each small town on the same day the Mulligan show is playing.

After buying a new hat in the town where each circus is performing, Kitty runs into Matt Mulligan Jr, now about twenty-years old. He invites her to an ice cream parlor. While the first draft script by Leslie ends there, one could expect that Kitty and Matt fall in love and that eventually their fathers reconcile with Jumbo becoming the star attraction of the circus.

The second approach Aleen Leslie took to the movie adaptation, dated January 18, 1944, began with both Kitty and Matt Jr. grown up. Both the Considine circus and the Mulligan outfit arrive in the same town on the same day. Matt is concerned that his father and the father's business partner are trying to ruin the Considine circus by deliberately playing the same locales. Frederick, Mulligan's partner, has written an anonymous letter to the income tax department to look into Considine's back taxes thinking that the letter will result in Considine having to sell his outfit to pay the taxes due. Mulligan could then take Jumbo away from Considine.

When the Considine circus arrives, Matt and Kitty resume their friendship. Matt contends that it is just a coincidence that the two circuses are always playing the same towns, but Kitty says that Matt's father is trying to ruin the Considine business which used to be called the Considine-Mulligan Circus.

As with the prior draft, this approach by Leslie stops there but again one can guess what happens in the rest of the story. In any event, *Jumbo*, as a movie, was not produced by MGM in the 1940s.

In 1950, *The New York Times* reported that Metro was planning to revive *Jumbo* with Judy Garland again considered for a lead role. Arthur Freed was to produce the picture with filming to begin in late 1951.[53]

Joseph Fields wrote a more extensive screenplay for this version of *Jumbo* dealing with the Mulligan and Considine circuses. The prologue opens with Shamus Mulligan as the ringmaster of Mulligan and Considine's Wonder Show with John F. Considine performing as a daredevil fire-eater. Kitty Considine, at nine years of age, is enamored with Matt Mulligan who sings "The Most Beautiful Girl in the World" to her.

After becoming irritated with Considine's fire eating act, Mulligan dissolves their partnership and divides the circus between them with Considine receiving Cleo, the elephant, who dies giving birth to Jumbo. Kitty is heartbroken over seeing Matt depart. His father wants to drive the Considine circus out of business.

Time passes. Both Kitty and Matt have grown up. Matt performs acrobatics while riding a horse in his father's circus. Kitty's father's circus is in financial trouble with his troupe going without pay for two weeks. Mulligan's Biggest and Greatest Show is taking business away from the Considine outfit.

While in Oklahoma, the two shows come face-to-face as each wants to parade through town. The performers from each circus begin to fight. After the town's mayor cancels performances of Mulligan's show, Mulligan vows to get Jumbo away from Considine.

Matt confesses to his dad his love for Kitty but leaves her when his father and John Considine resume arguing. Mulligan informs the federal government that his former partner owes back income taxes. The government plans to auction off the Considine circus. Mulligan is trying to get Jumbo. He catches Considine attempting to hide Jumbo from the auctioneers and successfully bids for the elephant and the rest of the circus. Matt seeks to console Kitty, but she wants to be left alone. She sings "Little Girl Blue."

John Considine seeks to start anew and decides to sell his house in Kentucky. At the railroad station, the Considine's meet twenty-four show girls who have been abandoned by their manager, and he decides to employ them in the new circus. When John and Kitty go to Kentucky to see their old home, they are startled to find that it has burned to the ground. However, Considine had it insured and so receives a check from the insurance company.

Matt has one of the clowns from the Considine circus teach him a routine that the clown does with Kitty thinking that he can do it with her in clown make-up to propose to her. He sings "My Romance," but Kitty refuses his proposal. After he leaves, Kitty reprises the song.

With the insurance money, Considine wants to buy back Jumbo and plans to open his new circus in Davenport on the same day Mulligan's circus is playing there. As the new circus is about to debut, police officers and the insurance man arrive and accuse John of burning down his own house for the insurance money. But the authorities permit Considine to premiere his new show before arresting him.

Kitty performs a number with the chorus girls featuring Jumbo's theme music. At the nearby Mulligan circus, Jumbo hears the music with tears flowing from his eyes. Jumbo escapes the tent running toward the Considine circus. Running amuck, the elephant creates havoc in the town.

When the insurance man finds that Mulligan insured Jumbo with his company and realizing all the damage the elephant has caused, he agrees to drop the arson charges against Considine if John stops Jumbo from doing more damage to the town.

Upon seeing Considine, Jumbo calms down and tears of happiness stream from his eyes. Mulligan suggests that both he and John merge their circuses into the Greater Combined Mulligan and Considine Shows. In the combined show, Kitty performs a high-wire trapeze act as part of the "Six Jet-Propelled Jerricho's." Matt masquerades as one of the trapeze artists. He and Kitty fall arm in arm to the net. He then throws his arms around Kitty and hugs her fervently.

This proposal also was never produced. Not until 1962 was a film adaptation of *Jumbo* made. That movie, *Billy Rose's Jumbo*, had yet another story line about the large elephant. Starring Doris Day as Kitty Wonder, Jimmy Durante as her father, Pop Wonder, and Stephen Boyd as Sam Rawlins, the son of circus owner, John Noble, the tale dealt with the Wonder Circus whose owner, Pop Wonder, likes to gamble leaving the circus in debt. Kitty employs Sam Rawlins as a performer and circus hand not realizing that he is really the son of John Noble who wants to take over the Wonder Circus. Buying up Pop's IOU's and with Sam's help, Noble gains control of the Wonder Circus. Sam falls in love with Kitty and begins feeling guilty about what he has done. He splits from his father and brings Jumbo back to join a new Wonder circus.

Chapter 3:

The Movie Roles That Might Have Been with Kathryn Grayson

Because of distinctly different singing styles, Metro often wanted to pair Judy, who was at the time described as a "jazz" singer, with the operatic voice of Kathryn Grayson. The two did appear in three MGM motion pictures – *Thousands Cheer* (1943), *Ziegfeld Follies* (1945), and *Till the Clouds Roll By* (1946).

In addition to the film projects described in this chapter, as will be noted in succeeding chapters, Kathryn Grayson was often a substitute for Judy Garland in several films in which the latter was unable to appear.

Judy Garland at a young age.

Eight Girls and a Horse – 1941

Edgar Selwyn was set to produce this planned film starring Judy Garland and Kathryn Grayson as two students at the Creative Arts Club for Girls in New York City.

Nadine Brewster (Grayson) wants to be a singer; Glenda Smith (Garland) seeks to become a comedienne. Nadine's tuition and board are three months past due, and she is trying to contact her father.

The treatment for *Eight Girls and a Horse* opens with a scene in a nightclub where Nadine is auditioning, singing "Zigeuner" from the operetta *Bittersweet*. She doesn't get the job because she is only sixteen.

Unbeknownst to her, her father, Pop Brewster, is down on his luck owning a race horse which is about to be put down. Pop bought the horse, Skylark, for $50 and hopes to make it a winner again but it has bad hooves. The trainer tells Pop's friend, Blackie Gilman, a bookie, who is at the racetrack with his girlfriend, Fay Fenton, that Skylark is a lost cause.

Pop Brewster dies of a sudden heart attack with Blackie then becoming executor of Pop's will. Pop's only asset is the horse.

Blackie visits Nadine's school to inform her of the bad news but can't bring himself to do that. Instead, he relies on Miss Lloyd at the school to relay the sad news to Nadine. Hoping to keep Nadine in school, Blackie informs Miss Lloyd that Nadine inherited a valuable race horse. Blackie, feeling sorry for the girl, wants to give her $1000 by purchasing the horse for that price.

Upon learning about the horse, Glenda persuades Nadine that Skylark is probably worth much more than $1000 and that the girls at the school should form a corporation to train Skylark and enter it into races. In addition to Nadine and Glenda, Valerie, who is studying to be an actress; Allison, learning to play the cello; Hannah, a tuba player; Sybil, a violinist; Marcia, a ballerina; and Karen, studying dancing, all become members of the corporation hoping to share in the horse's winnings.

The next day, they all go to Belmont race track to see Skylark. There they meet Allen Hardy, the son of stable owner and successful business man, George Hardy. Allen explains to Nadine that he knows how to treat the horse to make it a winner again. He takes the horse to his father's stable for salt water treatments.

Blackie, informed of what the girls are doing, goes to the Hardy stables. Nadine describes what she has in mind about racing Skylark. He obliges Nadine's wishes and becomes friends with her. However, after Blackie relays the truth about the horse's ability to win races, Nadine becomes upset.

Time passes, Allen says that the horse is in fine shape. All of the girls rise early and go to Belmont to see Skylark in a trial heat. The horse performs well and so is entered in its first race in a long time. Blackie is at the race track and offers Allen 100 to 1 odds on the chances of the horse winning the race. Allen gives him $50. The race is a photo finish with Skylark and Durango at the finish line. Skylark is declared the winner. Harley wins $5000 based on his bet.

However, the vet advises Nadine and the girls that Skylark will never race again. When the horse came up lame, the vet says that Skylark was raced too soon. Nadine informs Miss Lloyd of the situation informing her that she will have to drop out of school. Miss Lloyd responds that if Nadine could only stay in school until the end of the year, she may qualify for a tuition scholarship that would pay her expenses for a full year.

Meanwhile, Blackie is trying to establish a trust fund for Nadine. He subsequently learns that she has dropped out of school. He then attempts to find her.

Allen visits Nadine and asks her to appear on his father's radio program, *The Hardy Hour*, sponsored by his family's food company. She refuses, not wanting her relationship with Allen to get her ahead in show business. Inadvertently, she goes to an audition for *The Hardy Hour* and obtains the job singing on the show. She needs a guardian to sign her contract and asks Blackie to sign the document. When George Hardy learns that Nadine was the girl with the horse who his son was trying to push on him and whom he thinks doesn't have the social standing for a relationship with Allen, he bales out of the deal. When his father won't relent on the matter, Allen says he is through with Hardy Foods.

Allen rushes to Nadine who is depressed and feeling sorry for Allen's decision to give up his job. After leaving Allen, Nadine, not watching where she is going, is hit by a car. She is hospitalized but is expected to fully recover. Glenda says that Miss Lloyd wants Nadine to return to school.

Allen and his father visit the hospital. George Hardy asks Nadine to appear on the radio show he sponsors presumably meaning that her costs at the school will be covered and that she will become a successful singer.

Perhaps, when the actual screenplay for the proposed movie would have been done, the part of Glenda would have been expanded into more of a co-star role instead of a supporting one since Judy was, at the time, a bigger star than Kathryn Grayson. As a news article stated:

> There will be a great vying in singing in "Eight Girls and a Horse" when that picture is made at M.G.M., with present casting plans including both Judy Garland and Kathryn Grayson.
>
> Miss Garland, of course, is widely known and regarded as a heavenly caroler by a majority. For the type of half-blues work that she does, she puts more soul into the business than most. She has the power to move audiences.
>
> Miss Grayson, on the other hand, has had her innings in but one important feature so far seen, "Andy Hardy's Private Secretary," and proved that she possesses the sort of operatic brilliance that first drew the public to Deanna Durbin and which is typical of Susanna Foster.[54]

Two Sisters from Boston (aka An American Symphony) – 1941-1942

As Edward Schallert reported on March 11, 1942, "Joe Pasternak is to return to his musical productions. Such is the word from M.G.M., and the title of his feature sounds imposing. It is 'An American Symphony,' but that is only temporary." Schallert continued, "Judy Garland and Kathryn Grayson as sisters will be the stars. One will portray a popular warbler, the other an operatic. That will afford the needed contrast between their voices."[55]

The first outline for *American Symphony,* done by Herman Boxer and Carl Dudley in 1941, references only Judy Garland as the female protagonist. Judy's father in the story, Paul Carlson, is a once-renowned musical conductor who is now rehearsing an orchestra of children using instruments borrowed from a pawn shop. Judy Carlson, Paul's daughter, works at a settlement house supervising children's playtime.

She takes one of the children named Mary, who is sulking, to the Palmer mansion where Mary's father is the head butler. At the mansion, Judy meets handsome Bill Palmer. Instantly attracted to Judy, Bill decides to take music lessons from her father. Judy explains to Bill the problems her father is having as a teacher and conductor of a children's orchestra. She remarks that her dad's great ambition is to establish a music foundation to advance the talents of deserving children. Bill suggests that they go to the city council since it can help organize cultural societies. For the council to help, signatures of 4.5% of the city's population must be secured along with a reliable sponsor, and $5000.

Bill's mother becomes the sponsor and arranges a concert by the New York Philharmonic to raise the needed money. However, the charity concert will not be helmed by Judy's father but by the orchestra's regular conductor. Bill and Judy come up with a plan to have her father conduct the concert by delaying the Philharmonic's maestro's arrival at the concert hall. Judy's father is given tickets to the event along with the children in his orchestra.

When the arrival of the Philharmonic's maestro is delayed, Judy convinces her father to take over. At the same time, the children from Mr. Carlson's orchestra converge backstage to take their place behind the curtain. The curtain rises, and Carlson and the children begin to play.

Judy and Bill are in the audience gathering the needed signatures required by the City Council. The regular conductor arrives, likes what he is hearing from the children's orchestra, and has his musicians take their place to join with the children in the finale of the symphony.

Apparently, not liking this outline for *American Symphony*, Metro contracted for another one done by Laslo Benedek in December 1941 which included a role for Kathryn Grayson along with Judy Garland.

In this outline, Judy would have played Judy Burgson, working in a nursery for children during the day and singing in a nightclub in the evening which she keeps a secret from her parents. Her father, Oscar Burgson prefers his other daughter's, Kathryn, operatic style of singing. Kathryn is planning to audition for the wealthy Palmer family who sponsor a radio show.

During the audition at the Palmer's, Judy sneaks in and hides behind drapes separating the music room from the rest of the mansion. When the Palmer's son, Bill, notices her, he surprises Judy causing the drapes to come crashing down interrupting Kathryn's audition. Bill's father, who doesn't like Kathryn's singing style, uses the interruption to tell everyone his displeasure with the music.

Later, Bill arrives at the Burgson house to apologize for what happened at the audition. He informs the family that he is apologizing on behalf of his father which is not correct. Bill subsequently learns that Judy is singing at The Blue Jay nightclub in the evenings even though she tells her folks she is working at the nursery.

After the audition with Kathryn, Mr. and Mrs. Palmer had an argument about his objection to Kathryn's singing. They both decide to go on vacation in Florida. Bill takes charge of the upcoming Palmer radio show. He decides to feature both Kathryn and Judy on the presentation. Meanwhile, in Florida, Bill's father receives a letter from Oscar Burgson thanking him for the apology and for giving Kathryn a chance to appear on his radio show. Palmer hurries back home to find out what is going on.

On the *Palmer Hour*, Bill first presents Kathryn singing a song and then Judy performing the same number in a jazz style. The two girls conclude the number by singing a duet in an arrangement of the song for two voices. Since the applause for the sisters is tremendous, Mr. Palmer is congratulated by everyone for a great musical discovery.

Harriet Frank put together a treatment in February 1942 combining elements of both of the foregoing outlines, especially the second one. In the treatment, the names of the characters have been changed. Judy is now Judy Gershen; Katie is still her sister. Their father conducts a junior symphony orchestra.

Katie and the orchestra are auditioning for Frances Evans whose husband Robert doesn't appreciate operatic style music, preferring jazz. Their son, Peter, dates both Judy and Katie but falls in love with Judy. The two sisters, along with the father's junior orchestra, appear on the Evans radio show and are a hit

Metro subsequently engaged Felix Jackson, who wrote *Destry Rides Again* and *Mad about Music*, to do the screenplay with a totally different approach than the ones described above. About six months after the initial announcement of the project, the title was changed to *A Tale of Two Sisters.*

A year passes. Judy is dropped from the film. MGM announces that Kathryn Grayson would star along with Van Johnson in the planned motion picture. *The New York Times* noted that Alan Reed and Jimmy Durante would also appear in the film.[56]

Finally, the movie, now titled *Two Sisters from Boston*, opened in April 1946. Kathryn Grayson was in the film with June Allyson taking over the part originally targeted for Judy Garland. Grayson portrayed Abigail Chandler, from a conservative Boston family, who travels to New York hoping to become an opera singer. But having no luck in the field of opera, Abigail takes a job singing in a Bowery tavern. Rumors get back to her family in Boston about what Abigail is doing. Her mother and uncle decide to travel to New York to see Abigail perform. The young woman lies to her family saying that she really is an opera singer and is able to sneak into a performance at the Metropolitan Opera singing in the background. Martha, her sister, decides to help Abigail really become an opera singer. In the process, shy Martha steps into her sister's scandalous role at the beer hall and ends up meeting a young man named Lawrence (Peter Lawford) with whom she begins a romance.

The final version of this project really diminished the role that Judy Garland may have had and, in the process, made Kathryn Grayson the primary star of the film.

Week End at the Waldorf – 1944

In the mid-forties, MGM decided to do a musical version of its earlier hit *Grand Hotel.* Judy Garland as well as Kathryn Grayson, Jimmy Durante, June Allyson, and Xavier Cugat's band were announced as stars of the new feature, *Week End at the Waldorf.*[57] Except for Xavier Cugat, none of the actors mentioned appeared in the final film released in 1945.

In 1943, writer Edgar Allan Wood developed some ideas for *Week End at the Waldorf* as a musical. Wood is most noted for cowriting the legendary *Wizard of Oz* and 1938's *Everybody Sing* with Judy Garland.

One concept involved Lieutenant Commander Raceg checking into the hotel with his new wife, Yvonne (Judy Garland). Yvonne is a singer and motion picture star who had met the lieutenant while singing for the troops. She performs the number that she sang when her new husband first saw her. Yvonne's grandmother had sung at the old Waldorf Hotel in the 1890's.

The balance of Wood's suggested plot for the remake flashes back to the 1890's featuring famous performers that appeared at the hotel. Also, in the flashback is Mr. Preysing who asks for a secretary to come to his room. Miss Flamm (probably to be played by Kathryn Grayson), the stenographer, naturally can sing and dance. Another guest is Madame Grusinskaya, an opera singer, who also requests Miss Flamm's services. When Miss Flamm arrives at the Madame's suite, Gruninskaya insists that she appear at the Metropolitan Opera House that evening.

In the flashback, Yvonne, in make-up as her grandmother, also performs along with a young male singer, the lieutenant in make-up as another character. Obviously, this concept would have permitted the performance of several songs during the movie with Judy appearing as Yvonne as well as Yvonne's grandmother.

Wood's second proposed concept for a musical version of *Week End at the Waldorf* focused on a young Bostonian named Grayson, whose hobby is doing magic tricks particularly those involving taking items from another person without that person knowing and then surprising the individual when he returns them. Grayson checks into the hotel as does Lon Pratt, an older gentleman, wanting to spend a week at the facility to party. While registering, Pratt hears Viola Fenton singing and invites her to dinner.

Vocalist Hildegarde is giving a benefit at the hotel. Grayson, who is a big fan of the singer's, meets Hildegarde who becomes infatuated with the young man. Grayson also makes friends with Viola Fenton. Hildegarde is jealous of Grayson's attention to the younger singer, but eventually he confesses his love for Hildegarde. After Pratt strikes up a relationship with Viola, he learns that she is married.

Presumably, MGM thought that Wood's ideas were very thin for a musical remake of the film, and so *Week End at the Waldorf* underwent a metamorphosis from a musical to basically a romantic comedy with a dash of corporate wrongdoing thrown in. Actress Irene Malvern (Ginger Rogers) is at the hotel before the premiere of her new movie. Having devoted her life to her career, she is yearning to find the perfect mate. Chip Collyer (Walter Pidgeon), a war correspondent, is staying at the Waldorf for a rest before returning to Europe to cover World War II. Through a series of misunderstandings, when Irene encounters him in her room, she believes he is a jewel thief. Eventually the misconceptions are resolved with Irene falling in love with Chip as he returns to Europe.

Hotel stenographer, Bunny Smith (Lana Turner) desires to live on wealthy Park Avenue. She sees her chance working with hotel guest, Martin Edley (Edward Arnold), who is seeking to sign the Bey of Aribajan to a shady oil deal. At the same time, Bunny develops feelings for Capt. James Hollis (Van Johnson), who has shrapnel lodged near his heart and will have to undergo a dangerous surgery. One can guess with whom Bunny ultimately falls in love.

The only musical interlude in the film is when Xavier Cugat and his band perform a series of musical numbers. At one point in the making of this picture, Charles Boyer was under consideration apparently for the role that went to Walter Pidgeon, and Xavier Cugat was to play an FBI agent disguised as a band leader.[58]

Show Boat – 1944, 1945,1950

The original story line for the Broadway musical *Show Boat* concerned the relationship between Magnolia Hawks, the daughter of Cap'n Andy, the owner of the show boat called "Cotton Blossom," and a young gambler she meets, Gaylord Ravenal as well as the relationship between Steve Baker, the leading man of the show business troupe, and his wife and leading lady, Julie LaVerne.

When the show boat arrives in Natchez, Mississippi in 1887, a fight breaks out between Steve Baker and Pete, an engineer on the boat. After Steve knocks Pete down, Pete swears revenge revealing that he knows a secret about Julie. When Magnolia encounters riverboat gambler Gaylord Ravenal, she becomes attracted to him.

During rehearsals for the evening show, Steve and Julie find that the town sheriff is going to arrest them because Julie is a mulatto passing as a white woman even though her mother was black. Steve informs the sheriff that he also has black ancestors and so their marriage is legal in Mississippi. While Steve is not guilty of miscegenation, the couple must still leave the show since the state forbids blacks from performing for a white audience.

Ravenal is hired as the new leading man for the show boat with Magnolia as his leading lady. The two marry and eventually leave the show and move to Chicago. The two live off the proceeds of Ravenal's gambling but are soon broke. In 1903, Magnolia gives birth to a daughter named Kim. Ravenal leaves Magnolia and his new daughter depressed over his inability to support them. Friends of Magnolia help her find a job singing at a nightclub where coincidentally Julie is the featured performer. Steve has abandoned Julie who has developed a drinking problem. Julie secretly quits her job after hearing Magnolia audition so that Magnolia can gain employment. Magnolia becomes a great singing star after her father helps her win over the crowd at the club.

Flash forward to 1927, Cap'n Andy encounters Gaylord Ravenal and makes plans for him to reconcile with Magnolia. Magnolia is retiring from show business and her daughter has become a Broadway star. Magnolia greets Ravenal warmly and takes him back.

Metro bought *Show Boat* from Universal for $100,000 for Arthur Freed to produce the movie musical. Universal had made two versions of the stage musical – one in 1929 with Laura LaPlante and the other in 1936 with Irene Dunne.

In 1943, Arthur Freed and Oscar Hammerstein 2nd corresponded about the project. In response to Hammerstein's letter asking about mounting a stage revival of *Show Boat* and not wanting it to conflict with any movie version of the play that MGM would release, Arthur Freed replied, "We have not started work on the script, which would take at least four or five months, again with optimism. Preparation and shooting – six months, cutting editing and scoring – two months, previews, etc. – another month, prints, color work, release prints etc. – two or three months, trade showings, advertising, etc. – another three or four months; so add this up and you can see how long it takes to make a picture of this magnitude."[59]

In 1944, Louella Parsons wrote that Judy Garland was to star in the movie version produced by Arthur Freed in the role of Magnolia with James Melton, the likely prospect to play Gaylord Ravenal.[60] The columnist reported eight months later that Gene Kelly would play the role of the riverboat gambler with Judy as Magnolia. In the column, Freed said about the play, "I consider it the finest American operetta ever written and the music by Jerome Kern will live forever."[61]

A year later in 1945, Hedda Hopper wrote in her column that "After the Broadway opening of 'Showboat' next summer, Metro will revive it on the screen with Judy Garland, Gene Kelly, Gloria DeHaven, Walter Huston and Agnes Moorehead."[62] Nonetheless, the following year, Danton Walker wrote that "Gene Kelly turned down the Ravenal role in 'Show Boat,' opposite Judy Garland because he wants to direct the next Sinatra film."[63]

Four years later, in 1949, papers reported that the cast of the MGM film would include, in addition to Garland, Kathryn Grayson, Howard Keel, Frank Morgan, Marge and Gower Champion, and Ethel Barrymore. By the middle of 1949, *Variety* updated readers on the status of the project writing that Judy Garland would star as Magnolia when her health permits and that the picture would start production in about eight months. The article went on to say, "Miss Garland's reinstatement (by MGM) is expected when she recovers which doctors believe she will by that time."[64]

Variety subsequently reported on June 30, 1950, before the actual filming of the MGM version of *Show Boat* had begun, that Metro executives would meet in early July to decide the future status of Ms. Garland at MGM and that an announcement was expected that she now was in contention for the role of Julie LaVerne in the motion picture. "Exes at studio are understood to feel that Miss Garland will be able to undertake part at that time inasmuch as role is not a strenuous one. In addition, part could be wrapped up in around 21 days of lensing. Role has already been built up as it is, actress' numbers now slated to include "Old Man River" along with "Bill" and "Can't Help Lovin' that Man."[65] Evidently, the role of Magnolia for Judy was no longer under consideration.

Nevertheless, by August, 1950, *The New York Times* confirmed officially that Garland's name had been withdrawn from the project and that singer Dinah Shore, who had tested for the role of Julie, was being considered.[66] When the motion picture was finally released in September 1951, Ava Gardner starred as Julie LaVerne, Kathryn Grayson played Magnolia, and Howard Keel had the part of Ravenal.

Chapter 4:

The Young Adult Movie Roles That Might Have Been

At age nineteen, Judy Garland married orchestra conductor David Rose on July 27, 1941. After divorcing Rose in 1944, she married MGM director Vincent Minnelli on June 15, 1945. To show how strong the couple's bonds were to the studio, following is the menu for their betrothal dinner on March 1, 1945 given by the studio: Boula a la Mayer, Filet of Sole a la Loper (fashion designer Don Loper was the host for the dinner), Roast Sirloin of Beef a la Freed, Salade a la Gibbons (art director Cedric Gibbons), Baked Alaska a la Edens (music arranger Roger Edens), and Café Noir a la Ayers (costume and scenic designer Lemuel Ayers).[67]

During the period from 1940 to 1950, Judy made several musicals at Metro including *Meet Me in St. Louis*, *The Harvey Girls*, *Easter Parade*, and *In the Good Old Summertime*. Presented in this chapter are some young adult movie roles for which Judy was considered.

Pot O' Gold – 1940

On the radio show, *Pot O' Gold*, listeners could win $1000 if the host of the show, band leader Horace Heidt, phoned them and they answered. The series, which premiered in 1939, was immensely popular. James Roosevelt, son of President Franklin Roosevelt, decided that a movie about the show would be a sure hit for his first venture as a film producer.

Roosevelt evidently asked Louis B. Mayer to loan out Judy Garland to co-star in the planned film. Mayer rejected the request as he did a subsequent request from Roosevelt for Lana Turner to be in the movie. Roosevelt then settled on another actress as the female character, Molly

McCorkle. Jimmy Stewart appeared as Jimmy Haskell who works for his uncle C. J. Haskell (Charles Winninger) in the health food business.

As Sheilah Graham wrote, "Paulette Goddard has been signed by James Roosevelt to play opposite Jimmy Stewart in 'Pot O' Gold.' Judy Garland and Lana Turner had previously been announced for this role."[68]

The musical featuring the talents of Stewart and Goddard, not known for their singing abilities, began with Uncle Charlie Haskell visiting his nephew, Jimmy, at Jimmy's music store and encouraging him to come to work in the uncle's health food plant. Since Jimmy's music store is not doing that well, he decides to accept the job offer. Uncle Charlie hates music and so is less than thrilled when members of the musical McCorkle family, who are in Horace Heidt's band, practice outside the Haskell factory. C. J. calls the police to remove the music makers. His nephew, on the way to his uncle's office, encounters Molly McCorkle and the band. The band has received an ultimatum from the police to cease rehearsing. Jimmy throws a tomato at one of his uncle's lackeys but mistakenly hits his uncle in the face. Molly thinks Jimmy is a hero.

Jimmy rents a room in Molly's mother's boarding house and becomes a harmonica player with the band. Subsequently, he is arrested for assault and battery but is released on bail. By mistake, Jimmy is transported to jail where he runs into his uncle who has been arrested for contempt of court. The guards let Jimmy go. He promises his uncle that he will retrieve the uncle's wallet to pay his bail.

Jimmy returns to the boarding house where he is feted by the band with a song played on knives, forks, and spoons along with water glasses since the group pawned their instruments to cover Jimmy's bail. He sneaks out of the boarding house and goes to Uncle Charlie's home to retrieve the uncle's wallet. Back at the boarding house, Molly fantasizes about Jimmy and her in medieval times and sings "Do You Believe in Fairy Tales?" To Horace Heidt, Jimmy admits that he is indeed Charlie's nephew. He reimburses the band the $200 for his bail so they can get their instruments back.

Jimmy comes up with the idea for the band to play in his uncle's basement and pretend that no one hears any music but his uncle.

Convincing Uncle Charlie that he is going mad and needs a rest, the uncle heads to Canada for a vacation.

Jimmy invites Heidt's orchestra to play on the Haskell radio show where the band and Molly perform an elaborate production number for radio listeners who, of course, can't see the performance. Molly finally learns that Jimmy is really C. J.'s nephew and, in anger, announces that the Haskell radio program will give away $1000 each week. Jimmy finds a way to honor the announcement and comply with government laws by choosing phone directories at random using a "wheel of fortune." Once a directory is selected, a spin of the wheel identifies a page number from the directory and then a line on the page to finally select the person to call. *Pot O' Gold* becomes very popular, and Jimmy asks Molly to marry him.

Produced by James Roosevelt Productions, the film was released by United Artists on April 3, 1941. It was the one and only film to be made by James Roosevelt.

Coincidentally, Jimmy Stewart filmed *Pot O' Gold* at the same time he was making *Ziegfeld Girl* at MGM with Judy Garland, Lana Turner, and Charles Winninger. To say the least, *Pot O' Gold* was not the greatest movie Stewart ever made. In hindsight, MGM was correct in not loaning out Judy to make this film that included so many unremarkable musical numbers.

Claudia – 1941

"Judy Garland's itching to do 'Claudia' in pictures, and is doing daily trips to 'Uncle Louie's' office trying to talk him into letting her," so read an item in a fall 1941 Hedda Hopper column.[69]

Claudia started out as a novel by Rose Franken which she adapted into a Broadway play. The movie version was released in 1943 by Twentieth Century Fox and starred Dorothy McGuire in the lead role with Robert Young as her architect husband, David.

The film concerned a young, newlywed couple living on a farm in Connecticut. Claudia is naïve, financially irresponsible, and overly dependent on her mother, Mrs. Brown, for advice. Mrs. Brown is ill but doesn't want her son-in-law to tell Claudia about her condition. Meanwhile, a local playwright begins flirting with Claudia, and she decides to accept an offer to sell the farmhouse without discussing it with her husband.

Claudia explains to David that she permitted the playwright to kiss her to show her husband that other men find her attractive. She also sees how hurt her husband is when she announces she sold the farm thinking that he would believe that she is a smart businesswoman. Claudia then begins having dizzy spells and goes to a doctor who confirms her pregnancy.

Claudia's mother phones David informing him that her doctor advised her that the prognosis for her condition is dire. Claudia has listened to the phone conversation on an extension but pretends, when her mother arrives, that she is not aware of her mother's condition.

Claudia tells David that she does indeed want to remain on the farm. When Mrs. Brown visits, she feels that her daughter may be aware of her condition even though she hasn't told her. She realizes that Claudia will have the strength to let her go.

Claudia was one of the top ten grossing films for Fox in 1943 and so a sequel was commissioned titled *Claudia and David.*

Dragon Seed – 1942

Based on the Pearl Buck novel, *Dragon Seed* was a 1944 release from MGM telling the story of Jade Tan, played by Katherine Hepburn, who resided in a Chinese agrarian village invaded by the Japanese before World War II. The village inhabitants attempt to placate the invaders but with no success. Jade and her husband Lao Er Tan (Turhan Bey) along with other siblings of the Tan family whose patriarch is Ling Tan (Walter Huston) join the resistance and escape to the mountains where they manufacture guns and ammunition. They return to the village and organize a local resistance group. The wife of Ling Tan's cousin reveals to Wu Lien (Akim Tamiroff), the local merchant collaborating with the Japanese, details about the resistance group. Word of this revelation gets back to Ling Tan and Jade.

Jade goes to Wu Lien thinking of poisoning him but decides to poison the Japanese general in charge of the invading force. She places the poison in the sauce for the duck being served at a lavish meal. The general's staff eat the duck sauce and die. Wu Lien, whom the general believes is responsible for the incident, is shot.

Jade informs her husband of what she did. The two go back to the mountains but return once again to their village to instruct the villagers to burn their houses and crops so that the enemy has no food for the winter. Jade implores Ling Tan to help rid the country of the enemy so that the next generation of Chinese can live free. She and her husband return to the hills. Ling Tan decides to burn down his house and fields and accompany Jade and his son. His neighbors do the same. Jade's young son is the "dragon seed" for future generations to fight for their country's freedom.

Before Hepburn was selected for the project, several actresses were under consideration for the role of Jade. They included Greer Garson, Luise Rainer, and Hedy Lamarr. In August 1942, Louella Parsons reported, "Jack Conway, who will direct 'Dragon Seed,' after 'Assignment in Brittany,' is finished, will also test Judy Garland for the role of Jade. That is a surprise, for I thought Hedy Lamarr had the part all sewed up. I am not so sure Jade is right for Judy, who doesn't seem the type for the exotic young Chinese matron."[70]

Lamarr and Garson were eliminated as candidates for the role because they failed the Oriental make-up tests. One could always question why no Oriental actress was considered for the main part, but, after all, this was 1940's Hollywood. In any event, casting Judy in the role would have been a stretch for her at the time since, in her prior movies, she had never played an ethnic character.

The Story of Gaby Des Lys – 1943

In this planned biographical film, Garland would have appeared as actress/singer/dancer Gaby Des Lys, who entertained audiences in the early part of the twentieth century. Born Marie Elise Gabrielle Caire in 1881, she selected her stage name as a contraction of *Gabrielle of the Lillies.*

Appearing mainly on the stage, Des Lys did act in one American silent movie, *Her Triumph* in 1915. She also made a handful of features in France before she passed away in 1920.

Des Lys was popular as a dancer in Paris and London particularly known for dances like the Grizzly Bear, Turkey Trot, and one named after her – The Gaby Glide. As a singer, she recorded two songs in Paris, "Tout en Rose" and "Philomene."

In her personal life, she reportedly had a relationship with King Manuel II of Portugal who supposedly gave her a pearl necklace valued at $70,000.

A year before her death, she had contracted the Spanish flu and underwent several operations on her throat to cure an infection caused by the virus. Her death was due to complications from the infection.

In 1933, MGM bought a story titled "Gaby Deslys" written by Melville Baker and John Kirkland to turn into a movie, but the film company sold the story to Paramount a few months later. The Baker/Kirkland treatment was seen as a possible vehicle for Greta Garbo.

The treatment opens in 1921 with newspaper reports of Gaby Deslys' death and then flashes back to Vienna in 1910. Lilli Karvas is working as a waitress in the Froeliche Katz, a hangout for cadets from the Austrian Imperial Military Academy. She falls in love with one of the cadets, Max von Grunstahl. He decides to throw away his military career and marry Lilli, but reconsiders and, in the middle of the night, leaves Lilli without a word of farewell. She never really recovers from the shock of his departure.

Lilli drifts from one job to another ending up working in the chorus of a cheap cabaret. There she meets newspaperman Jimmy Harris to whom she relates her story of heartbreak. He tells her that she can stay at his flat on a platonic basis for as long as she wants.

During a chorus routine with other dancers, she slips and falls with the audience laughing at her misstep. Among those in the audience is King Manuel of Portugal who sends her a huge bouquet of roses as an expression of sympathy.

Jimmy, taking advantage of a tip he receives that revolution is brewing in Portugal among people dissatisfied with the king, shapes the incident of the flowers into a story that a woman is chiefly responsible for the king's shortcomings as a monarch. The story states that Gaby Deslys of Marseilles, France is that woman. The day after the story is published, Lilli awakes to find herself Gaby Deslys. Jimmy sees to it that Gaby is photographed with pearls given to her by a rich suitor. The pearls turn out to be some of the crown jewels from Portugal.

In the meantime, Max von Grunstahl has left his regiment determined to marry Lilli. Nevertheless, he is unable to locate her unaware that she is now using the name Gaby Deslys.

During the next nine years, Gaby stars in stage productions in Paris, London, and New York. She thinks that she has forgotten Lilli until Jimmy Harris reappears. She also encounters an American millionaire, Henry Chase, whom Gaby has half-promised to marry. When he finds Gaby in a harmless conversation with Jimmy Harris in her bedroom, he concludes that she is a harlot who will give herself to anyone. Chase shoots himself outside of Gaby's house.

She decides to go back to Vienna for rest and registers at a small hotel as Lilli Karvas. Gaby locates Max whom she still loves, and they spend time together. On the last night of their vacation, Max insists that they spend time at the upscale Hotel Metropole where Lilli is recognized as Gaby. Seeing a newspaper photo of Lilli as Gaby, he realizes that she is the notorious woman of the world. Nevertheless, whether she is Lilli or Gaby, he still loves her.

Gaby responds, "No, Max, it can't be. You'd always be reminded. You'd never really believe in me again. . . Just remember what you've told me - - about the things you want to do. Do them for me. Just as if I were with you."[71] During the night, she leaves him as he left her years ago.

In the final scene, Gaby lies dying in Paris attended by Jimmy Harris and her doctor. She instructs Jimmy to report that she refuses to have an operation on her throat because it would mar her beauty. Newspapers carry the story. Millions read of Gaby Deslys who "got her reputation by losing it;" the woman without a heart who never gave her love.

About ten years later, MGM writers, Alfred S. Reynolds and Irving Guttman, developed a treatment called *The Story of Gaby Deslys* which differed significantly from the Baker/Kirkland one. According to Hugh Fordin's book, *MGM's Greatest Musicals*, this was the first treatment dated March 12, 1943 intended for Judy Garland.[72]

The treatment opens with Phillipe Renoir and Henry Colbert trying to interest Raul Poirot in backing a show they want to produce. They entertain him at the Café Pierre in Paris, circa 1906. However, Poirot is more interested in viewing Gaby Deslys' performance than in discussing the show. They invite Gaby to their table where she mentions that she would like to achieve fame and wealth. She says that love is for adolescents and fools. She leaves the café with Poirot and presumably spends the night with him. He gives her 200 francs which she deposits in the bank. She then goes on a shopping spree at Cartier's but asks Mr. Cartier to put her purchases totaling fifteen hundred francs aside and she will pay for them in two weeks. Gaby begins dating Cartier.

Later she meets Phillipe Renoir again who is a newspaper columnist and asks him to do a publicity article about her hoping it will get her into the Folies Bergere. She becomes a member of the chorus but yearns for more success.

Newspapers cover a fight between Cartier and young Armand Dubois over Gaby at a Paris nightclub. She is pleased with the publicity and mentions that Dubois is richer than Cartier.

Thanks to continuing publicity from her devoted friend, Phillipe Renoir, Gaby becomes a headliner at the Folies. She also has a new lover, Armand Dubois, who showers her with jewelry. When Dubois is forced to leave Paris for a couple of weeks, Gaby takes up with even more wealthy, Ricardo Gomez, a good-looking Argentinian. When Dubois returns to Paris, Gaby has a hard time making both him and Gomez believe that each is her "only one."

At the Folies, Gaby's lead song is "I Sing the Glory of the Parisian Girls" which is a tremendous hit. She next meets Baron Ramon Crespi. For a while, she tries to date the Baron, Ricardo, and Dubois at the same time but soon realizes that she is in love with Crespi who buys her a small house in the suburbs. She confesses to Renoir that she would marry Crespi if he asked her.

The Baron is called back to his home country of Portugal. Gaby reads in the newspapers that the King of Portugal and his eldest son have been assassinated and that the Baron has now become king.

Time passes, and Phillipe Renoir secures financial backing for a play and leaves the newspaper business. Having conquered Paris, Gaby goes to London to perform, but her success there is interrupted by a throat infection. The Baron, now King Manuel of Portugal, is in London to attend the funeral of British King Edward. Learning of Gaby's illness, he hurries to her beside. They confess their love for each other but realize that Gaby could never be his queen. After Gaby regains her strength, her doctor counsels her that she is susceptible to such infections.

In 1910 there is another revolution in Portugal. King Manuel is exiled to England with the rumor that he lost the throne because of Gaby and the million dollar necklace he gave her while hunger and unemployment were rampant in his country. Gaby is heartbroken when she learns that the former king is getting married to someone else.

Gaby receives an offer to perform in the United States. Performing in *Honeymoon Express*, Gaby hires a dancing partner named Harry Pilcer. He develops a new dance for her called the "Gaby Glide" and becomes infatuated with her. She responds that she is interested in him only as a dancing partner. She invites him to return with her to Europe to perform.

Her new show in Europe, *A La Carte*, is another success. During the run of the show, Pilcer hears rumors of Gaby's affairs with men but refuses to believe them.

Gaby, in Paris at the beginning of World War I, entertains the French and British troops. Pilcer remains in love with Gaby, but his love is not returned. In London, a noted playwright announces that he will create a play for Gaby and produce it himself. The playwright doesn't want Harry to appear in the production. She has difficulty informing Pilcer of this. Pilcer finally realizes that the things he has heard about Gaby's affairs are true when he sees the playwright and a rich department store owner arguing over her. Pilcer leaves Gaby's employ and goes to work for Gladys Valise, who impersonates Gaby's act.

Renoir re-enters Gaby's life telling her that his last show flopped and asking to borrow money to put on a new show. Gaby agrees to appear in the show for almost no money. She also reunites with Harry Pilcer and confesses that she loves him. They become engaged, but Gaby wants to wait a year before getting married so she can make more money and then retire.

The war is still going on and Harry enlists when America enters the conflict. Gaby wants to buy a large house in France for the two of them and lots of children. Since he has been assigned as a translator to the U.S. Intelligence Headquarters in Paris, Harry is still able to appear nightly in performances with Gaby. The war ends, and Harry and Gaby agree to marry.

As perhaps inevitable, things do not work out as planned. With Harry having to report to Headquarters for an urgent job of translation, Gaby is caught in the rain and is taken home by a male friend, who becomes drunk at her place and spends the night – but not with her. In the morning, Harry returns to the house and sees the man leaving. Thinking the worst, he leaves Gaby and returns to America.

Gaby develops another serious throat infection. Learning of her illness, Harry returns to Europe. Before he comes back, Gaby makes up a will setting up a trust fund for an orphanage that she has been supporting for a number of years and authorizing the sale of her jewelry with proceeds to go to the poor. Harry returns as Gaby lies dying. Pointing to a picture of the orphanage for which she established the trust, Gaby says that she told him that their new house was for many children. As the camera pans to the picture of the orphanage, the audience would see happy children playing as the movie ends.

Even though no Gaby Deslys movie was made in 1943, MGM did not abandon the idea. In 1948, Robert Thoeren presented a third treatment about the life of Deslys to Arthur Freed. This one, titled *Gaby and Harry*, had the cooperation of Harry Pilcer as a technical advisor. Unlike the other treatments, Thoeren, who would later write the screenplays for *The Fighting O'Flynn* and *Captain Carey, U.S.A.*, focused almost exclusively on the relationship Deslys had with Pilcer.

It opens with Gaby appearing in a show for the Shubert organization in America. Her act consists of walking up and down a staircase and undressing behind a veil much to a let-down for the producers. Realizing this, she investigates what Americans consider to be a good show and sees Harry Pilcer perform for the first time.

She hires Pilcer to be her dance partner. Opening night of her show proves to be a success with Harry dancing as beautifully as Gaby looks. As much as Harry is infatuated with Gaby, she treats him as her personal valet running errands for her.

Before going back to Europe, much to everyone's surprise, she spends her last evening in America with Pilcer saying she likes him very much and invites him to return with her. Arriving in France, Gaby is welcomed by a huge crowd including a richly dressed Argentinian, Sr. Rodriguez, whom Harry dislikes.

Monsieur Vernon, the producer of the Folies Bergere, wants to feature Deslys in a new show with the financial backing of Rodriguez. Gaby insists that Harry be given a part in the show. Meanwhile, Rodriguez is jealous over newspaper reports that Gaby married Harry on the ship while traveling to Europe. She denies all such reports.

When Gaby fails to meet Harry at the appointed time, he attempts to find her, eventually locating her at dinner with Rodriguez. Trying to avoid a brawl, Gaby asks Rodriguez to leave. He departs in anger, while Harry threatens to return to America. After pleading with him not to go, Harry decides to stay. Gaby admits that she is not a good actress. She says that she is only successful if people talk about her affairs, jewels, and wealth. Harry responds that Gaby doesn't need scandals to stay on top. He will teach her to become a better performer.

Newspapers report the mysterious disappearance of Gaby from the limelight as Harry develops new dance numbers and teaches her. They try out their new act in a little theater with a small audience and Monsieur Vernon in attendance. Vernon is convinced that all of Paris will want to see Gaby's new act. Since Rodriguez has withdrawn financial support from Gaby's show, Vernon decides to finance it.

The day before the opening, disaster strikes with inspectors condemning the building as unsafe. Harry suggests that Gaby pay for the steel supports for the balconies to make them safe, but Gaby refuses. Gaby tells Harry that all of her money had gone to build a small hospital for Dr. Martel who treated her when she was young. Vernon tests the strength of the theater balconies by having heavy sandbags placed on them. They pass the test, and the show goes on. Harry and Gaby then tour the continent with the show.

Harry's father makes a surprise visit to Europe informing his son that Mr. Ziegfeld wants Harry to appear in a show in America. The father implores Gaby to let Harry take advantage of this opportunity. She says that she will miss him but that she won't stand in his way.

Reporters ask Harry's father for information about his son for a newspaper article. The resulting headlines say that Harry and Gaby are splitting up. Harry is irate at his father and decides not to go to America. The father leaves but remains in France for a period of time.

At the beginning of World War I, Gaby decides to stage a new show in London. Harry receives word that his father is in a hospital in Marseilles and goes to see him. The hospital is run by the doctor who cared for Gaby as a child. Harry's father is not really sick. He just wants his son to learn the truth about Gaby and the medical facility. The doctor says that Gaby has never contributed any money to the place. His father asks his son to return to America with him. But first Harry explains that he has to confront Gaby. Gaby is so happy to see him that Harry is unable to say anything about the hospital. Eventually, he mentions Dr. Martel. Gaby doesn't know how to reply. Harry says that no matter what her reply, he'll never believe her again.

The war is now a year old. Gaby is living alone in her house. Harry has joined the Lafayette Squadron to fight the Germans. Gaby wants to become a Red Cross nurse but is rejected due to her medical report. She decides to fund a recreation home for soldiers.

Harry is invited to a party a general is throwing for some of the brass. When he arrives, the general introduces him to Gaby. The orchestra plays the first bars of their best known dance number. Gaby steps on to the floor followed by Harry. The famous team is united. After the dance, the orchestra plays again. Harry leaves and numerous men take their turns dancing with Gaby.

The general tells Harry about the recreation hospital in Paris that Gaby established and that she donated money to its support under the condition that her contribution would remain anonymous. He also informs Harry that Gaby is ill, and, after all the dancing, has to be taken by ambulance to a hospital in Paris. Harry accompanies her. In the ambulance, he speaks of his love for her and reminisces about all the happy times they had together. She listens with half-closed eyes. Gaby then sleeps peacefully as the ambulance enters the grounds of the hospital Gaby has founded.

The Thoeren treatment dated May 2, 1948 was the final one done for Garland related to this never-made film project at Metro.

The Moon Vine – 1943

First performed on Broadway in February 1943, this comedy was written by MGM screenwriter, Patricia Coleman.

Based on an initial script, the story was set at the turn of the twentieth century in Mansfield, Louisiana, focusing on eighteen-year-old Mariah Means, a college student who strives to be an actress. Her best friend is Ellen Hatfield, the daughter of the president of the local college.

The Means family wants Mariah to marry Roscoe, a missionary in Australia to whom Mariah is engaged. Strother Means, Mariah's unmarried older sister, considers her to be undisciplined and not respectful of authority.

Ovid Carter, an acquaintance in the town, gives Mariah a copy of a theater magazine which she devours. Ovid is in love with Mariah, but, being the offspring of unmarried parents, the townspeople would frown on his asking any girl to marry him. Mariah is really in love with Danny

Hatfield, Ellen's brother, whom Mariah has never met. She has only seen his photo. Danny had run away from home to become an actor and entertainer.

Mariah comes up with the idea for Ellen to write a letter stating that Roscoe has died in Australia, thus freeing Mariah to pursue Danny. Who should then turn up in town but Danny Hatfield? Mariah meets him and agrees to keep the secret that he is an actor.

In love with Danny, Mariah informs her mother that Roscoe has died. Being a good actress herself, she goes into mourning for two weeks. The relationship between her and Danny blossoms. Danny says that when they are alone, her personality changes. "She is warm and sweet like a moon vine that opens after dark." He confesses that he loves Mariah.

A group of young men from the town, who like to serenade women, put on an impromptu show in front of Mariah's house observed by Ovid. She tells Ovid that Danny is a professional actor.

In a conversation with Ovid, Danny reveals that he fled a murder scene in New Orleans before coming to Mansfield. He is wanted as a witness in the upcoming trial of the accused. Ovid responds that if Danny doesn't testify, he is protecting all the prejudice and false morals that his father, Dr. Hatfield, has been fighting. Danny decides to become a witness despite Mariah's protestations. She asks Danny to leave her.

At a revival meeting, Danny confesses everything – that he is an actor and what he witnessed in New Orleans. Furthermore, he says that, after testifying, he will renounce show business and go to Australia to become a missionary.

Two weeks later, Danny returns to Mansfield after testifying at the trial with the town backing him one hundred percent. When he sees Mariah, they kiss. Mariah's grandmother informs her that she has received a letter from Australia. Danny asks Mariah to marry him but, feeling guilty about lying concerning Roscoe, she can't say "yes."

Danny points out that he has received an offer for the two of them to perform in a show but discarded the letter when he decided to go to Australia. Ovid advises Mariah to tell Danny the truth about Roscoe before Danny goes away. Ovid had sent the Australia letter to force Mariah to be honest. She finally explains to Danny about Roscoe and says she loves Danny. She and Danny decide to elope and take the job in the theater.

According to *The Billboard*, the stage production of *The Moon Vine* would "... probably make a good B movie."[73] Despite lukewarm reviews, the producer wanted to keep the show going for three weeks to encourage movie producers to adapt it for motion pictures. Reportedly, Paramount had invested in the play.

About the time the play opened on Broadway, Arthur Freed sent a memorandum to Judy Garland asking her to read the script and let him know what she thinks of it as a starring vehicle for herself.[74] Garland would have appeared as Mariah Means. It is not known if she ever replied to Freed's memorandum, but the play never became a movie.

Cabbages and Kings – 1944-1947

"The time has come, the walrus said,
To talk of many things,
Of shoes and ships and sealing wax,
Of cabbages and kings ..."

This quote from Lewis Carroll opens the screenplay by Stella Unger and Paul H. Rameau of a fantasy musical take-off on *Alice in Wonderland*. Since Unger was a lyricist, unlike most screenplays for musicals, the script for *Cabbages and Kings* includes the words for the songs.

Seventeen-year-old Alice Smith is graduating from high school. She is hoping to receive an award for Dramatic Arts but the award goes to another girl. After everyone departs the graduation ceremony, Alice stays behind. Disappointed at losing the award, Alice speaks with the school's janitor, Lem. He remarks that no one gets everything they want all the time but everybody receives some happiness some of the time. He then points out to Alice the novel, *Alice in Wonderland*, saying that there is a lot of truth in it and that it is her turn to go crashing through the looking glass.

Alice starts working in retail sales but is terminated for various reasons. Her third job is for Bandorf's on 5th Avenue in their accounting department. She helps an important customer of the store, Mrs. Bagly-Ellerton, by locating a special bottle of perfume. As she accompanies the customer in an elevator to have the perfume bottle wrapped, the elevator becomes stuck between floors. Alice is fired again.

Seeking consolation and having no confidence in her abilities, Alice goes to Coney Island trying to find Lem who has left a note stating where he is. She stops at the House of Fun entranced by the voice of King Coney, a carnival barker.

Coney gives Alice a dime so she can enter the fun house. Inside, she bumps into one of the mirrors and disappears falling through space. She lands on a chess board lawn framed by beautiful gardens with the chess pieces called "gremlins" performing everyday tasks.

Alice is led to the center of the lawn by the Queen. The King and Queen say they want to help Alice and that all of her fears exist only in her mind. The King hands her an address card for her to obtain another job.

Alice goes to the address which is an advertising agency where she is hired as a receptionist by the Duchess. Mr. Dee is the boss; Manny, the mad hatter assists Mr. Dee. The boss is depressed because a potential client has not shown up for his appointment. With Alice at the receptionist's desk, Lemmy Turtle arrives saying he wants to manufacture wonder lamps to make dreams come true. He asks Alice what her dreams are. She responds that she would like to sing on the radio.

Mr. Dee, the Duchess, and Manny are thrilled to meet Turtle, the client for whom they have been waiting. Turtle tells the group that he wants to sink millions into his lamp project. The slogan for the product will be "Turtle's wonderlamp will make your dreams come true for a dollar ninety-eight." He seeks to use radio to sell his product and sponsor the show with Alice singing. Alice auditions, but the only song she can think of singing is "Silent Night." As for an announcer on the show, when Alice suggests King Coney, Mr. Dee launches a city-wide search for him.

Turtle's Wonderlamp Program starring Alice Smith and King Coney goes on the air with Coney showing up at the last minute. He improvises the opening and introduces Alice as America's Dream Girl Number One.

Women in the audience rush the stage to mob King Coney tearing off his clothes. He achieves instant fame. Photographers ignore Alice and only want to take pictures of Coney.

The media hail Coney as the new radio discovery. Turtle advises Alice to fight for recognition as well as for Coney's love since Alice is infatuated with him.

Dee informs Alice and Turtle that the International Television Company wants her and Coney to make a test film for them. Because Alice is so depressed over Coney and the media ignoring her, Turtle says that the test should be canceled, but, when he mentions that maybe another girl could be hired to take Alice's place, she perks up and goes for the test.

At the TV studio, when Coney sees Alice all dressed up, he is impressed. The director is smitten with her. For the test, the duo sing "There's a Brand New World Around the Corner" in a big production number.

At the end, Coney kisses her. She gives him a smack on the face and runs off.

Later, Coney asks Alice why she hit him. She replies that he has been acting arrogant and conceited and is in love with himself. He leaves. Alice sings and fantasizes dancing with Coney. Coney admits to himself that Alice may have been right about him being conceited. He seems to have fallen in love with Alice.

At a tea party given by Lady Kemble for Alice, Turtle plays the piano and Alice sings. Coney confesses his love for Alice as they kiss.

At that moment, two police officers arrest Alice for taking the perfume bottle that Mrs. Bagby-Ellerton had purchased. In the courtroom, a version of the court in *Alice in Wonderland*, Coney defends Alice. He makes a liar out of Bagby-Ellerton and questions Alice about the incident. She says that she is only guilty of having a heart full of dreams. The jury finds that no crime was committed.

Back at the House of Fun on Coney Island, Alice is lying on the ground unconscious. She regains consciousness and realizes that it was all a dream. She had tripped and hit her head against a fun house mirror and fell into an excavation underneath the House of Fun. She gives Coney a kiss. In the middle of the bystanders, Lem appears and leads her away from the fun house. She says that she has fallen in love and states that she will never be afraid of anything again.

Coney follows them and tells Alice that he is studying the law at night school. He asks her for a date.

Blind pianist Alec Templeton contributed to the music for the planned motion picture. MGM purchased the screenplay for around $100,000 in 1944 and, at one time, wanted to title the film, *Alice from Brooklyn*. Later that year, newspapers reported that Judy Garland, Jimmy Durante, and Van Johnson would play the main characters with Judy as Alice Smith, Durante as Lem and Mr. Turtle, and Johnson as King Coney.[75] While the story was a take-off on *Alice in Wonderland*, the character of Alice Smith, who spends much of the screenplay in a fantasy land, may remind Garland fans of a similar film Judy starred in – *The Wizard of Oz*.

Three years after the studio bought the screenplay, Templeton was asked about the status of the planned film. He stated that "Already MGM has over $300,000 invested in it. June Allyson was cast as Alice, supported by Jimmy Durante and Gene Kelley (sic)."[76] *Variety* reported that Cyd Charisse would have a featured role in the project to be produced by Joe Pasternak and directed by George Sidney.[77]

Cabbages and Kings was originally intended as a Broadway musical. MGM purchased the rights to the play from producer Mike Todd when he was about to be inducted into the Navy.

Even with the change in cast, the movie was never made.

The Girl from Rector's – 1945

Various stars were considered for this never-made film adaptation of the stage play, *The Girl from Rector's*. First, Lana Turner and then Ann Sheridan were reported to play the lead in the motion picture adaptation. And then Lucille Ball was a candidate for the main role. The role called for a girl who can sing. Lucy told gossip columnist Sheilah Graham, "But, I can dub a song better than any one else in the business," in response to the report that Judy Garland would receive the role.[78]

The movie was to be directed by Jack Cummings with a screenplay by Dorothy Kingsley from the play written by Paul M. Potter.

Rector's, a fancy restaurant in New York City, turned "Broadway into Paris" during the 1890s and 1900s and introduced lobster, champagne, and supper dances.

The play translated from a French farce focused on Richard O'Shaughnessy Van Arsdale, a playboy bachelor living in New York City being mentored by his friend Andy Tandy on how to party. Richard was dating Loute Sedaine, the girl from Rector's, who like Tandy, enjoyed drinking and carousing.

After Tandy leaves Richard's apartment, Aubrey Muboon, a professor at Chicago University and Richard's cousin, visits Richard to discuss the professor's upcoming marriage to a Battle Creek, Michigan socialite, Marcia Singelton. Muboon had argued with Marcia's mother, Mrs. Copley, who then called off the marriage, and Aubrey wants Richard to fix things with his prospective mother-in-law.

Richard attempts to apologize to Mrs. Copley and her daughter on behalf of Aubrey when they stop by his house, but he ends up talking the mother and daughter out of the impending marriage. Mrs. Copley suggests that Richard become her daughter's fiancé. He confesses that he does love Marcia, and she consents to marrying him.

Richard doesn't want to tell his cousin what happened, but he does explain the situation to Tandy. Also, he doesn't want to inform Loute that their relationship is over thinking that she will be in Buffalo for a while and that, when she returns, he will already be married. However, Loute unexpectedly returns to Richard's place as does Aubrey now knowing that his cousin will be marrying his former fiancée.

Richard travels to Battle Creek for his wedding. The couple is married by the town's mayor, but Mrs. Copley insists that, before the marriage can be consummated, a religious ceremony also must occur. Mrs. Copley invites her cousin, Judge Caperton, to the ceremony. Her husband and Marcia's stepfather, who has been in Martinique surveying his sugar plantation, will also attend.

Who should show up at the Copley house but Tandy and Loute? Tandy turns out to be General Witherspoon Copley who had really been in New York City (not Martinique) using the name Andy Tandy. Loute is Judge Caperton's rarely seen wife, Juliette, who also had been in New York. Loute has been the model spouse of a man she sees about one month out of the year telling him that she spends most of her time in Europe working on charitable causes. Richard is startled to see Tandy, and Loute faints when she sees Richard.

Richard is concerned that when Loute recovers, she will reveal everything and say that he belongs to her. Tandy asks Loute to invite Richard that evening to dinner at a roadhouse to entrap him.

But before the roadhouse meeting, Aubrey stops by the Copley house after receiving a special invitation from Mrs. Copley. He sees Loute and informs Mrs. Copley that Loute is the girl from Rector's for whom Richard has a special affinity. Mrs. Copley thinks that Aubrey is mad particularly after he spies Mr. Copley and says that Copley is a friend of Richard's and a comrade of Loute's.

Loute then accompanies Richard to dinner at French Charley's to test his love for Marcia. Mrs. Copley, her husband, and her daughter, and the professor all go to the place as well. Richard informs Loute that their love affair is over despite Loute coming on to him. Tandy (Mr. Copley) masquerades as the restaurant's waiter, the judge as the bellboy, Mrs. Copley as the cashier, and Marcia and the professor as honeymooners. All deny to Richard who they really are. Fed up with the charade, Richard departs the dining room. The professor tells Loute that he still wants to catch Richard kissing her thinking that Marica will then divorce Richard and marry him.

Tandy has rented rooms in the establishment for everyone. When they all go to their rooms, Loute decides to change rooms with the Copley's maid leading to a comedy of errors. The judge, Loute's husband, enters what he thinks is her room only to find the maid. Tandy enters Loute's room mistaking it for his wife's. Richard then seeks to talk with Loute. He gives her a good-bye kiss, goes to Marcia's room, and tells her he loves her. The professor, hoping to find Richard kissing Loute gets Mrs. Copley to accompany him to what he thinks is Loute's room only to find the maid and the judge. After the judge claims to his wife that he is innocent, she forgives him. All relationships are in good standing except for the professor and Marcia.

While not a musical, songs in the original play included "Baby Doll," Loute's nickname, and "Haste to the Wedding."

Young Bess – 1945-1949

In 1945, Metro bought the film rights to *Young Bess,* a novel by Margaret Irwin about the early years of Elizabeth I of England before she became queen. A July 1945 column by Sheilah Graham noted that Angela Lansbury would be ". . . a natural for the movie lead in 'Young Bess.'"[79]

A script was completed by Jan Lustig and Arthur Wimperis in 1946 with Deborah Kerr then testing for the lead role in 1947. A May 1948 report stated that Robert Taylor, Deborah Kerr, and Elizabeth Taylor were testing for the main roles in the movie with Elizabeth Taylor now being considered for the role of young Bess. By August 1948, Walter Pidgeon and Janet Leigh were being auditioned for the main roles. Filming of the movie kept being pushed back.

In January 1949, columnists reported that James Mason was being sought for the lead male role in the picture and that he wanted Judy Garland to play young Bess. As E.V. Darling wrote about this choice: "I rate myself one of Judy's greatest admirers. I have been interested in her ever since I saw her play in that great college background film titled, "Pigskin Parade.'" He stated further, "However, I can't see her as young Queen Bess. I believe the part should go to an English actress. Still I could be wrong. That fellow James Mason is a shrewd judge of things theatrical."[80] As with other stars considered for the film, neither Mason or Garland got the roles.

The movie, not made until 1953, eventually starred Jean Simmons as the daughter of King Henry VIII and Ann Boleyn and a future queen. The feature opens with the death of Elizabeth's cousin, Mary Queen of Scots, with Elizabeth then ascending to the crown.

The film flashes back to Elizabeth's formative years after her mother had been beheaded, and she has been banished from the palace. Whenever Henry VIII remarries, Bess is brought back to the palace to meet her new stepmother, but is normally banished again until Henry marries his sixth wife, Catherine Parr who takes Elizabeth under her wing.

When the king passes away, both Bess and her stepmother depart the palace when young Edward, Elizabeth's half-brother, becomes king under the protectorate of Ned Seymour. Bess falls in love with Admiral Tom Seymour, Ned's brother, but he loves Catherine Parr and they marry.

Nonetheless, Bess continues to have feelings for Tom Seymour and he for her. Learning about the situation between her husband and Bess, Catherine explains that she needs Tom and will not let him go. Later, Catherine dies, and Tom goes out to sea. When he returns, he visits Bess. Tom Seymour is then arrested for treason by his brother and is executed. Young King Edward dies, Ned is executed, and after Mary dies, Elizabeth becomes queen.

James Mason and Judy Garland would eventually star in a film together – 1954's *A Star Is Born.*

Forever – 1946

Judy Garland was set to star in this emotional love story written by Mildred Cram. If the film had been made, it would have been Judy's first picture after the birth of her daughter, Liza.

According to Hedda Hopper's column, Judy's co-star in the project may have been Gregory Peck.[81] Music and lyrics were to be written by Richard Rodgers and Oscar Hammerstein.

The story line from the Cram novel concerned a young man named Colin preparing to be born once more – this time as an Englishman. The concept is that after people die, they remain as they were, but, then, before rebirth, they begin to change to assume the adult form of their next life.

Colin travels to France to meet a novelist in the afterlife who can tell him about England. He eventually meets Julie in a meadow on the outskirts of Chaminox, France. She is the loveliest girl he has ever seen. Julie's mother has just married and will give birth to her in nine months. Julie and Colin kiss and are together for several magnificent days. Colin explains that when reborn, they will find each other in twenty-seven years.

Colin is born in a small town called Devonshire. He grows up and attends Eton and then goes to college to become a lawyer. He dreams of visiting Chaminox and, after turning twenty-six, he remembers that he is to marry a pretty girl.

Meanwhile, Julie, living in Philadelphia, is experiencing the same dreams about France as is Colin. However, Julie is married to a successful banker, Bunny Wilson. Wilson's bank decides to send him to Paris on business. While Bunny is working in Paris, Julie drives to Chaminox and visits a field in the countryside where she encounters Colin. They think they have seen each other before. The couple kisses and forgets almost everything about their current lives except their love for each other. Julie thinks she must leave Chaminox and return to Paris to be with her spouse. The next day, she returns to the field to say "good-bye" to Colin but can't leave him.

Colin's client, whom he had been trying to contact, gets in touch with him and asks him to go mountain climbing in the Alps. Colin promises Julie that he will see her later that day to go dancing at their hotel. Julie receives a note stating that her husband will be driving to Chaminox that day to see her. Bunny wants Julie to drive with him to Geneva to meet a client of his. Bunny drives very fast on mountain roads and ends up plunging their vehicle into a river. While he survives, Julie does not. She awakens in her hotel room and discovers that she is deceased.

In the afterlife, Julie is reunited with Colin who himself was killed in a mountain-climbing accident. The two spirits find each other on the dance floor of the hotel, but their memories begin to fade. Colin pulls Julie close to him. Julie lifts her head to Colin and says, "This is forever."

The screen rights to the Mildred Cram novel were originally purchased by actress Janet Gaynor as a starring vehicle. In the mid-1930s, Gaynor sold the rights to MGM. Metro thought of Norma Shearer and then Joan Fontaine for the lead before considering Judy Garland.

Notes to Arthur Freed about *Forever* indicate that the climax of a film, based on the Cram work, should focus on the lovers seeking to fulfill their life and love by returning from death into this life and not with Julie and Colin seeking fulfillment of their love in the afterlife.[82]

The issue of reincarnation also seems to have been a problem in adapting the novel for the screen. A letter to Voldemar Vetluguin of MGM states that, ". . . the idea of filming 'Forever' was dropped because of difficulties encountered in bringing the reincarnation theme to the screen. Because of opposition to such a religious theme by various church groups, this is completely understandable."[83] The idea was to downplay the concept of reincarnation and instead base a potential movie on similar emotional experiences that are passed on from mothers to their offspring resulting in the two lovers searching through their lives for one to love.

Pride and Prejudice – 1947-48

MGM wanted to produce a musical adaptation of Jane Austen's novel with Judy Garland in a starring role. According to columnist Hedda Hopper, Garland informed her that she planned to spend a year in England with her then husband Vincente Minnelli and her daughter Liza. "The chief purpose of the trip is to remake 'Pride and Prejudice' in its original setting. Judy will star in it, and Minnelli will direct."[84] In addition to Judy, Lucille Bremer and Peter Lawford were to appear in the film. The latter would no doubt have the role of Fitzwilliam Darcy with Judy as Eliza Bennet.

Obviously, in planning to spend time in England for *Pride and Prejudice*, Garland didn't realize that the screenplay for the remake was set in eighteenth century America.

Sally Benson, who had written *Meet Me in St. Louis*, was initially commissioned to write the screenplay for *Pride and Prejudice*. Arthur Freed was to produce the motion picture with Richard Rodgers and Oscar Hammerstein II doing the music.

The script focused on the Bennet family living in Meryton, outside Philadelphia in the mid-1850's.[85] Mr. and Mrs. Bennet resided on a small estate called Longbourne with their five daughters – Lydia, the youngest, Kitty, Mary, Eliza, and Jane, the oldest. All the daughters are looking for marriage prospects. They sing a number called "Dying on the Vine" about too many berries that die on the vine because there's no one to pick them, and when there are too many girls and no men to choose them, they, also, die on the vine.

Mr. Bennet receives a letter from William Collins who, according to Bennet's father's will, will inherit Longbourne after Mr. Bennet dies. Mrs. Bennet is concerned that her and her daughters will then be homeless. Collins, a clergyman, has arrived in Philadelphia and will be visiting the Bennet's. He is in Philadelphia with his patroness, Lady Catherine de Bough, and is looking to marry.

While Jane and Eliza are picking flowers in the garden for the guest room, Charles Bingley and Fitzwilliam Darcy stop by. The sisters assume that one of the gentlemen is Collins. The two men introduce themselves and ask for directions to Netherfield Park. Bingley has bought the place and intends to live there with his sister, Caroline, and with Darcy.

Bingley fixes up Netherfield and invites everyone from Meryton to attend a ball. Mrs. Bennet thinks that Bingley is a good marriage prospect for one of her daughters. She wants her girls to take up singing and dancing to impress him. Professor Peale agrees to give the girls singing lessons.

Eliza tells her father that Jane is interested in Bingley and that Mary could have Mr. Collins. Nevertheless, he encourages Eliza to think of Collins as a marriage prospect for herself. Mr. Bennet sings "A Bird in the Hand" based on the saying "A bird in the hand is worth two in the bush." Eliza replies that if you have your mind set on one bird in the bush, a bird in the hand is too tame.

When the invitation to the Bingley ball arrives, the girls get ready for the dance which includes a cotillion where each man invites a girl to dance with him.

At the ball, Bingley dances with Jane. Darcy dances with Caroline Bingley but keeps his eyes on Eliza who is dancing with Captain Wickham, a young soldier. Mrs. Bennet wants Eliza to dance with Darcy instead. Darcy thinks that Eliza is tolerable but not attractive enough for him. Overhearing this, Eliza leaves the ballroom and enters the living room where Professor Peale is at the piano. Captain Wickham and Darcy also come into the room where Jane begins singing about the type of resting spot she wants when she passes away.

At the end of the song, Jane invites Eliza to also sing. She chooses the same song but performs it in Spanish thinking no one will know it is the same. However, Darcy understands Spanish.

After Eliza's song, Wickham reveals that he knows Darcy. Wickham's father had managed the estate for Darcy's father who had willed that Wickham should receive a sum of money and a clerical living upon his death. Darcy, according to Wickham, did not abide by his father's wishes.

Caroline Bingley wants to marry Darcy, but he still has eyes for Eliza. The cotillion part of the ball begins with a song about the type of dance partner Darcy is seeking. Again, Bingley dances with Jane; Professor Peale with Mary; and two officers with Kitty and Lydia. Both Darcy and Wickham approach Eliza. She chooses Wickham for the dance.

When the Bennet's return home, they find that Mr. Collins has arrived and is sleeping in the guest room. The next morning, they all meet Collins. Jane receives an invitation for dinner that night at Netherfield. Mr. Collins takes Jane and Eliza for a walk in the village where they encounter Darcy and Bingley. When Jane learns that Bingley will be having dinner with Darcy in Philadelphia that night, she is very disappointed. Darcy and Bingley leave and sing a song about an evening in Philadelphia, dinner at the Mansion House, and nothing like being young and single and having a high old time.

After returning home, Jane tells Eliza that she doesn't want to go to Netherfield for dinner if only Caroline will be there. Eliza encourages her to go but to pretend that she's coming down with a cold so she can spend the night there. To make it convincing, Eliza plans to have Jane get caught in a downpour on the way to Netherfield.

Mr. Collins speaks to Eliza and asks her to marry him. She declines the proposal. He replies by saying that he will continue to propose to her until she answers "yes." He commences a song describing how life would be like with him. The song indicates the ideal life his wife will have as she is called upon to cook, clean his clothes, write his letters, and keep in good with the right people.

The following morning, Mrs. Bennet wants her husband to convince Eliza to marry Collins. He remarks that her mother will never speak to her again if Eliza doesn't marry Collins and that he will never speak to Eliza again if she does marry him.

A groom from Netherfield stops by to tell the Bennet's that Jane is really sick from a cold. Eliza rushes to Netherfield to see her sister and stays at the estate until Jane recovers. That night, Darcy asks Eliza to dance with him while Caroline plays the piano.

Time passes. Jane feels better. Bingley, Darcy, Jane, Eliza, and Caroline have a picnic. Jane and her sister prepare to return to Longbourne.

Eliza, who plans to have a party at Longbourne for everyone, has a Maypole erected. Mr. Collins announces that he will take the occasion to say he is engaged to Eliza. Jane and Eliza bribe some local children to dance around the Maypole. Darcy, the Bingley's, Mr. Collins, and Professor Peale all attend the affair along with the Bennet's neighbors.

The children reluctantly begin their Maypole dance with the sisters singing about the dance. At the end, the children walk away from the pole. Eliza then begins dancing with Darcy, Jane with Bingley, Lydia dances with Wickham, Mary with the professor, and Kitty with one of the young soldiers. After the dance, Collins runs after Eliza who falls into Darcy's arms as he hides her from the man. Darcy and Eliza subsequently argue about Wickham and his pursuit of Lydia. Collins returns from his search for Eliza and informs Darcy he plans to marry her and that Jane expects to be engaged to Bingley. Darcy walks away and describes to Bingley what Collins told him.

Later, Jane receives a message from Caroline Bingley that she, her brother, and Darcy are leaving Netherfield and going to Philadelphia. Jane is devastated by the news. Mr. and Mrs. Bennet along with Eliza and Jane decide to depart for Philadelphia as well. Mr. Bennet arranges for Mr. Collins to stay with their neighbors, the Lucas's, while they are away. The Lucas's happen to have a marriageable daughter named Charlotte. Before they leave, Collins gives Mr. Bennet a letter of introduction to his patroness, Lady Catherine.

After a month staying at the Mansion House hotel in Philadelphia, the Bennet's invite Caroline Bingley to their suite. She informs the Bennet's that Darcy's sister has arrived from England and that her brother plans to marry Georgianna Darcy. After Caroline leaves, Jane faints. A doctor is called who says that Jane is too sick to travel back to Longbourne. The Bennet's also receive news that Mr. Collins is marrying Charlotte Lucas.

Darcy stops by the hotel suite to see Eliza. He says how much he loves her and asks for her hand in marriage. He confesses that he did inform Charles about Jane's intentions for marriage. Eliza rejects his proposal. When he asks why, she brings up his treatment of Captain Wickham. He says that Wickham is unscrupulous and then leaves.

Later, Eliza attends dinner at Lady Catherine's where she meets Guy Fitzwilliam. He asks her why she is so prejudiced against Darcy. He informs her what Darcy thought of Jane trying to marry Bingley and that, if one of the Bennet daughters didn't get a proposal, another one would surely. Aghast at the comment, Eliza leaves and returns to the hotel only to be told that Lydia has eloped with Captain Wickham.

Upon hearing the news of the elopement, Mr. Bennet goes after the couple to prevent the marriage. Jane, Eliza, and Mrs. Bennet return to Longbourne, but, before they go, Eliza encounters Darcy who tells her that he had no idea that Jane was really in love with Bingley. He then informs her that Wickham received 3000 pounds from him and wanted to use it to study law – not seek a clerical living. Wickham had spent the money frivolously. Wickham also asked Darcy's sister to elope with him, but Darcy prevented that.

Christmas Eve and Eliza, Jane, and their mother are back at Longbourne. Mr. Bennet returns with news that Lydia has married Wickham. Through Mr. Darcy's efforts, Mr. Bennet gave the couple $50,000.

Lady Catherine visits the Bennet's to speak with Eliza about Darcy. She wants to know if Darcy has asked Eliza to marry him. She asks Eliza to promise her that she will not marry Darcy. When Eliza refuses to make such a promise, Lady Catherine leaves.

Mummers stop by the Bennet's along with Professor Peale, dressed as Father Christmas, who sings a song about old Father Christmas. Bingley is also there and sings about himself as a Turkish Knight. Professor Peale bends tenderly over Mary. Wickham stands with his arm around Lydia. Jane looks lovingly at Charles, while Eliza and Darcy look longingly into each other's eyes. Kitty is the only daughter without a man.

Evidently, Metro did not consider the script by Sally Benson to be acceptable, and so the studio assigned Sidney Sheldon to redo it. Sheldon completed only a partial script. It did not differ dramatically from the one Benson had done.

He did suggest one song be sung by Eliza as she walks through the family garden before Collins' arrival thinking about his proposal of marriage. He suggests that Eliza sing about how things will be when women are running the world. [86]

The Sheldon effort did add a little more humor to the tale of the Bennet daughters. For instance, when Darcy and Bingley first stop by the Bennet estate to ask for directions, Eliza assumes that one of the men is Mr. Collins and talks about his offer of marriage. Darcy quickly clears up her confusion.

In any event, Metro never produced a musical version of *Pride and Prejudice*.

The Actress (Years Ago) – 1947

"Judy Garland and Spencer Tracy will star in the movie version of *Years Ago*, with Garson Kanin directing – for Metro of course! Spencer is the spirit behind the deal and when Kanin was recently in Hollywood he went to town on selling him the idea of himself for the Frederic March role, and Judy for the part played by Ruth Gordon in the play. . .",[87] so reported Sheilah Graham in an April 1947 column.

Written by actress Ruth Gordon, the Broadway play was an autobiographical account of Gordon's dreams of becoming a theater actress.

Ruth Gordon Jones wants to drop out of school to pursue an acting career in New York City. But her father wants her to continue her education and become a physical education teacher. He explains to Ruth that if she receives her high school diploma, he will then support her during her first few months in New York thinking he can give her the bonus he expects from his factory job. When he confronts his boss about the bonus, his boss fires him. Ruth is determined to go to the city even without her dad's money. Her father gives her a treasured spyglass he kept from his days as a seaman to sell in New York City in order for Ruth to have enough funds to pursue her acting career.

The film, retitled *The Actress* and directed by George Cukor, was released in 1953 with Jean Simmons – not Judy Garland as Ruth and with Spencer Tracy as her father.

Romance on the High Seas – 1947

The working title for this Michael Curtiz production was *Romance in High C*. The movie concerned a husband and wife, Michael (Don DeFore) and Elvira (Janis Paige) Kent, each jealous when either spouse looks at a member of the opposite sex. They suspect each other of cheating on them. After a series of vacations cancelled because of business emergencies at Michael's firm, the Miracle Drug Company, Elvira books a trip to Rio De Janeiro. Subsequently, she finds that the travel agency mixed up her passport photo with that of nightclub singer Georgia Garrett (Doris Day). Again, Michael says he is unable to go because of business. The mix-up of passport photos offers Elvira the opportunity to spy on her husband in New York to see if he is having an affair, while she sends Georgia, posing as her, on the ocean cruise. Michael, suspicious of his wife willing to travel alone, hires a private detective, Peter Virgil (Jack Carson), to go on the cruise to shadow Elvira who is really Georgia.

While on the ocean voyage, Georgia and Peter eventually fall in love. Naturally complications ensue with Peter, feeling guilty about falling in love with the woman he was hired to watch, and Georgia trying not to tell her current boyfriend, Oscar Farrar (Oscar Levant), that she is impersonating another woman. Concerned about what is actually occurring on the cruise, Michael and Elvira each separately fly to Rio, arriving at different times. Michael sees a billboard in the hotel lobby that Mrs. Kent is scheduled to sing in the casino. When Michael visits the hotel room registered to his wife, he sees Georgia, but returning later to the same room, he encounters his wife. All confusion is finally cleared up with Elvira introducing Georgia in the casino as the singer and Peter and Georgia as well as Michael and Elvira all back together.

Judy Garland was the first choice to play Georgia Garrett. But MGM refused arrangements to loan her out to Warner Brothers which distributed the motion picture. Also, evidently Curtiz had second thoughts about Judy given reports of her behavior during the making of *The Pirate*.[88] Doris Day made her movie debut in this film. *Romance on the High Seas* was released in 1948.

The Stratton Story (aka Monte Stratton) - 1947

Based on a true story about baseball player, Monte Stratton, this biographical film was announced in 1947 with Van Johnson playing Stratton and Judy Garland as his wife Ethel. As Sheilah Graham reported in her column, "Van Johnson has never worked with Judy Garland in all the years they have been at Metro. But this is being taken care of – Van hopes."[89]

Monte Stratton from Texas has a knack for pitching a baseball. He lands a tryout with the Chicago White Sox and is given a contract in 1934. Stratton falls in love with a young woman named Ethel and proposes marriage. Later, Ethel gives birth to a baby boy. In the 1938 off-season, Stratton accidently shoots himself in the right leg while hunting in Texas.

His leg has to be amputated. Supported by his wife and with an artificial limb, he learns to walk again, begins practicing his pitching, and makes a successful minor league comeback in 1946.

The motion picture was released on May 1949. Neither Johnson nor Garland played the leads. June Allyson had the role of Mrs. Stratton, while Jimmy Stewart appeared as Monte Stratton. In the same year that *The Stratton Story* was released, Judy did star in a feature with Van Johnson – *In the Good Old Summertime.*

Peg O' My Heart – 1948

To be produced by Joseph Pasternak, *Peg O' My Heart* was to star Judy with Robert Stack as her co-star according to Louella Parsons in her November 28, 1947 column, "Hollywood Today."

In 1951, MGM announced that Debbie Reynolds and Carlton Carpenter instead of Garland and Stack would appear in the lead roles of this venture.

Peg O' My Heart, written in 1912 by Hartley Manners, as a starring vehicle for his wife, Laurette Taylor, concerned a poor Irish girl who comes to live with her English aunt and her cousins – the Chichester's.[90]

Widow Mona Chichester and her offspring – Ethel and Alaric, learn from the newspapers that the bank in which their life savings has been deposited has gone under. At the same time, Margaret O'Connell comes to stay with the Chichester's after Mrs. Chichester's brother, Nathaniel, dies. A lawyer for Nathaniel informs Mrs. Chichester that her brother left an estate of 200,000 pounds. While he left no money to his sister, he did provide for a niece who is the child of Mrs. Chichester's late older sister. To anyone who undertakes the education of Margaret, who prefers to be called Peg, 1000 pounds a year will be paid. If, at the end of one year, Peg is found to be unworthy of further education, she will be returned to her father in America and given 250 pounds a year. But if Peg is able to continue her education, she will receive 5000 pounds a year upon reaching age twenty-one. Nathaniel wished that his sister be first approached about making a lady out of Peg.

Knowing that the Chichester family is now penniless, Mrs. Chichester considers making a home for Peg and educating her in order to receive 1000 pounds. Nathaniel's lawyer, Mr. Hawkes, will visit on the first day of each month to evaluate the progress that Peg is making.

Peg meets Jerry, a lord and one of Alaric's friends. Jerry was with Uncle Nathaniel when he passed away.

A month goes by with Mr. Hawkes due to return for his first evaluation. Mrs. Chichester doesn't know what to say to him since every tutor she has hired for Peg has resigned. Jerry stops by to ask Peg to a dance which Mrs. Chichester forbids. Nonetheless, wanting to go to the dance, Peg sneaks out in the middle of the night to meet Jerry.

When Peg returns, she sees Ethel with a bag packed planning to run off with a married man who says he loves her. Peg informs Ethel that the man is no good having flirted with Peg. The two females attempt to sneak upstairs, but Peg falls down creating a commotion and waking the rest of the family. Peg tries to cover for Ethel by telling Mrs. Chichester that she went to the dance. Peg threatens to leave and return to her father in America.

The next morning, Alaric informs his mother that he thinks that Peg is a lost cause and that he will have to find work to support the family. His mother tries to convince Alaric to marry Peg pointing out that, when she is twenty-one, she will be receiving 5000 pounds a year. Alaric agrees and proposes marriage to Peg when she awakens. Peg laughs at him refusing the marriage offer. Alaric is relieved.

Hawkes arrives for his evaluation. He recommends that Peg continue her training with the Chichester's. Nevertheless, when Peg refuses, he agrees to book passage for her on the next ship to America.

Jerry visits and reveals that he is the executor of the uncle's will and intends to inform Peg of all of the will's provisions despite protests from Hawkes, Alaric, and Mrs. Chichester. Ethel explains to Peg that the only income the family has is from the stipend they will receive for Peg's training. However, Jerry advises the family that the bank in which the Chichester's had all of their money will re-open meaning that they won't be penniless. In the end, Jerry proposes to Peg, and she accepts.

The film was never produced in the late 1940s or in the early 1950s.

Annie Get Your Gun – 1949

Metro purchased the screen rights to this Broadway play from Irving Berlin hoping to make it a starring vehicle for Judy Garland after she completed *In the Good Old Summertime.*

The story concerned the on-again, off-again romance between Frank Butler, the sharpshooter in Buffalo Bill's Wild West troupe and Annie Oakley who, after winning a shooting match between her and Butler, is asked to join Buffalo Bill's show. Frank and Annie become romantically involved until Buffalo Bill gives Annie top billing. Subsequently, Annie is adopted by Chief Sitting Bull and receives a letter from Frank ending their relationship. Frank joins a competing Wild West show, the Pawnee Bill troupe. Annie and Frank eventually get back together, but Frank becomes jealous of Annie and argues with her over who is the better sharpshooter. The two decide to settle their argument in a shooting match. Chief Sitting Bull persuades Annie to deliberately lose the match to Frank so he can regain his pride. She does, and Frank proposes marriage to her.

Arthur Freed named Busby Berkeley as director of the movie despite the fact that Garland and Berkeley had a bad relationship when he worked on *For Me and My Gal* and *Girl Crazy*. During the last week of March 1949 and the first week of April, Judy recorded "I've Got the Sun in the Morning," "I'm an Indian Too," "You Can't Get a Man with a Gun," "Doin' What Comes Natur'lly," "Let's Go West Again," and "The Girl that I Marry." With her co-star Howard Keel who played Frank Butler, she recorded "Anything You Can Do I Can Do Better" and "They Say It's Wonderful" as well as "There's No Business Like Show Business" with Frank Morgan and Keenan Wynn in addition to Keel.

Stating that she wasn't feeling well, Garland began missing filming sessions for the picture. Evidently, around this time, Judy sent a note to Arthur Freed saying, "I can't thank you enough for the beautiful flowers nor for the wonderful, wonderful note on Monday. Glad you miss me – but I'll be back." She signed the note "Annie."[91]

Judy in scenes from Annie Get Your Gun.

In early May, when Arthur Freed looked at twelve days of filming on the project, he indicated that Berkeley had no conception of what the film was about. By May 5, Busby Berkeley was replaced as director with Charles Walters taking over. A few days later, on May 10, with continuing delays in shooting the film, Judy was removed from the project and placed on suspension. On May 29, the star entered Peter Brent Brigham Hospital in Boston, Massachusetts hoping to cure her dependence on prescribed medications.

Evidently, a contributing factor in Judy Garland's problems in making *Annie Get Your Gun* was that she had to portray a character in Annie Oakley that was totally foreign to the parts she had played in her previous MGM films. According to Charles Walters, "She (Judy) couldn't decide whether she was Ethel Merman, Mary Martin, Martha Raye, or herself."[92].

Strictly Dishonorable – 1950

Based on a 1929 Broadway play by Preston Sturges, MGM wanted Garland to co-star in *Strictly Dishonorable* with Ezio Pinza. The story, set in New York City in the late 1920s, concerned an opera singer named Augustino "Gus" Caraffa played by Pinza who encounters his biggest fan – a young woman from Mississippi, Isabelle Parry. When Gus insults the singing talent of Marie Donnelly, the wife of newspaper owner, Harry Donnelly, Harry vows vengeance on Gus hoping to ruin his career. He hires a news photographer to take photos of Gus which he then edits to show the singer in embarrassing situations.

While performing as an extra in Gus's opera, Isabelle creates a disaster on stage bringing down the curtain on the opera. With her fiancé, Henry, she goes to Gus's apartment to apologize to him. Gus's agent, Bill Dempsey, believes that Harry Donnelly hired Isabelle to make the opera singer look bad. Isabelle apologizes to Gus and ends the engagement with her jealous fiancé. Dempsey hires a photographer to take a picture of Gus and Isabelle kissing hoping to plant a story in the papers about the young woman before Donnelly can publish his own story. Dempsey and Gus discover that Isabelle was not hired by Donnelly, but, before they can send the photo to the papers for a favorable story about the singer, Donnelly's men steal the photograph. Dempsey suggests that Gus and Isabelle marry to show the public that Gus was really kissing his wife.

When Donnelly learns that Gus and Isabelle are newlyweds, he recruits Lili, Gus's former girlfriend, to have her sue Gus for breach of promise. Lili wants Gus to annul the marriage. He signs the annulment papers and moves into Dempsey's apartment. Isabelle and Gus's mother work together to have Gus and Isabelle reconcile. In the end, they do and go to Niagara Falls for a honeymoon.

According to columnist Sheilah Graham, the motion picture was scheduled to begin filming in November 1950 with the hope that Judy, after leaving the production of *Annie Get Your Gun*, would be well enough to resume making motion pictures by then.[93] Janet Leigh was hired to replace Garland in the feature which was released in July, 1951.

A prior version of Preston Sturges' stage play was filmed by Universal in 1931 with Paul Lukas as Gus and Sidney Fox as Isabelle. It adhered more closely to the play than did the 1951 MGM film.

Opera singer Augustino Caraffa meets Isabelle in a hotel speakeasy. She is engaged to her domineering boyfriend, Henry. After finding that Isabelle danced with Gus while he was out of the room, Henry commands that Isabelle leave with him. She refuses, and they break up.

Gus befriends Isabelle and takes her to his apartment in the hotel. He tries to seduce her but is interrupted by an elderly judge who lives in the apartment above Gus's. Isabelle falls in love with the opera singer. That night, Gus sleeps in the judge's apartment leaving Isabelle in his. The next morning, Gus realizes that he is in love with Isabelle and, despite Henry trying to make amends with Isabelle, she agrees to Gus's marriage proposal.

Since Ezio Pinza was a singer and Paul Lukas was not, MGM apparently revised the story line of its version of *Strictly Dishonorable* to feature Pinza performing opera and operetta type numbers. One wonders if the studio would have made further changes to the story if Judy Garland and not Janet Leigh had played Isabelle making the female lead a singer as well.

Chapter 5:

The Musical Roles That Might Have Been with Fred Astaire and Gene Kelly

While at MGM, Judy starred in two movies with Fred Astaire – *Ziegfeld Follies* and *Easter Parade* and in four films with Gene Kelly – *Ziegfeld Follies*, *For Me and My Gal, The Pirate*, and *Summer Stock*. Described in this chapter are additional features that might have been – some with Astaire and some with Kelly.

Fred Astaire with Judy Garland.

Anchors Aweigh – 1942

Judy was announced as starring with Gene Kelly in MGM's musical *Anchors Away*. As Louella Parsons opined, "As for Judy, the Navy certainly won't object to her being the gal the gobs all fall for (in the movie, of course). Until her health suffered she was one of the most popular visitors at Navy base camps. If I were a fortune teller I'd say that the little Garland girl is coming under a favorable star again after a bad year."[94]

Due to the success of the Garland-Kelly film *For Me and My Gal*, Metro wanted the pair to appear together again in *Anchors Aweigh*. But the project was delayed until 1944 prompting the studio to replace Judy with Kathryn Grayson.

Directed by George Sidney from a screenplay by Isobel Lennart and produced by Joseph Pasternak, *Anchors Aweigh* told the story of two Navy sailors – Joe Brady (Gene Kelly) and Clarence Doolittle (Frank Sinatra) on a four-day leave in Hollywood. When a little boy named Donald is found wandering around the streets wanting to join the Navy, the police ask Joe and Clarence to convince the boy to return home. At his house, Joe and Clarence babysit the boy until his Aunt Susie (Kathryn Grayson) returns. Susan explains to the two sailors that she has been seeking work in music and wants to perform with Spanish conductor, Jose Iturbi. To impress Susan, Joe tells her that Clarence is a personal friend of Iturbi's and can arrange an audition for her. After the two fail to speak to Iturbi, Joe and Clarence want to confess the truth. When Susan runs into Iturbi at the studio commissary, he has no idea about any audition. Susan wants to phone Joe, with whom she is falling in love, to castigate him, but Iturbi stops her and agrees to a screen test which turns out well.

Anchors Aweigh may very well be best remembered for an animated sequence in which the Gene Kelly character dances with Jerry, the mouse, from the *Tom and Jerry* series of cartoons.

The Belle of New York – 1943- 1945

Originally, this movie would have starred Judy Garland with Fred Astaire in a tale about a playboy who falls in love with a young Salvation Army worker. *The Belle of New York* started out as a Broadway musical with Edna May playing a worker for the Salvation Army and then became a silent feature starring Marion Davies. Arthur Freed was to produce the film for MGM beginning in spring 1944 with Van Heflin co-starring.

Newspapers reported in 1943, that Garland had started to take dancing lessons from Renee de Marco to prepare for her role in the project.[95]

During rehearsals for the film, Judy dropped out of the project. Kathryn Grayson was then announced as the star of the picture along with Keenan Wynn and Lina Romay. Hedda Hooper subsequently announced that Metro had canceled the project.[96]

The original musical concerns Violet Gray, a Salvation Army worker, who becomes heir to a fortune belonging to eccentric Ichabod Bronson. When Bronson, President of the Young Men's Rescue League and Anti-Cigarette Society, discovers that his son, Harry, intends to marry an actress, Cora Angelique, he decides to make Violet the recipient of his wealth. However, Violet, who is in love with Harry, wants him to inherit his father's money. Violet performs a risqué Folies Bergère number causing Ichabod to change his will back to Harry as heir. Harry then falls in love with Violet.

Around the time Judy was interested in the female lead role in the project, Irving Brecher did a screenplay for the proposed film dated July 24, 1944. Judy's character was named Angela; Fred Astaire's character, Charlie Hill. Angela is a volunteer for the Salvation Army and is better known as the "Belle of New York." She is completely dedicated to her work and is distressed because most of her converts are more interested in her than in saving their souls. When Angela meets Charlie, she thinks the fun-loving playboy only wants to mock her and so is very distant with him. However, he is "so happy that he walks on air about five or six feet off the ground. As he realizes that for the first time in his life he is in love, he rises higher and higher, now walking over the house-tops."[97]

Eventually, Charlie is convinced that he can find happiness with Angela if he teaches her to be a little bad while she teaches him to be a little good.

MGM subsequently revived the project with the film being released in 1952. Fred Astaire and Vera-Ellen had the main roles in the motion picture adapted by Chester Erskine from the play by C.M.S. McLellan. Vera-Ellen appears as Angela Bonfils, an attractive female working at a mission house sponsored by the Daughters of Right, which seeks to reform indigent men. Astaire's character, Charlie Hill, is a wealthy womanizing bachelor who is about to marry a female sharpshooter, Dixie McCoy. Before the ceremony, Charlie encounters Angela and is instantly infatuated with her; she not so much with him. Leaving the sharpshooter at the altar, Charlie visits Angela proclaiming his love for her. She replies that he should seek employment before allowing him to join her movement.

Charlie messes up the jobs he gets including a messenger for Western Union, a sanitation worker, and a street car driver. After traveling on a street car with Charles, Angela begins falling in love with him, and she consents to marriage.

The night before the wedding, male friends of Angela stop by Charlie's apartment and convince him to toast the bride. He becomes inebriated and misses the wedding. Charlie says he is selfish and undependable, and Angela falls out of love with him signified by no longer feeling her body rise in the air.

Missing Charlie, Angela has the notion of acting like a frivolous woman to begin a new relationship with him. She dresses in a form-fitting gown, starts smoking, and goes to a casino where Charlie is a singing waiter. When Charlie sees her, he is worried when she orders champagne. He gives her sparkling soda. After Charlie starts a fight with a man hitting on Angela, Charlie again says he loves her. As their bodies rise in the air, the two are in love as the crowd sings "When I'm Out with the Belle of New York." In the final scene, the couple appears in wedding attire still dancing in the air.

The movie had mostly forgettable songs but great choreography, as one expects from a Fred Astaire film.

Yolanda and the Thief – 1944

Garland had wanted to play the female lead in this MGM musical directed by her husband at the time, Vincente Minnelli, but was persuaded that the better role for her would be the main role in *The Harvey Girls.*

The film starred Lucille Bremer in the role of Yolanda Aquaviva that Garland had wanted. Yolanda, having been raised in a convent, can now go out into the secular world and manage the estate and fortune she has inherited. Victor Trout (Frank Morgan) and Johnny Riggs (Fred Astaire) are two grifters running from authorities. They are in Patria, a South American country, that does not have an extradition treaty with the United States. Johnny learns that Yolanda is on the same train as he and Victor. Yolanda is returning home but knows nothing about managing money. When Johnny and Victor go to the Aquaviva estate, Johnny overhears Yolanda praying to her guardian angel for guidance in carrying out her new responsibilities. He arranges to meet Yolanda, pretending that he is her guardian angel and calling himself Mr. Brown. She pledges to follow his advice.

During a technicolor dream, Johnny imagines marrying Yolanda. Upon visiting her estate, Johnny has her sign a power of attorney and steals bonds from her safe worth $1 million. When she realizes what she signed, her aunt says that is the first step to marrying Mr. Brown. After Johnny dances with Yolanda at a festival in the country, he says "good-bye" to her and explains that she can now manage her affairs on her own. He returns the bonds with a love letter and attempts to leave the country by train. However, Yolanda's real guardian angel, Mr. Candle (Leon Ames), prevents the train from crossing the border and advises Johnny to become Yolanda's husband. He returns to her, and they marry.

Yolanda and the Thief was released in 1945. In that same year, Judy married the director of the film, Vincente Minnelli. Among the correspondence in the Arthur Freed Collection is an undated thank-you note from Judy to Freed stating that "The Yolanda goods arrived today and almost took my breath away. It is a beautiful present including the inscription and I am very proud of it. My deepest thanks."[98] What specifically the gift and the inscription were is unknown.

Take Me Out to the Ball Game – 1946

Gene Kelly and Stanley Donen developed the story line for this musical in 1946. The concept was that Kelly and Frank Sinatra would star as baseball players during the period 1905 to 1915. Kelly would be a short stop; Sinatra, a second baseman, and Leo Durocher, a first baseman. The trio would be called O'Brien, Ryan, and Shaughnessy. O'Brien and Ryan really wanted to be entertainers instead of ball players. Problems arise when C.B. Higgins is willed the baseball team. Higgins turns out to be a woman played by Kathryn Grayson.

The idea was presented to Arthur Freed who decided that Judy Garland should play the female owner of the team instead of Grayson. George Wells was assigned the task of developing a screenplay for the picture with Garland.

As Gene Kelly's biographers described, "Judy's continuing drug problems and absenteeism on other films, however, led to this idea being dropped. Freed then thought of June Allyson, but she was pregnant and declined. Esther Williams, who had been very successful in a string of movies in which she swims, was next."[99]

The original screenplay written by George Wells between October 10, 1946 and February 14, 1947 about a baseball team named the "Wolves" included the characters of Eddie O'Brien (Kelly) and Dennis O'Ryan (Sinatra). The team's manager was Michael Gilhuly; Slappy Burke was the team's trainer.

O'Brien and O'Ryan are performing their vaudeville routine in Pottstown, Illinois and have yet to join the Wolves for spring training. They plan to play one more season with the team before becoming full-time vaudevillians.

Upon arriving in Florida for spring training, the two players learn that the ball club has been inherited by K. C. Higgins, a distant relative of the late owner, J. B. Newhouse. Higgins arrives the next day by train.

As Wells describes in his screenplay,

> On the train steps stands Katherine C. Higgins, (Judy Garland) in a trim traveling dress and carrying a small valise. She glances about for a moment and then steps off the train, heading for the hack stand. Slappy has changed his course and is moving toward her – his head turned away. They bump violently. Katherine's valise is torn from her grasp, the contents spilling out on the platform.[100]

At the hotel, Eddie and Dennis meet Katherine not knowing that she is the team's new owner. Eddie asks Katherine, "On the trip down you didn't happen to run into a little fathead by the name of Higgins, did you?" Katherine responds, "A little fathead." Dennis, "Yeh, the new owner. Some lame brain from Providence, Rhode Island."[101]

Before Katherine informs them of who she really is, Eddie and Dennis reveal that they break training rules staying out late at night and that Gilhuly is none the wiser.

The following day, Katherine gives Eddie pointers on batting showing that she is knowledgeable about baseball. Later, at the team's favorite restaurant, she joins the team for dinner and sings an Irish jig with Dennis and Eddie. She also threatens Eddie with fines if he stays out late at night on the town. Attempting to lighten her up a little, he begins to romance her. She reveals that her full name is Katherine Catherine Higgins. He calls her Casey.

Dennis also attempts to woe Casey by ignoring her hoping that will pique her interest in him. She concludes that he may be heartbroken over breaking up with a girl.

In the locker room, after the Wolves lose a game to the Pirates, K. C. advises each player on what they can do to improve their performance. The Wolves begin winning games. Nevertheless, Eddie is having trouble on the field. Slappy suggests that Eddie is restless – too much training and not enough relaxation. K. C. takes Eddie out dancing where they waltz with Casey singing and kissing Eddie. Eddie's game improves.

K. C. and the team are invited to a charity ball for the Boys' Club by Joe Chandler, a gambler who bets on sports. At the event, Casey realizes that it is not really a ball for charity. A dancer, Sherry Dawn, entertains by asking the players to dance with her. She had previously met Eddie and Dennis when they were doing their vaudeville routine. She likes Dennis.

Eddie and Casey miss the train to the team's next game when Eddie injures his leg. Eddie confesses that he is in love with Casey and asks her to join him on the vaudeville circuit so they can be close to one another. Just as the two are growing fond of each other, Casey discovers that Eddie faked his leg injury so they could be together. She assigns Eddie to a minor league farm team. The Wolves begin losing games.

Sherry has been following the team around the country trying to rekindle her relationship with Dennis. Dennis finally admits that he loves Sherry. Casey asks Eddie to rejoin the Wolves and concedes that she has missed him.

Chandler, who has been observing the team's climb in the standings close to winning the pennant, sends a note to Eddie offering him a job in a show he is presenting at a new night club. He wants Eddie and Dennis to leave the team right away meaning that the two would miss the pivotal last game of the season. Eddie would like to take the job; Dennis doesn't want to leave the team.

Eddie goes to Chandler's office telling him that the deal is off. Chandler divulges that he has bet that the Wolves will lose their next game. Eddie leaves and joins his team.

Sherry advises Dennis that if Eddie plays, Chandler's men will kill him. Doing a comedy skit before the game, Dennis knocks Eddie unconscious so that he can't play. The Wolves begin losing the game. Casey, Sherry, and the players go into the stands to take care of Chandler's henchmen. Eddie is revived and hits the ball winning the game three to two.

The final scene of the planned film shows a theater marquee reading:

The Wolves Frolics

Featuring

O'Brien and O'Ryan
Those Two Nifty Wolves in Blue

On the stage of the theater, a production number involves all the team's players finishing with a foursome of Casey, Eddie, Dennis, and Sherry.

With changes to many of the names of the main characters, the story line of the final film with Esther Williams playing the role of K. C. Higgins is similar to that of the original script by George Wells. The main difference is that the gambler, in the movie named Joe Lorgan, convinces Eddie to be a full-time performer for him. Eddie begins rehearsing his act at night while still attempting to play ball during the day. Casey finds out what Eddie is doing as his performance with the team suffers. She suspends him, but with the help of a group of children, he rejoins the team. Lorgan plots to keep Eddie from playing in the final game, but he eventually returns to the field to hit a game-winning homerun.

Cimarron (musical) – 1947

Judy was to co-star with Gene Kelly in a musical remake of this Western film that had originally starred Irene Dunne and Richard Dix in 1931. The movie was based on the novel by Edna Ferber. The RKO-produced feature, *Cimarron,* chronicled the settling of the Oklahoma territory from the late 1880's to the early 1900s through the lives of husband and wife, Yancey Cravat (Dix) and Sabra Cravat (Dunne), and their son Cimarron who married a Native American.

Vincent Lawrence wrote a treatment and a screenplay for the MGM remake of *Cimarron* dated September 29, 1942 that opened with a scene set in Osage, Oklahoma in 1927. Friends and colleagues are celebrating the election of the editor and owner of the local newspaper, *The Wigwam*, to Congress. Sabra Cravat, in her sixties, is the new congresswoman, and her general manager, Jessie Ricky, begins to reflect on her life and career with two U.S. Senators who have come to congratulate Sabra on her election.

In 1886, Sabra's husband, Yancey Cravat, participated in a land rush on Indian Territory opened by the federal government for white settlement. Yancey is a leading citizen from Wichita, Kansas, who runs a newspaper in that town and initially just wants to cover the land-rush story for his newspaper. Nevertheless, he becomes caught up in the excitement of the land rush and stakes claim to some property for ranching.

Back in Wichita, he tells his young wife about what he did and they agree, despite Sabra not knowing much about pioneering, to move to Osage with their young son, Cimarron. Sabra is appalled by the decrepit nature of the town and its lawlessness. Yancey is confronted by Lon Yountis, a tough man in the town, who asks if he is planning to run a newspaper like he had in Wichita. The guy who owned the paper in Osage had been murdered. Initially, Yancey says that he is interested only in ranching but later changes his mind and decides to re-start Osage's newspaper.

Shortly before the first issue of the paper, a group of citizens calls upon Yancey to help establish a church in Osage. Yancey heads the effort and holds a meeting of townspeople. He chooses as his text, "There is a lion in the streets," and talks about the murder of the former owner of the paper saying he knows who the culprit is. Just as he is about to divulge the name, Yountis fires at him. Yancey fires back seriously wounding Yountis.

As years pass, both the town and the paper grow. Sabra gives birth to a daughter named Donna. Yancey's restlessness grows looking for new fields to conquer. Sabra organizes a ladies' society to raise money for churches and schools. Some of the women in the group want to rid the town of the madame named Dixie Lee who manages the local saloon.

When news comes of another land rush on the Cherokee Strip authorized by President Cleveland, Yancey is intrigued. Reluctantly, she allows her husband to participate in this new land grab.

Another five years pass by. Sabra has kept the newspaper running while raising her son and daughter. Yancey finally returns. He tells her about the Cherokee Strip, the gold rush in Alaska, but really doesn't have anything to show for his absence. He now wants to join Teddy Roosevelt and his Rough Riders. Yancey realizes that his relationship with Sabra has changed, but she remains unmoved.

Yancey postpones joining the Rough Riders for a week in order to be with his wife. During this period, Yountis and his gang return to rob the bank. Yountis is killed by Yancey, and the rest of the gang is driven off.

After the end of the Mexican War, Yancey comes back to Osage once again. This time he is a war hero covered with metals. Oklahoma is admitted to the Union. Sabra is upset that her son, Cimarron, is in love with Ruby, a Native American who wants to marry him. Sabra forbids the marriage, but Yancey allows Cimarron to go ahead with it. Meanwhile, Yancey is disappointed that his daughter has become something of a snob.

Oil had been discovered in Oklahoma with a lot of Osage's citizens becoming wealthy, including Dixie Lee, who leaves town. Now that Oklahoma is a state, many people want Yancey to be its first governor. But he decides to leave for adventure and excitement at the Panama Canal.

Yancey Cravat has now been gone for twenty years. Except for his service in World War I, nothing has been heard from him. Sabra still maintains his name as editor of *The Wigwam*.

Sabra leaves the paper's office to go on a tour of the oil fields with the two senators. As they enter the oil fields, a big gusher comes in but something has gone wrong. The gusher has come in ahead of time forcing up a torpedo of nitroglycerin. An oil worker caught the torpedo preventing a big explosion. The man is critically injured. Some of the workers call the man "Old Yance." Sabra springs from her car and rushes toward the gusher. She kneels beside the man crying out "Yancey! Yancey!" He looks up at her saying, "Sabra! I got to see you!" Yancey dies in her arms, his pioneering spirit undimmed.

Persuaded by the success of Rodgers and Hammerstein's *Oklahoma* on Broadway, Metro announced in July 1944 that singer James Melton would have the lead male role in the musical version of *Cimarron*. Whether Lawrence's screenplay would have been used by the studio as the basis for the musical or not is unclear.

Nothing more was heard about the *Cimarron* musical until early 1947 when columnist Erskine Johnson reported, "MGM writers are cooking up a musical version of 'Cimarron,' with Judy Garland and Gene Kelly in the Richard Dix-Irene Dunne roles."[102]

Making a musical version of *Cimarron* was still being considered by MGM in 1948 with the announcement in the September 6, 1948 edition of *The Los Angeles Times*, that the studio was thinking about starring, who else, but Kathryn Grayson in the feature to be produced by Arthur Freed. Nevertheless, according to Freed, this musical project just never came together.

Metro finally did remake *Cimarron* in 1960 with Glenn Ford and Maria Schell in the lead roles. However, this version was not a musical - simply a revised version of the 1931 film.

Finian's Rainbow – 1947

Louella Parsons in her October 11, 1947 column announced that Arthur Freed had seen *Finian's Rainbow* in New York and wanted Louis B. Mayer to purchase the film rights to the musical. The columnist went on to note that Judy Garland would play the female lead, Sharon McLonergan, with Mickey Rooney as the leprechaun, Gene Kelly as Woody Mahoney, and Barry Fitzgerald as Finian McLonergan. While this plan never came to be, *The New York Times*, almost a year later, reported that Mickey Rooney was behind an effort to bring the musical to the silver screen. A producer for the stage play indicated that "Rooney wants to form his own independent unit at Metro and he is anxious to play the role of the leprechaun with his father, Joe Yule, who is now appearing as Finian, repeating that part in the movie."[103] This initiative also failed.

In the original musical, Irishman Finian McLonergan and his daughter Sharon arrive in Rainbow Valley near Fort Knox. Sharon is homesick for Ireland and sings "How Are Things in Glocca Morra." Finian believes that millionaires bury their gold near Fort Knox which is what he wants to do with a crock of gold he has stolen from a leprechaun called "Og."

In Rainbow Valley, the tobacco sharecroppers are at risk of losing their land because of back taxes. The farmers want Woody Mahoney who has a sister, Susan, a mute, to fight for them against the local sheriff and State Senator Billboard Rawkins who is represented by Buzz Collins. When Woody doesn't have the funds necessary to pay the interest on the back taxes, Finian pays the balance endearing Sharon and him to the sharecroppers. Sharon explains to everyone her dad's philosophy of following your dreams by singing "Look to the Rainbow."

When Finian buries the pot of gold, he encounters Og who says that without his gold he will slowly become mortal. Sharon and Woody come by looking for her dad. Distracted by the moonlight, they perform "Old Devil Moon."

When two geologists inform Senator Rawkins that gold has been detected in Rainbow Valley, he seeks to drive Finian and the farmers off the land.

The next day, when Og and Sharon meet, he confesses his feelings for her. But Sharon is in love with Woody. The sharecroppers celebrate the relationship between Woody and Sharon, while Og informs Finian that he loves Sharon. Og also warns Finian that if he makes three wishes near the gold he buried, the gold will disappear forever.

Senator Rawkins arrives to tell Finian and the farmers that, by living with black people, they are breaking the law and must vacate the land. Sharon, while standing near the hidden gold, says to the Senator that she wishes he were a black person. He turns black and is chased off the property by the sheriff.

After Woody says to the sharecroppers that there is gold on their land and that the Shears-Robust company has offered them all charge accounts, the farmers use their accounts instead of trying to find the gold. As the sharecroppers unpack all the items that they financed through their charge accounts, Sharon and her dad sing, "When the Idle Poor Become the Idle Rich."

Shears and Robust wonder when the gold will be found to pay off the charge accounts, but Woody and Finian say that there is no need for the gold since the news of it has led to large investments in their tobacco brand.

Woody's sister Susan discovers the hidden gold and takes it for herself. Senator Rawkins, hiding in the woods, meets Og and describes what happened to him. Og uses his own magic to make the Senator a nicer person. Rawkins then meets up with a group of black gospel singers who are going to sing at Woody and Sharon's wedding. However, Buzz Collins and the sheriff interrupt the wedding to arrest Sharon for witchcraft in turning the Senator into a black man. Finian promises that Sharon can change Rawkins back. He intends to use one of the wishes standing near where the gold was hidden but discovers it missing.

Finian finds the almost human Og with Susan with whom he has now fallen in love. He informs Og that Sharon is in danger. When Og reveals that he doesn't know where the gold is, Finian runs off. Susan knows where the gold is but can't speak. Not realizing that the gold is under his feet, Og wishes that Susan could speak. Understanding that only one wish is left and thinking that, if he uses it to save Sharon, he cannot be a leprechaun again, Og is not sure what to do. Susan kisses him, and Og wishes that Rawkins be white again.

The sharecroppers welcome Og and Susan. But Finian has lost his pot of gold. Understanding that both his daughter and Og have found their dreams, Finian goes off again in search of his own rainbow.

Finian's Rainbow finally reached the big screen in 1968 starring Fred Astaire as Finian and singer Petula Clark as his daughter Sharon.

Lovely to Look At – 1948

This planned remake of *Roberta* was originally to star Judy Garland, Gene Kelly, Frank Sinatra, and Betty Garrett. Harry Ruby and George Wells were working on a modern story line based on the Alice Duer Miller book, *Gowns by Roberta*. The motion picture would feature songs by Jerome Kern.[104]

Garland was to begin this project after completing *Annie Get Your Gun*. Since she was on suspension from MGM for failure to show up to work on that film, June Allyson reportedly was to replace her on *Lovely to Look At*. When the film was released in 1952, none of the stars noted above were in it. Instead, Kathryn Grayson appeared in the role intended for Garland along with Red Skelton, Marge and Gower Champion, Ann Miller, and Howard Keel.

Red Skelton played Al Marsh, a producer who, along with Tony Naylor (Keel) and Jerry Ralby (Champion), are attempting to find funding for a Broadway play. Al receives a letter from Paris stating that his aunt has passed away and left him a share in a dress salon in France. Thinking that he can sell his share and have enough funds to back his play, Marsh with Naylor and Ralby head to Paris accompanied by Bubbles Cassidy (Miller) who finances the trip. Upon arrival, the men find that the dress salon is bankrupt and needs to be fixed up before Al can earn money from it. Tony and Jerry meet Stephanie (Grayson) and Clarisse (Champion), the other owners of the salon. Al, Tony, and Jerry decide to present a fashion show hoping to bring in more business as Tony falls in love with Stephanie and Jerry with Clarisse. Al develops a relationship with Bubbles.

The original treatment done by Wells and Ruby in December 1948 for Judy Garland and Gene Kelly indicated that Kelly would play Tony Taylor of "Tony Taylor and His Troubedors" the leader of a band that hasn't made it to the big time. They are performing at the opening of a supermarket, while the band seeks to play at nightclubs like the one owned by Barney Mitchell in Manhattan. Also in the band are drummer Peewee and singer and base fiddle player, Al Wodzscynzkic, whose name is changed by Tony to Al Marsh. Presumably, Frank Sinatra would have appeared in the role of Marsh. Betty Garrett would have played Bubbles, and Judy would be Stephanie, the co-owner of "Roberta's."

An agent viewing their performance suggests that Tony needs to have a backer with maybe $30,000 or $40,000 to get started in the big time. The story line of the rest of the planned film would have been similar to that of the version released in 1952.

If Judy had the role of Stephanie in the film, she would have sung such songs as "Smoke Gets in Your Eyes," "Lovely to Look At," "The Touch of Your Hand," "Yesterdays," and "You're Devastating."

The Barkleys of Broadway – 1948

In 1948, Garland and Fred Astaire were set to star in an original musical, written by Betty Comden and Adolph Green, about a husband and wife acting team who were, at times, competitors with one another in their acting endeavors. When a young English playwright persuades the wife to display her talent in a drama, the husband becomes resentful as his wife strives to become a serious actress. Garland was thrilled with the script. Songs were written by Harry Warren and Ira Gershwin.

The initial title of the project was *You Made Me Love You* from the song of the same title that a young Judy Garland had sung to a photo of Clark Gable. Judy began rehearsals on the picture on June 14, 1948 shortly after her twenty-sixth birthday. However, during the second week of rehearsals, she began missing work due to illness and other reasons.

Several inter-office memorandums from Hugh Boswell, production manager for *The Barkleys of Broadway*, to various MGM executives including Arthur Freed during the summer of 1948 chronicle Ms. Garland's excuses for not coming in to work on the film:

> At approximately 12:45 pm, this date (June 22, 1948), Miss Garland phoned Mr. Worsley to say that she was still ill and would not be able to come in for dress rehearsal.

> Miss Judy Garland had a fitting call in wardrobe at 11:00 A.M. today, Wednesday – 6/30/48. She phoned assistant director, Mr. Worsley, at 9:40 A.M. to report that she had a slight attack of intestinal flu. Not too bad, but bad enough so that she would not be able to come in for a fitting, stand on her feet for any length of time, and still be able to make her broadcast tonight. (The "broadcast tonight" refers to *The Tex and Jinx Show*, a radio program hosted by husband and wife, Tex McCrary and Jinx Falkenburg, on which the cast of the film *Easter Parade* appeared.)

> Miss Garland was called for a wardrobe fitting at 11:00 A.M. today, Tuesday, July 6th, 1948. At approximately 10:20 A.M. she phoned wardrobe department and had fitting postponed until 2:30 this afternoon. At 11:45 A. M., she called wardrobe department again, to say that she had a sick friend, and could not come in at all today.
>
> Miss Garland was called for an 11:00 A.M. fitting in Wardrobe, today Thursday, 7/8/48 At 10:40 A.M., her secretary called wardrobe, who had the call transferred to me. Miss Garland's secretary informed me that Miss Garland was ill, and would not be in today.
>
> Miss Garland had a call at 2:30 P.M. for a wardrobe fitting, today, Friday, 7;9;48 At approximately 11:45 A.M. she called Mr. Freed's office to say that she had to go to the doctors last evening, and would not be in today.
>
> Miss Garland had a call for a wardrobe fitting at 11:00 A.M. – today, Saturday. 7/10/48. At 9:20 A.M. her secretary phoned Mr. Ryan, to say that she was very ill, and would not be able to come in. However, she hoped to be able to come in on Monday.
>
> Miss Garland had a wardrobe fitting call for 10:00 A.M. today – Monday – 7/12/48. She called Mr. Freed's office at approximately 9:20 A.M. to say that she would not be in.[105]

Arthur Freed had a telephone conversation with Garland's physician, Dr. Schelman, who stated that the star could possibly work four or five days under medication and then, after a rest, work again for a few more days. As Freed stated in a memo for the record, "(The doctor) . . . was of the opinion that if she didn't have to work for a while it might not be too difficult to make a complete cure but that her knowledge of having to report every morning would cause such a mental disturbance within her that the results would be in jeopardy."[106]

On July 18, MGM formally suspended Judy Garland from the project and replaced her with Ginger Rogers reuniting the actress with Fred Astaire after an absence from the screen for nine years. Their last picture together had been 1939's *The Story of Vernon and Irene Castle.*

Judy Garland spent the remainder of the summer of 1948 resting and regaining her strength.

Give a Girl a Break – 1950

This MGM production was originally intended to star Fred Astaire, Gene Kelly, Judy Garland, and Ann Miller.[107] Released in 1953, the picture actually featured Marge and Gower Champion along with Debbie Reynolds, Helen Wood, Kurt Kasznar, and Bob Fosse.

The plot centered on three actresses vying for a role in a Broadway musical revue after a temperamental star leaves the project. The revue's composer, Leo Belney (Kasznar) would like a young ballerina, Joanna Moss (Wood) for the role; Bob Dowdy (Fosse), a "gofer," wants Suzy Doolittle (Reynolds); and the producer (Larry Keating) seeks Madelyn Corlane (Marge Champion). Corlane just happens to be the former dance partner of Ted Sturgis (Gower Champion) who is directing the musical.

Joanna, Suzy, and Madelyn all do well in their auditions. Joanna lands the part but, when rehearsals get underway, she is not doing well. Subsequently, she announces that she is going to have a baby and leaves town with her husband who has accepted a new job as the head of the English Department at an out-of-state university.

Madelyn is offered the role next, but she has left town and cannot be contacted and so the part goes to Suzy. The revue and Suzy are a hit. After the show, Ted walks out of the theater and sees his former partner Madelyn who tells him that she wanted to find out if it was show business or Ted that she missed. They run into each other's arms and kiss.

While presumably Judy Garland would have played the Madelyn Corlane role, it isn't clear in which roles Fred Astaire and Gene Kelly would have appeared.

Royal Wedding – 1950 -1951

After her suspension from Metro for *Annie Get Your Gun* and after her release from the hospital in Boston, Judy returned to film another musical at MGM, *Summer Stock*. The film was completed by March 1950.

Judy was next assigned to the musical *Royal Wedding* which originally was to star June Allyson and Fred Astaire. When Allyson became pregnant, Garland was asked to replace her. The film concerned a brother and sister dance team, Tom and Ellen Brown, who sail to England to perform at a London theater during the festivities surrounding the wedding of Princess Elizabeth to Prince Phillip. During the voyage to England, Ellen begins a romance with Lord John Brindale but keeps it a secret from her brother. In London, Tom meets Anne Ashmond, and they also begin a secret romance. Ellen and Tom reveal their respective romances to each other but decide not to marry in order to keep their successful act together. But the siblings realize that they cannot be happy unless they marry the objects of their affection. They do so immediately and end up celebrating their marriages on the same day as Elizabeth and Phillip are wed.

In May 1950, Judy began rehearsals for the movie. However, by June, Judy told director Stanley Donen that she could not rehearse full days and still be in condition to begin filming the picture. Arthur Freed agreed to have her rehearse only in the afternoons, but then the star indicated that she couldn't rehearse at all on June 17. On June 19, MGM issued a memorandum to staff stating that Garland's contract had been suspended effective June 17 and that no further requests for her services were to be made. This effectively ended the actress' association with MGM. Jane Powell took over her role of Ellen Brown. The motion picture was completed on October 5, 1950 and released on March 23, 1951.

Brigadoon – 1951

After being terminated by MGM for missing work in *Royal Wedding*, Judy may have made a return to the studio in the Lerner and Lowe musical, *Brigadoon,* with Gene Kelly. Writing in *The Los Angeles Times*, Edwin

Schallert reported, "Though it has usually been assumed that Kathryn Grayson would automatically become the feminine star in 'Brigadoon' when that is produced by MGM with Gene Kelly as the male star, I hear that Alan Lerner Jr. and Frederick Lowe have ideas about suggesting Judy Garland for this plum assignment, because of her enormous success during her Palace Theater engagement in New York."[108]

Brigadoon was another fantasy musical Broadway show that Metro brought to the silver screen. When Tommy Albright (Kelly) and Jeff Douglas (Van Johnson) are on a hunting trip in Scotland, they become lost in the woods and happen upon Brigadoon, a village that rises out of the mist every hundred years. Tommy falls in love with Fiona Campbell. They learn that if anyone ever leaves the village, the place will disappear forever and that any outsider who wants to stay in Brigadoon must love a village resident strongly enough to accept the loss of everything in the outside world.

Fiona's sister, Jean is marrying Charlie Dalrymple, but the ceremony is interrupted by Harry Beaton, who says he will leave Brigadoon to make it disappear since he is in love with Jean. Trying to cross the bridge to the outside world, Harry fights with Tommy and then Harry is accidentally shot dead by Jeff.

Fiona confesses her love for Tommy and he vice versa allowing them to stay in Brigadoon. However, when Tommy tells Jeff that he intends to marry Fiona, Jeff replies that Tommy can't just leave the real world behind. They both leave Brigadoon. But Tommy has second thoughts and, still in love with Fiona, he and Jeff head back to the place. The village miraculously re-appears, and Tommy returns to Fiona.

Vincente Minnelli directed the picture with Cyd Charisse appearing as Fiona Campbell, the role for which Judy was under consideration.

Chapter 6:

The Musical Roles That Might Have Been After MGM

As Arthur Freed remarked about Ms. Garland, "Judy hasn't a mean bone in her body; but she's got more comebacks in her than anyone in the profession. Never count her out."[109] Her biggest comeback in the 1950s was the 1954 musical drama *A Star Is Born*, directed by George Cukor and produced by her then husband, Sid Luft, in association with Warner Brothers. Here are other musicals in which she might have starred after being terminated by Metro.

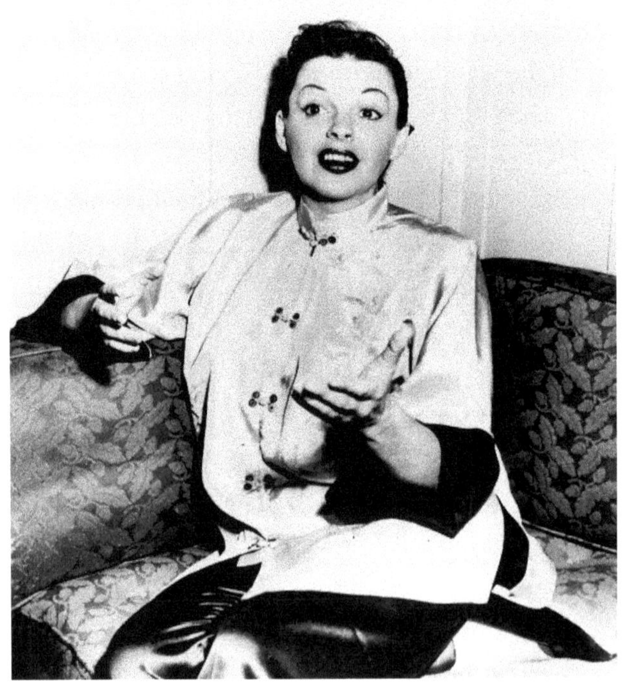

Judy Garland, backstage at the Curran Theater in San Francisco,. confirming to reporters that she recently married Sid Luft on June 29, 1952.

The U.S.O. Story - 1950

Originally titled *Stars and Stripes Forever*, this planned feature was designed as a vehicle for the talents of legendary entertainer Al Jolson. Singer/actor Jolson performed in U.S.O. shows during World War II and the Korean conflict. He passed away on October 23, 1950 at age sixty-four from a massive heart attack. After Jolson's death, this movie project was then considered as one for Judy Garland with a new title, *The U.S.O. Story*. Jerry Wald and Norman Krasna were to produce the film for RKO.

Herbert Baker, who later scripted TV variety shows for Danny Kaye, Perry Como, and Frank Sinatra, wrote two treatments for the Jolson project. Al Jolson is heading a U. S. O. tour in the South Pacific. The troupe includes Hoagy Carmichael, Frank Fontaine, six chorus girls called the Stars and Stripes Sextette, and singer Jeanne Daniels. Brief biographies of each of the chorus girls are presented as the group flies from Guam to Okinawa where Jolson knows General Flanagan in charge of the base. Jeanne Daniels is a young Hollywood star who has made five hit movie musicals. She is debating whether or not to leave the tour to marry her boyfriend back home.

General Flanagan is somewhat depressed because he is being forced to retire at age sixty-four, and a new young Brigadier General is flying in to replace him.

The major change in the second treatment is that the girl singer is renamed Wanda Hendrix instead of Jeanne Daniels. She thinks of leaving the show to start a new movie but really doesn't want to depart. Jolson tells her that the movie has been delayed. Her real reason for wanting to stay with the U.S.O. is because her divorce is becoming final soon, and she doesn't want to return to the States just yet. However, she then finds that she is pregnant.

With the death of Al Jolson, the movie's story line could have focused on the Jeanne Daniels/Wanda Hendrix character with Judy taking that role. Alternatively, a script could have been developed with an entirely different story featuring Judy Garland.

The latter appears to be the case. On August 23, 1950, Dorothy Manners noted that the planned RKO film was now titled *Let's See the Girls* with Jane Greer in the lead – not Judy Garland. Columnist Edith Gwynn then announced in a November 12, 1950 article that *Let's See the Girls* was to be a film glorifying the U.S.O. tours with Dinah Shore, Jane Russell, and Marlene Dietrich starring – no mention of either Jane Greer or Judy. Newspaper reports also stated that the producers have been promised the full cooperation of the Defense Department in making the motion picture at Army camps and military sites with the producers agreeing to donate a percentage of the profits to the U.S.O.[110]

Variety reported in its January 10, 1951 issue that a deal for Judy Garland to star in this film was being held up by Howard Hughes, owner of RKO, because of his insistence that Judy's agent, Abe Lastfogel, give Hughes options on further pictures with the singer. The article also reported that Wald and Krasna would begin filming sequences in March featuring various entertainers who went overseas with the U.S.O. during World War II and that a seven-minute tribute to Al Jolson would be included in the picture.[111]

In the end, no motion picture about the U.S.O. produced by Wald and Krasna ever came to be.

Kiss Me, Kate – 1951

British producer Alexander Paal sought to obtain the rights to Cole Porter's musical, *Kiss Me, Kate*. Paal wanted to make a Technicolor version of the Broadway musical with Judy Garland and actor John Carroll as the leads. The story concerned an out-of-town tryout of a musical version of Shakespeare's *Taming of the Shrew* starring and directed by Fred Graham along with his former wife, Lili Vanessi, in the role of Kate. Both egocentrics, they discover that they still love one another despite the fact that Lili is now engaged to a powerful senator and Fred is having an affair with a young actress.

Louella Parsons reported that Judy would remain in London for the filming which was scheduled to begin in July 1951. If there was a delay in obtaining the rights to the musical, then Garland would return to Hollywood and come back later to begin the production.[112]

A film adaptation of *Kiss Me, Kate* was released in 1953. Made by MGM, the movie had Kathryn Grayson and Howard Keel in the lead roles.

Paint Your Wagon – 1952

After being forced out as the head of Metro, Louis B. Mayer started his own production company. One of the first properties he purchased for a film was the Broadway musical, *Paint Your Wagon*. Warner Brothers bid $300,000 for the screen rights; Paramount went to $350,000. Mayer offered $200,000 along with 5% of the profits which won him the rights to the work.

The play with music by Frederick Lowe and book and lyrics by Alan J. Lerner ran on Broadway in 1951. Set in California during the gold rush days, the story concerned miner Ben Rumson whose sixteen-year-old daughter, Jennifer, discovers gold. Laying claim to the land, prospectors start flocking to the new town of Rumson. Jennifer ends up being the only girl in the town. She falls in love with Julio Valveras who is forced to live outside Rumson because of his Mexican heritage. Learning of Jennifer's attraction to Julio, Ben sends his daughter to school in the East. She returns after a period of time to find her father thinking of moving on. Nevertheless, as others leave the town to go to another gold strike, Julio returns to see Jennifer, and Ben decides to stay in Rumson.

Initially, MGM thought of making the film version of the musical with Spencer Tracy, Kathryn Grayson, and Fernando Lamas in the main roles. But when the rights were purchased by Louis B. Mayer, reports were that the movie would be made by him as a Cinerama production with filming to begin June 8, 1953. Deanna Durbin was to be the lead female in the project.

Subsequently, Judy Garland was rumored to be the leading candidate for the top female role in the proposed picture. As reported at the time, "Some time ago it was hinted that Alan J. Lerner and Frederick Lowe, who wrote the musical show, were favorable to her starring in the screen version, and though they haven't been heard from lately, it's not unlikely that Mayer himself would prefer the singing star who formerly worked for him at MGM and whose talent he has always rated altitudinous."[113]

Judy's husband at the time, Sid Luft, confirms that Mayer thought the original play, *The Painted Wagon*, would be perfect for Garland. Luft wrote, "I told Mayer I would read the play and discuss it with Judy. Judy said 'Not *The Painted Wagon*, Sid.' I had to agree."[114]

John Lee Mahin was to do the script for the screen adaptation, while Alan Jay Lerner and Arthur Schwartz were to write the music and lyrics. The composers did create eight songs for the musical – "Bonanza!," "Californey Never Looked So Good," "Kentucky," "Noah Was a Wisdom Man," "Over the Purple Hills," "Paint Your Wagon," and "There's Always One You Can't Forget."

If the film had been made, apparently an actress named June Roselle and not Judy Garland would have gotten the main female role. Roselle later understudied Florence Henderson in the Broadway musical *Fanny*, which, as pointed out in the Appendix, originally was to star Ms. Garland.[115]

Bloodhounds of Broadway – 1952

Vaudevillian George Jessel produced this movie based on the Damon Runyon stories about a Broadway bookie named Robert "Numbers" Foster who has his girlfriend, Yvonne Dugan, lie about his activities when testifying before a State Crime Investigation Committee. Numbers got that nickname because of his amazing skill at calculating math problems in his head. He had left New York to go to Florida during the investigation.

With the investigation closed, he and his colleague Harry "Poorly" Sammis drive back up North. Missing a turn-off on the highway, they encounter twenty-year-old hillbilly Emly Ann Stackerlee singing a hymn over her grandfather's grave. In her initial appearance in the movie, Emly Ann looks similar to Dorothy from *The Wizard of Oz*. She has pigtails tied with blue ribbons and wears a blue gingham dress. Numbers thinks Emly

Ann has a lovely singing voice. He and Poorly take Emly Ann and her two bloodhounds, Nip and Tuck, to New York. Numbers drops the singer off at the apartment of Poorly's sister, Tessie, who gives her a makeover.

Numbers decides to find Emly Ann a job at a nightclub. However, Yvonne Dugan, jealous of Emly Ann, threatens to inform a new crime investigator, Inspector McNamara, that Numbers has transported a minor across state lines. Numbers is becoming attracted to Emly Ann and no longer loves Yvonne. He arranges an audition for Emly Ann before Hollywood agents hoping that she will go to Hollywood to further her career so she doesn't compete with Yvonne. Emly Ann performs a hillbilly song in the audition as well as singing and dancing to a more sophisticated number.

After Emly Ann confesses her love for Numbers, he does the same in return. When Yvonne learns of this, she goes to McNamara to give truthful testimony about Numbers' activities. McNamara visits Emly Ann to make an offer that if Numbers testifies before Yvonne does, he will have to serve only a year in prison. Emly uses her bloodhounds to track down Numbers to inform him of the offer. He testifies before the crime committee and pays the back taxes that he owes. After a year in prison, Numbers becomes a cashier at the nightclub where Emly is the star attraction.

According to Hedda Hopper, producer George Jessel made a pitch to the studio, Twentieth Century Fox, for Judy Garland to play the role of Emly Ann.[116] Scott Brady was cast as Numbers. Ultimately, Mitzi Gaynor landed the Emly Ann role, and Marguerite Chapman played Yvonne Dugan.

At the time, Mitzi Gaynor was twenty years of age – the same as her character's age. Judy Garland would have been age thirty.

14 Fifth Avenue – 1952

14 Fifth Avenue or *Meet Me in Manhattan* was supposed to be a sequel to *Meet Me in St. Louis* written by Sally Benson. According to a phone conversation reported by Louella Parsons,

"Sally Benson telephoned from New York to tell me that she is writing '14 Fifth Avenue,' the story of the Smith family, whom I knew so well. Sally was the youngest Smith...

Over the telephone she said that she's going to do a series of stories on the Smiths with her sisters, Rose, Esther, Agnes, herself and her mother and brother, of course, and she wishes that Judy Garland could play Esther in '14 Fifth Avenue,' . . ."[117]

Writer Fred Finklehoffe was also involved with this project. *Variety* reported, "Finklehoffe and Miss Benson are collaborating on the script and Finklehoffe will produce. Much of the film will be shot on location in NY, with interiors slated for filming here, probably at Motion Picture Center, where Finklehoffe made 'At War with the Army.'"[118]

This project never resulted in a motion picture.

Saratoga Trunk (musical) – 1954

Judy was considered for the role of Clio Dulaine in this proposed musical remake of another Edna Ferber classic – *Saratoga Trunk*. The original non-musical version of the Ferber novel starred Ingrid Bergman and Gary Cooper.

According to Louella Parsons, Judy's husband Sid Luft would produce the movie in conjunction with Warner Brothers.[119] Music would be written by Jule Styne and Alan Jay Lerner. Luft confirmed this in an article in *Variety* saying that Jack Warner was so satisfied with Judy's comeback vehicle, *A Star Is Born,* that the singer immediately made an offer to appear in a musicalized version of *Saratoga Trunk*.[120]

The original 1946 film focused on two individuals in the 1870's who each wanted to avenge injustices suffered by their parents. Clio Dulaine, the bastard daughter of an aristocratic New Orleans father and a French woman, wants to avenge her mother's mistreatment by her father's family. Clio's mother accidentally killed her daughter's father when he tried to prevent her from committing suicide. Clio and her mother were exiled to Paris. Clio returns to the United States where she meets Clint Maroon. They are instantly attracted to one another. Clint is seeking vengeance against Raymond Soule, a railroad man, who ruined Clint's father.

For her part, Clio intends to marry a wealthy man to prove that she is just as good as her father's family, the Dulaines. The Dulaines eventually pay Clio $10,000 and bury her mother in a New Orleans cemetery. Clio then joins Clint in Saratoga where she schemes to marry railroad tycoon Bartholomew Van Steed who owns a railroad, the Saratoga Trunk, which is worth millions since it connects coal regions with New York. Raymond Soule is attempting to steal the railroad from Van Steed. Clint offers to save Van Steed's railroad in exchange for partial ownership of the line.

In the end, Clio realizes that she loves Clint more than Van Steed who wants to marry her. Having saved the Saratoga Trunk for Soule, Clint's railroad shares have made him very wealthy.

Warner Brothers never turned *Saratoga Trunk* into a musical. Nevertheless, Morton DaCosta adapted Edna Ferber's book into a Broadway musical with songs by Johnny Mercer and Harold Arlen. The show opened in December 1959 with Carol Lawrence playing Clio Dulaine and Howard Keel as Clint. The show ran for only eighty performances.

Alice Adams (musical)– 1956

As early as 1950, columnist Sheilah Graham noted that Judy Garland is very interested in starring for Jerry Wald and Norman Krasna in a musical version of *Alice Adams*.[121]

In that year, Judy did do a radio program, *Theatre Guild on the Air*, that featured an adaptation of the Booth Tarkington novel. Co-starred with Garland were Thomas Mitchell as father Virgil Adams and Ann Shoemaker as mother Emma Adams.

The radio version begins with Alice Adams picking violets for a corsage to wear at an upscale party since she is unable to afford a corsage from a florist. Alice works at the local historical society for $18 a week. Her father, currently off work due to sickness, is a blue-collar worker for J. A. Lamb. Alice's dad would like her to become a stenographer so she could make more money, but her mother likes her daughter working at the historical society hoping that she can meet a wealthy prospective husband. Mrs. Adams would also like her husband to find a better job to earn more money.

Since Alice doesn't have a date for the party, Emma Adams asks her son Walter to take Alice to the dance. The party is given by an acquaintance of Alice's who is better off financially than Alice's family. At the event, Alice admires wealthy Arthur Russell, who is a distant relative of Alice' acquaintance, Mildred Palmer. He asks Alice to dance with him. But she asks Walter to take her home after Arthur finds Walter shooting craps.

A few days later, when Alice sees Arthur in town, he asks her to walk with him. She tells him that her father likes spending money on her. Arthur asks Alice to go with him to another upscale party, but she begs off saying that she has to stay with her sick father.

Emma Adams brings up the subject of a glue formula that her husband had developed while working at J.A. Lamb's. His boss claims rights to the formula, but Mrs. Adams says that her husband improved upon it and that he should go into business for himself making the glue.

Arthur and Alice begin dating steadily. Virgil decides to quit Lamb's and start a glue factory. Emma invites Arthur to dinner at the Adams' residence so he can meet the rest of the family. On a hot July day, the Adams serve Arthur heavy food, the cook is outspoken, and the dessert melts. Also, after word gets around town about Virgil's new business using a formula he developed while working for J.A. Lamb, Lamb comes to the Adams' residence during the dinner to see Virgil. When Arthur leaves the dinner, Alice thinks that their relationship is over.

Virgil finds that his son took $300 from his account at Lamb's which the auditors discovered. However, Lamb really wants to talk with Virgil about his new business. Lamb says that he is opening his own glue factory to compete with Virgil's

Alice tells Lamb that everything is her fault since her father thought that she was unhappy and that he had to make more money. Lamb goes back to speak with Virgil about him joining Lamb in his glue factory.

Alice sees Arthur on the porch of her house not really having left her. He proposes marriage.

Actor Eddie Albert was to be Judy's co-star in the musical remake of the 1935 RKO feature that starred Katherine Hepburn and Fred MacMurray.

Wald and Krasna had signed a deal with Howard Hughes, then owner of RKO, to produce sixty pictures for the studio, among them was to be a new version of *Alice Adams*. Supposedly, Oscar Hammerstein and Richard Rodgers were approached about doing the music and lyrics for the film, but the proposed feature never came to fruition.

Born in Wedlock – 1956

Judy Garland and Sid Luft purchased the screen rights to *Born in Wedlock* by Margaret Echard as a potential starring vehicle for Ms. Garland. The title of the novel was originally *Babes in The Woods*.

After the lengthy production of *A Star Is Born*, news circulated in Hollywood that Judy was regarded as "untouchable" by major film studios. Luft responded that his wife was being made a "patsy" by the industry and the press because of the $4.5 million cost of *A Star Is Born*. He stated that "Hardly a day goes by that we do not receive a script from a major film company asking if Judy would be interested." Furthermore, he indicated that "Anything we do in the future, we want to be sure we control the situation completely. That includes the details of financing, the script, the whole works."[122]

Luft wanted to follow that policy in adapting *Babes in the Woods* for the screen. Garland would have starred as Sylvia Barth, a singer and dancer in a burlesque show who was the widowed mother of two young daughters – Jean and Katie Linda Barth.

Her husband, from a wealthy family, had died relatively young, being disowned by his family for marrying an entertainer. Sylvia performs at the Gayety Theater in Birmingham, Alabama, while her daughters stay home alone in a one-room apartment most of the time. In a diary, Katie Linda chronicles her experiences growing up. The novel unfolds from her perspective.

After the Gayety Theater is raided by the police, Sylvia escapes arrest and, with her daughters, leaves town. They go to a man, Charles Walker Fairchild, who is a fan of Sylvia's from the theater. Fairchild, a lawyer, lives in a big house in Ellenwood. In that town, Sylvia and her offspring learn that Matilda Barth, their late father's sister also resides there. For years, she has been trying to gain custody of Jean and Katie. The daughters begin to grow fond of Mr. Fairchild. His wife Kathy is in a sanitarium having had a mental breakdown ever since she lost her baby years ago.

Eventually, Matilda Barth has Jean and Katie brought to her house unbeknownst to their mother with the intent of taking custody of them deeming Sylvia, as an entertainer, unfit to be their mother. While at their aunt's place, the sisters learn that Mr. Fairchild's wife has died. Matilda has the idea that she should marry Fairchild to ensure that she'll have permanent custody of the children.

Meanwhile, Walker Fairchild wins the Democratic primary for Congress in his state meaning that he will most likely be elected to Congress in the general election since, at that time, Alabama was predominately a Democratic state. Fairchild marries Sylvia who says she wants her daughters back. He tells the girls that he will pick them up after school one day and take them home to their mother.

After Sylvia is reunited with Jean and Katie, society people in Ellenwood still ignore her, given her background, despite the fact that she is married. Walker Fairchild and his new wife begin attending church to hopefully win over the citizens of the town.

When a show comes to town, Sylvia and her daughters attend a performance and meet Mr. Darcy who was in love with Sylvia when she appeared at the Gayety Theater. The daughters believe that their mother may leave her husband and run away with Darcy since Sylvia is depressed over most of the town's reaction to her and the lack of excitement in Ellenwood. One day, after school, when Jean and Katie can't find their mother at home, they go to Fairchild's office to tell him that their mother is missing. He and the daughters find Sylvia at an empty dance pavilion where she was about to dance with Mr. Darcy. Instead, she begins dancing with her husband. Walker Fairchild pledges to adopt Jean and Katie as his own daughters which he does.

Initially announced as a feature film for Garland in 1956, Judy wanted Luft to ask Henry Ford II about financing the preproduction costs of the planned film. As Luft describes in his book about his marriage to Garland, "I wasn't racing to talk to Henry about the movie business. I thought I understood Ford's character: he was a hard-driving businessman who was not about to gamble change on a Hollywood film."[123] After Judy cajoled Ford by telling stories about old Hollywood and mentioning the proposed movie, Ford simply smiled and ordered another round of cocktails. He never did put up any money for the project.

A subsequent report in 1958 indicated that Luft would produce a stage version of the novel with an unknown in the lead and then make a film adaptation with Judy in the main role. The project was renamed *Gayety Girl* to focus on the Sylvia Barth character instead of *Born in Wedlock* which, as described above, dealt more with Sylvia's daughter Katie Linda. Fred Finklehoffe was working on the screenplay for the movie to be filmed in England in 1961. Songs and a background score were to be added to the proposed film, but it was never produced.

All About Eve (musical) – 1957

The 1950 movie, *All About Eve,* dealt with a two-faced female, Eve Harrington (Anne Baxter), who worms her way into the lives of veteran stage actress Margo Channing (Bette Davis) and her acquaintances. After a performance in Channing's latest play, *Aged in Wood*, by Lloyd Richards (Hugh Marlowe), Eve, a big fan of Margo's, is introduced to the actress by Channing's friend Karen Richards (Celeste Holm), the spouse of the playwright. Margo befriends Eve after hearing Eve's story about growing up poor in Wisconsin and losing her young husband during World War II. Margo hires her as a personal assistant.

As Margo's maid Birdie (Thelma Ritter) observes, Eve studies Margo like she is a play or a book or a set of blueprints. Eve also takes an interest in Margo's boyfriend, Bill Sampson (Gary Merrill), a director. Margo becomes increasingly put off by Eve's behavior as guests arrive for a party for Bill with many of them complimenting Eve.

Eve petitions Karen to ask her husband to be Margo's understudy in her current play. Margo goes into a tirade upon learning that Eve is now her understudy. Bill tries to calm Margo by saying that he loves her and that she is paranoid about Eve.

Returning from a weekend with the Richards, the car in which Margo is riding runs out of gas because Karen left the gas tank virtually empty. Margo misses that night's performance with Eve filling in. Eve is excellent in Margo's part. Theater critic Addison De Witt (George Sanders) writes a column about Eve describing her struggle to become an actress and the reluctance of older actresses, i.e., Margo Channing, to encourage Eve's talent.

Margo is irate about the column. Eve resigns as Margo's understudy, while Bill and Margo make plans to marry.

Karen meets with Eve where Eve pleads with her to ask her husband Lloyd to be the lead in his new play. She threatens to have Addison write a column about how Karen had made Margo miss the performance in which Eve shined in the role. Given her impending marriage, Margo says that she doesn't want the role in Lloyd's new play which Eve then gets.

Eve informs Addison that Lloyd is going to divorce Karen and marry her. Eve surmises that Lloyd will write great plays for her. Addison replies that he will not permit Eve to leave him. He says that she belongs to him and threatens to divulge that he knows her true background. Her name is really Gertrude Slescynski and that she was paid $500 to leave her home town because of an affair that she had with her boss at a brewery. She had never been married let alone to a soldier who died in World War II. If she leaves him, he will print all of these details in his column.

Later, after receiving an acting award, Eve returns home to find a young girl there who is a big fan of Eve's - an aspiring actress who would like to become her assistant.

Columnist Walter Winchell reported in early 1956 that Ethel Merman was contemplating appearing in a musical version of *All About Eve* playing the Margo Channing role. Merman denied the report.[124]

On August 6, 1957, columnist Mike Connolly wrote, "Hollywood is Remakeville this season. Now 20th - Fox is blueprinting a musical remake of 'All About Eve' with Judy Garland in the role originated by Bette Davis and Peggy King singing Anne Baxter's role . . ."[125] Peggy King, a pop vocalist, had been signed by MGM in 1952 but mostly appeared on television in the 1950s including on *The George Gobel Show*.

A few weeks later, Hedda Hopper reported that Susan Hayward would do a musical remake of *All About Eve* for Twentieth Century Fox beginning in spring, 1958.[126] About ten years later, Hayward did take over a role intended for Judy Garland in the motion picture, *Valley of the Dolls*.

A musical version of *All About Eve* never materialized in the late fifties. It wasn't until 1970 that Lauren Bacall starred on Broadway as Margo Channing in *Applause*, the musical based on the short story that resulted in the Bette Davis film.

South Pacific – 1955

In a 1955 news article by Emily Belser, Garland stated that she hoped to do the movie version of *South Pacific*.[127] Legal entanglements involving the Broadway musical apparently prevented her from doing the film version until at least 1956.

The original Broadway musical with music by Richard Rodgers and lyrics by Oscar Hammerstein II, opened in 1949. The story line centered on an American nurse, Nellie Forbush stationed in the South Pacific during the second World War who meets and falls in love with Emile de Becque, a French plantation owner who has mixed-race offspring. The subject of racial prejudice is a main theme of the play.

In the end, Mitzi Gaynor played Nellie Forbush in the film with Rossano Brazzi as Emile de Becque. The movie was released in 1958.

Irma La Douce – 1961

The original musical play, *Irma La Douce*, included fifteen songs in a tale about Irma, a Parisian prostitute, who falls in love with

Nestor, a poor law student. Nestor is jealous of Irma's customers and decides to become her pimp and exclusive client. Disguising himself as Monsieur Oscar, a wealthy old man who asks Irma only for companionship, he provides her with enough funds to become her sole partner. He soon exhausts himself from his numerous jobs, studies, and making love to Irma. Irma thinks that Oscar is not getting his money's worth from her and so seduces him more passionately than she ever did with Nestor. His reaction is to kill off his alter ego. Nestor is then convicted of murder and sentenced to prison. He learns that Irma is pregnant and escapes prison proving to the judge that he impersonated Oscar. He is able to witness the birth of his child on Christmas Eve.

Columnist Dorothy Kilgallen wrote that "Academy Award winner Billy Wilder would like to get Judy Garland for the star spot in his film version of 'Irma La Douce,' although it seems odd casting to those who have only seen the Broadway version and have no idea what he has in mind."[128]

The Mirisch Corporation purchased the screen rights to the Broadway play for $350,000, Mirisch assigned legendary director Billy Wilder to the project. Wilder knew that musicals were not his strong suit. *The Emperor Waltz,* which he had directed, bombed at the box office. Wilder apparently wanted Garland for the film thinking he would include some of the songs from the Broadway version. But eventually all the numbers from the play were removed for the film.

As I.A.L. Diamond, who wrote the screenplay for the movie version, put it: "We saw the show in Paris and liked the twist – the double identity of the pimp who becomes a patron only to become jealous of himself – but we didn't like the show. Here was a musical with only one girl in it who dances only one dance. The songs stopped the action and seemed to have nothing to do with the story."[129] Diamond ended up rewriting the script with only one sentence of the original play remaining.

Jack Lemmon and Shirley MacLaine starred in the final version of the film released in 1963.

A Tree Grows in Brooklyn (musical) – 1962

Judy was mentioned as a possibility for the Cissy role in this proposed Twentieth Century Fox adaptation of the 1951 Broadway musical version of *A Tree Grows in Brooklyn*. Mike Connolly announced in his column that "Judy Garland is 20th-Fox's No. One choice to play the footloose Aunt Cissie (sic) in the studio's musical remake of 'A Tree Grows in Brooklyn'."[130] The column also noted that Robert Goulet would play the male lead.

However, Connolly also reported that producer Jerry Wald wanted Polly Bergen to play Aunt Cissy and that Judy had been signed by Twentieth Century Fox to play the mother, Katie Nolan, in the project.[131]

The musical by Betty Smith and George Abbott based on Smith's novel had music and lyrics by Arthur Schwartz and Dorothy Fields.[132]

Set in Brooklyn around the turn of the twentieth century, the story focused on Katie, her sister Cissy, her boyfriend/husband Johnny, and their daughter Francie. The play opened with nineteen-year-old Katie, who lives with her sister, meeting singing waiter Johnny Nolan. Katie's sister Cissy is living with Harry whose real name is Oscar, but Cissy has called all of her live-in boyfriends Harry since that was the name of her first one. The original Harry left her to go back to his wife.

Cissy has misgivings about Katie becoming involved with Johnny. Nevertheless, he asks Katie to marry him and then obtains a permanent job. Cissy tells Harry that she'll be awfully lonely when her sister marries Johnny. Harry proposes marriage to Cissy and wants to have children, but Cissy is not able to get pregnant.

Johnny and Katie marry and later Katie gives birth to Francie. Johnny works periodically but enjoys booze more than steady employment. To support the family, Katie takes a job cleaning their apartment building.

One day, Cissy announces that she is going to have a baby. She tells Katie that the baby will be hers but someone else is carrying it for her – an unwed mother. She enlists Katie and Johnny's help to sneak the baby in while keeping Harry busy by pretending to be in labor. The baby is born but has to be delivered to Cissy. Katie and Johnny are at Cissy's apartment when Harry comes home from work. While Harry is in the kitchen getting something for Cissy, she has Katie and Johnny retrieve the infant from around the corner and sneak it into the bedroom. Cissy and Harry name their new son Oscar for Harry's real name.

Twelve years pass. Francie is now thirteen. Johnny and Katie are still together despite his lack of steady employment and his drinking problem. Cissy and Harry also remain together with Oscar Jr. being twelve.

Cissy's "first" Harry is coming by to see her. His wife has died, and he wants to rekindle his relationship with Cissy. Upon seeing him, Cissy realizes that he is not the good-looking man she once knew fifteen years ago. Her current Harry returns home seeing the first Harry there and announces that he is through with Cissy and leaves.

Time passes. Unknown to his wife and daughter, Johnny has been employed playing piano in a house of ill-repute. He thinks he has won a piano for Francie being chanced off at the house. But when the madame informs everyone that no one who works for her is eligible for the drawing, Johnny protests and is fired.

After the incident, Johnny vows to get a regular job working on building the Lincoln Tunnel. Days later, Cissy bumps into Harry (Oscar), confesses that she loves him, and invites him to return to her. She informs Harry that she is going to have a baby (for real this time).

Katie is advised that Johnny has died at work.

Months pass; Cissy has given birth to a daughter, and Francie is graduating from the eighth grade. Before he died, Johnny had given money to Cissy to purchase flowers for Francie's graduation which are presented to her on that day with a card written by her dad.

Despite the various reports on Garland's involvement in the planned musical version of *A Tree Grows in Brooklyn*, the project never became a reality.

Say It with Music – 1963

Variety reported in May 1963 that Irving Berlin was working on a picture for Metro called *Say It with Music* to be produced by Arthur Freed and directed by Vincent Minnelli: "Berlin assured film won't be his life story and that he won't be portrayed on the screen. Freed can use as many of his established songs as he wants to, Berlin said, adding that he retains ownership of all his songs, including those already used in pictures, except for a handful. He will write new songs, too, but the exact number remains to be decided." The article went on to state, "Story of 'Say It with Music' will embrace the 'Golden Era' of the 1920's, according to Freed. . ."[133]

In June 1963, Hedda Hopper noted that Berlin had Judy Garland in mind for the film with Robert Goulet also starring. A few days after the Hopper column, *Variety*, on June 28, 1963, confirmed that Goulet was being considered for the lead in the project but there was no mention of Judy as his co-star.

Looking for a way to incorporate Irving Berlin's extensive songbook into a film, Arthur Laurents wrote a screenplay titled *Say It with Music* that, as noted by Berlin, was not an autobiography but instead built around the theme of the battle of the sexes from the 1910s to the 1960s. Despite changes over that time period with women receiving the right to vote, world wars, women pursuing careers, the thesis of the screenplay is that women basically want love and marriage while men don't want to be tied down with one woman.

The lead characters in the work are George, a bachelor and head of his own company, who loves women but is never going to marry one, and Martha, who after ending a relationship with George, seeks to imitate his dating habits. The story follows their various relationships through the decades showing the different styles of dress and settings, but, according to the script, "the more things change, the more they stay the same."

In the 1920s, George meets Elsie, a suffragette, whom he asks to dinner. They dance and sing "Say It with Music." He takes her to his place. They talk about equal rights. He takes her to bed. George gives her the key to his apartment. She says that she wants to marry him, but he doesn't believe in marriage.

Flash forward to the 1960s with Martha, who doesn't have a career but keeps busy seeking a man to marry. She is dating George. It's raining outside. Nevertheless, she wants to go to a society party. He wants to stay in and make love singing "It's a Lovely Day." Martha joins him in singing the number. It stops raining, and they go to the coming-out party.

At the affair, the scene shifts to John, an acquaintance of George's, who is looking for a girl named Mary. Mary stutters, and so men avoid her – but not John. The only way Mary can stop stuttering is by singing her sentences. John and Mary perform "Falling in Love is Wonderful" with George and Martha joining them in the number.

After the party, George and Martha are at her place with Martha preparing breakfast. She says that George has never told her that he loves her prompting George to sing about love leading to marriage and then divorce. The song ends with George declaring that he could never be faithful to any woman.

The next scene is at a modern art gallery owned by John during different time periods. Martha, trying to emulate George, is dating a variety of men. George is infatuated with a model from a painting. When John introduces Mary to George, Mary loses her stutter as she talks with him.

John's father advises him against marrying Mary, while Mary's mother wonders why John has not asked her daughter to marry him. John starts to sing "Won't You Play Me Some Jazz" with Mary countering him with "Won't You Play a Simple Melody." Mary then sings "What Will You Do When I'm Far Away?" John performs "Shaking the Blues Away," and Mary sings "Remember the Night" as the two grow further apart.

The next scene is set in 1950 at the Rivera Hotel. George is with Chantal, a ravishing French girl. Martha, at an adjoining table, is with a handsome Yugoslavian. Neither George nor Martha understands the language of their partners. Martha and George begin to perform "Anything You Can Do I Can Do Better."

Later, George meets Francine, a chorus girl, who used to be called "Helen." Martha is with a guy named Frank singing "A Pretty Girl Is Like a Melody." Next, Martha, elegantly dressed like a musical comedy street walker, sings "Lady of the Evening."

Focusing on Francine again, she meets George after her show. The two argue over George not taking her career seriously enough. She wants to be a star. He responds that she is not talented enough. This scene is followed by a show business montage through the decades including the following numbers: "When the Midnight Choo-Choo Leaves for Alabam," "Mandy," "Top Hat, White Tie and Tails," and "There's No Business Like Show Business."

After the montage, the scene returns to Francine and George talking about her career. George leaves her since there is only one star in his relationships and that star is, of course, him.

As George leaves, he bumps into Martha on the elevator. Both are worn out by their lifestyles. He asks her to have coffee with him. But, when the elevator door opens, a man is waiting for Martha to go out with him.

George departs the elevator and walks to his apartment singing "All Alone, I'm So All Alone." At his apartment, he picks up the phone asking the operator to dial Butterfield 8 . . .

The apparent initial draft of the Laurents screenplay ends thusly. The Laurents script does mention Judy Garland – not as one of the women romanced by George but in a cameo singing "There's No Business Like Show Business" in the montage described above.

Notes to this draft screenplay indicate the names of several stars who were considered for roles in the planned film. Laurents states that Frank Sinatra would play the lead male character with George Chakiris as the second male lead, perhaps as the character John described above.[134] Julie Andrews may have appeared as Martha who is described in the notes as a character who enters a man's world to act like a man pursing promiscuity with several sexual conquests. Ann-Margret was considered for the role of the chorus girl who wants to be an actress. A character played by Sophia Loren may have been added to the script as a partisan fighter during World War II who sleeps with the Sinatra character. Shirley MacLaine and Brigitte Bardot were also mentioned as possibilities for roles as women having affairs with Sinatra.

The Laurents script was rejected as a basis for *Say It with Music*, probably not because of its sexism. Writer Leonard Gershe was then hired to develop a different approach to incorporating Irving Berlin's songs into a story line.

Gershe's screenplay, dated May 20, 1965, opened with a musical prologue with performers singing about a dozen of Berlin's songs. Images were to be displayed on the screen encompassing various time periods from the 1900s to the 1960s. The story line was built around the song, "Always the Same" based on the idea that "No matter how much modernization changes our lives, the human element - emotion and motivation – always remains the same."

The principal characters in the story are Willie Braden, an entertainment mogul who heads Braden Broadcasting, and Diana Forbes, a reporter for *Time* magazine. There is also an on-screen narrator who provides commentary on the story as well as interacting with the characters at various times. About Braden, the narrator says that while Willie has vision and foresight for business, he lacks an understanding of the human element.

Publicity-shy Willie Braden has never been married and lives a solitary life concentrating on his business affairs. For a special issue of *Time* about entertainment, Diana Forbes is given the assignment to interview Braden. She finally lands the interview and discovers that Willie claims that he will never fall in love since everyone he has ever loved has left him. He had six sets of parents by the time he was eleven, and things did not work out with the girl he had wanted to marry.

In addition to several Berlin compositions sung by the characters, there are musical montages in the script. One covers fifty years of the different phases of the entertainment industry ending with "There's No Business Like Show Business." Another shows Willie and Diana in various European capitals as their relationship with each other develops.

In the end, the couple falls in love, and Willie proposes marriage. The narrator ends the story singing "Always the Same."

The team of Betty Comden and Adolph Green made a third attempt at bringing *Say It with Music* to the silver screen. Their screenplay dated February 14, 1966 featured stories about the love affairs of three women. in different time periods. Jenny Clark, a graduate student in sociology, was a product of the 1960s; Jane Claremont, a wealthy single lady from 1913, became socially conscious; and Jill Jameson was a showgirl from 1925. Each story was interwoven throughout with the script skipping back and forth in time.

Jenny Clark, who had written a master's thesis on the search for identity in the sixties, meets with Victor Roxbury about turning it into a book. To make the book more appealing to the public, she comes up with the idea of herself taking on a new identity and becoming a celebrity. She dresses up in a special outfit and crashes a party celebrating the opening of a special museum exhibit. The stunt makes the newspapers, and she subsequently becomes a magazine cover model and fashion icon. Jenny begins dating Victor, her publisher. He is concerned that the image Jenny created for herself is becoming real to her. After confessing that he loves Jenny, the couple appears to be headed to marriage.

Jane Claremont comes from a conservative family whose father runs a newspaper. He fires several female employees for dancing the Turkey Trot during their lunch hour. When the former employees picket the Claremont estate, Jenny becomes caught up in the protest. She meets Will McCoy, a budding artist and journalist. After dating Will, Jenny seeks to be more socially active and volunteers at a settlement house. She informs her father that she will be marrying Will. Her father thinks he can get the couple to break up by offering Will a job at his newspaper which Will refuses. Jane and he do end their engagement. Nonetheless, in the end, the two reconcile.

Jill Jameson is a showgirl appearing in the Music Box's *Revue of 1925* who meets comic actor Larry Wallace. She is a big fan of Larry's work, but they argue when Larry says that he wants to do dramatic roles instead of comic ones. They begin seeing each other frequently. His dramatic debut in a film will soon premiere, but Jill doesn't want him to give up his screen character that made him famous. As with the other screenplays for *Say It with Music*, a show business cavalcade is presented ending, naturally with "There's No Business Like Show Business."

Larry wants Jill to marry him. She doesn't want to give up her blossoming career. Larry's picture in which he appears in a dramatic role opens to negative reviews. She tries to console him but to no avail. But in the end, they get together headed toward wedded bliss.

In the final scene, a commentator states that while many things change in the United States, the ways of love and love songs remain the same.

While there was no mention of Judy Garland in a cameo role in this take on *Say It with Music*, nonetheless, as was the case with the Arthur Laurents' script, there is a scene where the Jenny Clark character meets Fred Astaire at a party and imagines herself dancing with him.

Little Me – 1963

In the screenplay written by Larry Gelbart, writer Patrick Dennis, a character who is never seen on screen, visits Belle Poitrine to help write her autobiography. Belle relates her life story to Dennis while engaging in various luxurious activities at her estate.

Belle was born in Drifters Run, the poor section of Venezuela, Illinois. Her mother, whom Belle thought was a nurse because she made people feel better, was really a prostitute. In Drifters Run, Belle encounters Noble Eggleston, the handsome son of a wealthy family who is immediately attracted to her and invites Belle to his sweet sixteen party given by his mother.

At the party, Noble introduces Belle to his mother as being from the "wrong side of the tracks." Mrs. Eggleston wants Belle to leave as soon as possible. Belle understands that she must acquire wealth, culture, and social position to be accepted by Noble's mother. Noble promises to wait for Belle while she leaves Venezuela to acquire such.

Before she leaves her small town, Belle confronts the miserly banker of her town in front of the townspeople who are asking for additional time to make their past due payments. In response to Belle's complaints about him, he tears up the mortgages and asks what he can do for her. He gives her money to go to Peoria. The banker, Mr. Pinchley, begins spending every weekend with Belle in her Peoria hotel room. He asks her to marry him despite that fact that he is an octogenarian and she a teenager. He promises to leave her wealth, culture, and social position.

However, she squeezes him so hard upon learning of his promises that the gun in his pocket goes off, killing him.

Belle is jailed, but the Buchsbaum Brothers learn of her fate and book her as a vaudeville act agreeing to make her a star. Noble testifies at her trial claiming that she is the sweetest, kindest soul he has ever known. Belle is acquitted and goes on the vaudeville circuit. But she is fired weeks later when the Buchsbaum Brothers find a new headliner who had shot her millionaire husband at their wedding.

Belle becomes a camera girl at a nightclub. Noble happens to meet Belle at the club and announces that he is engaged to Ramona, a girl from a wealthy family that his mother chose for him. Belle is about to jump from a ledge over her despair about Noble, when a Frenchman, Val, who is appearing at the club, saves her. Subsequently, Belle meets George Musgrove, an acquittance from Venezuela, who happens to own the nightclub. George leaves her pregnant as he joins the military to fight in World War I.

Later, Belle meets and marries Fred Poitrine who is in the Army. After he goes off to war as a clerk-typist, he perishes from a serious digit wound. Belle gives birth to a baby girl.

Noble, also fighting in World War I as a pilot, is shot down and listed as missing. Belle decides to go to France to search for him. While in a German POW camp, he learns that Belle is in France and escapes.

In the meantime, Belle sees Val in a military hospital suffering from amnesia. She helps him recover his memory. Belle then runs into Noble who asks her to marry him. She accepts but backs out of the engagement when Val regresses thinking that Belle has jilted him. Belle ends up marrying Val. The two tour Europe with a new vaudeville act.

Feeling homesick, Belle and Val book passage to America on the SS Gigantic. Noble is also abroad the vessel. He is now both a judge and a surgeon, a husband and a father, married to Ramona. Nevertheless, he confesses to Belle that he still loves her.

The ship crashes into an iceberg with Noble, being the perpetual hero, taking over from the crew the task of evacuating the ship. He is so perfect that he teaches the non-swimmers on board how to swim in two minutes. Everyone on the ship is saved except, alas, for Val who, after hearing Noble tell Belle that he still loves her, gets amnesia again and forgets how to swim. Belle sues the steamship company for the loss of her luggage and her husband and settles for $2 million. Meanwhile, Romana loses her family's wealth in the 1929 stock market crash. Mrs. Eggleston has her son's marriage annulled upon learning that Ramona is no longer rich.

The Buchsbaum Brothers are now making movies and ask Belle to partner with them since they need her money. They form Vita-Belle Pictures with Belle as their main star featured in movie adaptations of classic novels like *Moby Dick*. Belle becomes the wealthiest woman in America.

A Prince from a small country in Europe makes Belle a countess for agreeing to marry him. But thinking that he is dying and not wanting him to suffer, Belle poisons his wine unaware that he is recovering from his sickness.

Noble asks Belle to marry him as he becomes the governor of both North and South Dakota. However, he is impeached and removed from office after Belle encourages him to drink to their happiness. Having never drunk alcoholic beverages before, he becomes a drunkard and disappears before they can tie the knot.

Belle's daughter returns and has fallen in love with Noble Eggleston Jr., and they marry. The elder Noble, sobered up, finally returns to Belle, and they walk off hand-in-hand into the sunset.

As reported in March 1964, Judy Garland wanted to play the part of the older Belle Poitrine in the movie adaptation of the Broadway musical to be directed by Joe Layton.[135] An interesting casting choice would have been Judy as the older Belle and her daughter, Liza Minnelli as the younger Belle Poitrine.

While Larry Gelbart wrote the screenplay, the film, to be produced by Embassy, was never made apparently because of the relative failures of other musicals, at the time, such as *Star* with Julie Andrews and *Doctor Doolittle* with Rex Harrison.

Chapter 7:

The Musical Roles That Might Have Been with Bing Crosby or Frank Sinatra

Although Judy never appeared in a movie with Bing Crosby, she made numerous appearances on the early 1950s radio series, *The Bing Crosby – Chesterfield Show*. Garland did appear in a movie with Frank Sinatra – *Till the Clouds Roll By*, although they were not in the same scene.

Judy and Frank Sinatra

Just for You (aka Famous) – 1951

The trials and tribulations of a show business father and his offspring were the theme of this motion picture that was released in 1952. The film starred Bing Crosby as the father and Jane Wyman as his girlfriend.

In 1951, newspapers reported that Judy Garland would co-star in the movie with Bing. For example, Jack Lait, Jr. wrote:

> I said a few weeks ago that Judy Garland and Bing Crosby had planned to star in a movie together but that Judy had dropped the idea because she feared it might impair her health.
>
> In any case you hadn't heard, she has changed her mind, and the project will probably come off as scheduled. Tentative title for the epic is "Famous," and I hope the thing goes through if for no other reason than that Cole Porter has agreed to write the musical score.[136]

Nevertheless, Hedda Hopper reported earlier that, while Crosby wanted Judy to sing several songs on the motion picture, his co-star would most likely be Celeste Holm raising the question if Garland would have appeared as Crosby's girlfriend or in another role.[137] Also, Cole Porter apparently was never contacted directly by Paramount Pictures to do the score for the film. Harry Warren composed the score.

The story line of the picture concerned a widowed songwriter named Jordan Blake, played by Crosby, becoming concerned that he has neglected his children – Jerry (Robert Arthur) and Barbara (Natalie Wood), after he dismisses a song written by Jerry as "trite" and after learning that his daughter and her governess have ended up in night court over a drunken disagreement with a cop. Carolina Hill (Wyman), Blake's girlfriend, urges Jordan to take both of his offspring to a resort to bond with them, but things do not always go as planned.

Jordan tries to satisfy Barbara's desire to become a student at an exclusive girls' school. Jerry falls in love with Carolina Hill and writes a really lovely number about her, "A Song to Carolina." Unaware that his son has feelings for Carolina, Jordan marries her. Jerry's pride is badly hurt, and he disappears. Eventually, Jordan finds that Jerry has enlisted in the military. Father and son reconcile at a military installation in Alaska when Jordan is on a USO tour. Jordan sings Jerry's song about Carolina.

In an early synopsis of a November 1950 version of the screenplay written by Charles Brackett, Walter Reisch, and Richard Breen, the head mistress of Barbara's girls' school is described as a "most efficient young woman" who is greatly attracted to the Bing Crosby character.[138] In the final film, legendary actress Ethel Barrymore appeared as the head mistress. Obviously, the description of the character had been changed meaning perhaps that the part, as originally written, may have been one for Judy Garland as a special guest star in the film. This may clarify the comment noted above by Hedda Hopper that Judy would not have been Bing's co-star in the movie.

The Pajama Game – 1955

Sheilah Graham reported that Garland was asking Warner Brothers for the film rights to this Broadway musical.[139] She hoped to play the part of Katherine "Babe" Williams, the leader of a Union Grievance Committee, who works at the Sleep-Tite Pajama Factory. The factory has just employed a new factory superintendent, Sid Sorokin. Predictably, Babe and Sid develop affection for one another despite the fact that Babe represents the workers and Sid, the management. The union stages a slowdown in an effort for higher wages. When Babe kicks her foot into the machinery at the factory causing a breakdown, Sid fires her. However, once Sid accesses the company's books and sees that profits are sufficient to grant the workers raises, peace is restored at the plant, and he and Babe reconnect.

Numbers sung by the character Babe Williams included "I'm Not at All in Love," "There Once Was a Man," "Hey There," and "7 ½ Cents." Lyrics were done by Richard Adler and Jerry Ross. The book was written by George Abbott and Richard Bissell.

The film of *The Pajama Game* was released in 1957 with Doris Day as Babe Williams and John Raitt as Sid Sorokin. Stanley Donen and George Abbott produced the movie. If Garland had starred in the project, Frank Sinatra may have played the Sorokin role.

Carousel – 1955

In a 1955 newspaper article, Sid Luft indicated that his then wife, Judy Garland, ". . . turned down 'Carousel'. . ." in order to do a nationwide concert tour. He stated, "If a part isn't good for her, she doesn't have to do it. And it was hard to find a movie script to follow 'A Star Is Born.'"[140] However, correspondence from the Darryl F. Zanuck Papers at the Margaret Herrick Library paints a somewhat different picture of Garland being considered for *Carousel*.

A June 16, 1955 memo from Zanuck to Buddy Adler, George Stephenson, and Henry Ephron states, in part, "Everyone here in New York is absolutely enthusiastic about the combination of Judy Garland and Frank Sinatra and that includes Oscar and Dick. However, no one is prepared to urge me to take on the responsibility in connection with Judy." The memorandum continues, "When I return I have already told (George) Chasin that I will agree to meet with her and I am going to make very tough conditions with great protection for us – if I decide after meeting with her that we are going to use her."[141]

Unknown is if a meeting between Judy and Zanuck actually occurred. If it did, perhaps after hearing Zanuck's conditions for making *Carousel*, Garland turned down the offer as Sid Luft stated. Nevertheless, on June 29, 1955, Darryl Zanuck sent a cablegram to Buddy Adler indicating that he was ". . . definitely not interested in Judy Garland . . ." and that negotiations should start with Shirley Jones for the lead female role.[142] In the same message, Zanuck stated that Adler should make a deal with Frank Sinatra but, apparently, Sinatra's asking price for the project was too high and so Gordon MacRae was signed for the male lead.

Based on the Rodgers and Hammerstein hit Broadway musical, the film, set in 1880, tells the story of Billy Bigelow, a carousel barker, and

Julie Jordan, a young mill worker, both living in Boothbay Harbor, Maine. They fall in love and then are fired from their respective jobs – Billy because he flirted with Julie to the dismay of Mrs. Mullins, the jealous carousel owner; Julie because she stayed out after curfew imposed by the mill owner. Billy and Julie marry. Billy learns from his wife that she is pregnant. Not being able to obtain a job, he plots with Jigger Craigin, a friend of the wealthy mill owner, to rob the owner. The mill owner foils the robbery. Billy, cornered by the police, climbs on top of a pile of crates which collapse, and he falls on his own knife, mortally wounded. Julie rushes to him as he lay dying.

Fifteen years later in the afterlife, Billy is told that he can return to Earth for a single day to make amends. Billy finds that his daughter, Louise, has been constantly taunted over her father's criminal past. Billy attempts to cheer her up, but Louise is frightened. Julie glimpses him for a brief moment and senses that Billy has returned to Earth for a reason. Billy requests that his Heavenly Guide give him permission to attend Louise's high school graduation. Billy gives both Louise and Julie the confidence they need and the knowledge that he did love Julie.

The motion picture featured such iconic numbers as "If I Loved You," "June Is Bustin' Out All Over," and "You'll Never Walk Alone." The film was released in 1956.

Manhattan Tower – 1956

As reported by columnist Louella Parsons, "An ambitious plan to star Bing Crosby, Judy Garland and Bob Hope in a motion picture version of 'Manhattan Tower,' Gordon Jenkins' album, is being worked on by agent Jimmy Saphier."[143]

"Manhattan Tower" was originally released in 1946 on two 78-rpm records. In 1956, the concept album was expanded to a forty-eight minute version. The album, using sound effects, narration, dialogue, and original songs describes the story of Steven who is visiting New York City and staying in an apartment building overlooking Manhattan. He visits Philly's Bar and Grill in the city where he meets a pretty woman named Julie.

She sings about a "Happiness Cocktail." Steven teaches her the mambo singing "I'm Learnin' My Latin." Their romance develops with the songs "Once Upon a Dream" and "Never Leave Me." The couple rides in a hansom cab through Central Park. When Steven confesses that he loves Julie, they duet on "Repeat After Me." The couple agrees to meet the following day in Washington Square. Upon observing a wedding in Greenwich Village, Julie says that marriage is not her cup of tea right now and sings "Married I Can Always Get." Julie and Steven then visit the Statue of Liberty with its inscription set to music. Next, they attend a party with Steven singing "New York's My Home." Afterwards, he doesn't want to leave the city for his home town, but Julie tells him he should leave and says "goodbye."

In October 1956, Helen O'Connell, Peter Marshall, Phil Harris, Ethel Walters, and Cesar Romero starred in a ninety-minute television adaptation of "Manhattan Tower." Steven and Julie were played by Marshall and O'Connell with Phil Harris appearing as a bartender, Cesar Romero as a Latino dance teacher, and Ethel Waters as a Sunday school teacher taking her class to visit the Statue of Liberty.

This TV special was supposedly a prelude to the movie project with Crosby, Hope, and Judy. While Bing and Garland would have played the man and woman who fall in love, it is not clear what role Hope would have had in the film. Perhaps a special role would have been written for Mr. Hope or one of the existing roles, such as the bartender or dance teacher, would have been expanded to accommodate the comedian.

Judy Garland did later work with Gordon Jenkins on at least two albums. *Alone*, a studio album, released in 1957, and *The Letter*, a concept album, with actor John Ireland.

By the Beautiful Sea – 1961

Hedda Hopper reported that MGM director Charles Walters wanted to direct Garland in a film version of the Broadway musical, *By the Beautiful Sea*. The film was to be produced by Roger Edens with Bing Crosby co-starring. *Variety* also indicated that Pearl Bailey may be cast in the movie as a woman who runs a boarding house owned by the Garland character when the latter is on the road.[144]

In the planned movie adaptation of this 1954 Broadway musical written by Herbert and Dorothy Fields with music by Arthur Schwartz, Judy Garland would have appeared as Lottie Gibson, a vaudeville performer who, with her father, owns a theatrical boarding house by the sea on Coney Island. Lottie is in love with Shakespearian actor Dennis Emery (presumably to be played by Crosby). She persuades him to room in her boarding house where, just so happens, his divorced wife and daughter, known as "Baby Betsy" although she is seventeen, are residing. In order to win child parts on the stage, Betsy's mother instructs her daughter to dress as a thirteen-year-old.

Lottie wants to lend money to Dennis to help him out of his financial straits but finds that her father Carl has invested the money in a Coney Island attraction. Lottie decides to win the prize for making a parachute jump from a balloon on the 4th of July.

In disguise, Lottie wins the prize, but the money is not enough. However, her father also wins money for being shot out of a cannon, and so she ends up with the funds she needs.

Baby Betsy, out of jealousy, tries to break up the romance between her father and Lottie. Lottie presents Betsy with one of her dresses. When Betsy puts it on, she looks seventeen and thanks Lottie. Lottie and Betsy go off to the midway together where Betsy is romanced by Mickey, a singing waiter, and Lottie by Dennis.

The movie was never produced.

Chapter 8:

The Biographical Roles That Might Have Been

About Judy, a news article said, "'She's wonderful,' the Hollywood people sigh. 'But a man would have to be out of his mind to get involved with her.'" The item went on, "Maybe, but Hollywood, with its present shortage of compelling names, can ill-afford to do without Judy. She's been barred, blackballed, blasted, but every time she bounces back. 'Never again, the producers swear after each picture, and then Judy scores in Las Vegas, at the Palace, or London's Palladium, and Hollywood offers come pouring in."[145]

The report from 1956 continued, "But now they want her – to do Helen Morgan's life story, to do Laurette Taylor's life story." In the 1950s and 1960s right up until her death in 1969, Judy's name was mentioned in conjunction with several noteworthy biographical motion picture projects.

Some of These Days – 1953

In January 1948, MGM purchased the screen rights to *Some of These Days*, the autobiography of Sophie Tucker which had been published in 1945. Although Metro denied the report, Sophie Tucker stated that Judy Garland and John Garfield would play the leading roles in the planned movie based on the autobiography.

Theodore Reeves was to do the screenplay for the project which would have been produced by Pandro S. Berman.

Sophie Tucker was a singer in vaudeville and also made some appearances in Broadway plays as well as in movies. Born in 1886, she married Louis Tuck after graduating from high school and singing in her father's restaurant. Sophie expanded her last name to "Tucker" and, after giving birth to a son, decided to separate from her husband and pursue a show business career in New York City.

She began performing in blackface after overhearing a music promoter say to his assistant, "This one's so big and ugly the crowd out front will razz her. Better get some cork and black her up."[146]

Tucker worked her way up from singing in small venues throughout the Northeast to appearing in burlesque shows to finally getting a chance to sing in the Ziegfeld Follies. Once, for an appearance in New York, her trunk was delayed in reaching the theater, and so she didn't receive her makeup in time to put on blackface. She sang without the makeup and was a hit meaning she could perform as herself in the future.

Her singing act usually consisted of a comedy song, a novelty number, and then a "hot" song like "There's Company in the Parlor, Girls, Come on Down." Sophie was initially billed as "The Mary Garden of Ragtime." "Some of These Days" became her theme song when her maid introduced her to its songwriter.

After her first husband died, she married vaudevillian Frank Westphal, a piano player, who developed an act with her. As she recounts in her autobiography, appearing at the Palace Theatre in Chicago, Frank and she had a big argument. He left the theater. Come show time, he was nowhere to be found. "The curtain went up. Still no Frank. I got madder and madder. Maybe, too, I was a little scared. Coming up the hard way, as I have, has given me respect for the law of show business, which is that a performer shall be there and ready when his call comes. Two minutes to go, and along came Frank. With him was the crumbiest-looking bum you ever laid your eyes on." She went on to recollect, "I was ready to let all fireworks loose, but Frank shushed me: 'Hold everything, Soph. The bum goes on in the act with us.'"[147] The guy accompanied the two playing the mouth organ, and the act was a hit. Since she made more money than Westphal, this doomed their marriage, and they divorced.

To freshen her act, Tucker formed a small band, "Five Kings of Syncopation," and labeled herself as "The Queen of Jazz." The act eventually broke up when the band demanded more money. She then formed a new act with a pianist, a violinist, and a dancer. Eventually, Ted Shapiro, her long-time accompanist joined her.

Sophie married a third time to Al Lackey, one of her biggest fans who became her manager. She introduced a song, "I'm the Last of the Red Hot Mamas," which became her new moniker.

Tucker appeared in her first feature, Warner Brother's *Honky Tonk* in 1929. She didn't think much of the film. A few years later, she was signed by MGM as the next Marie Dressler and made *Broadway Melody of 1937*, appearing with Judy Garland. Around that time, Tucker predicted that Judy would be the "Hot Mama" of the future. She further commented that Judy understands the value of lyrics and possesses one of the finest voices she had ever heard.[148] After making *Thoroughbreds Don't Cry*, also with Garland, Tucker returned to Broadway.

One may speculate that if a motion picture had been made with Garland as Sophie Tucker, it would have focused on Tucker's early years in entertainment. While their singing styles were not the same, Judy, no doubt, could have done a reasonable facsimile of Tucker's way of presenting a song. What would have been more interesting is how MGM might have made Garland up to look more like Tucker who was a hefty blonde. If MGM took Tucker's suggested casting to heart, John Garfield would probably have played Frank Westphal in the film.

The Fabulous Fanny - 1953

In April 1953, columnist Lyn Connelly reported, "Judy Garland will do 'The Fabulous Fanny' based on the life of Fanny Brice."[149]

Born on October 29, 1891, entertainer Fanny Brice was not only a comedienne but also a singer, theater performer, and film actress. She headlined the *Ziegfeld Follies* in 1910 and 1911 and later was hired again by Flo Ziegfeld for the Follies in the 1920s and 30s. In 1921 she introduced her signature song, "My Man." Brice starred on

Broadway in the plays, *Fioretta*, *Sweet and Low*, as well as *Billy Rose's Crazy Quilt*. In the movies, she starred in *Be Yourself!* and in *Everybody Sing* with Judy Garland. She had a long-running radio comedy, playing a mischievous youngster named Baby Snooks. Brice passed away on May 29, 1951.

Shortly after her death, writer Norman Katkov authored a biography of Brice titled, *The Fabulous Fanny: The Story of Fanny Brice*. The book was based on notes Brice had left before she died hoping to author her own autobiography. Katkov also included reminiscences from many of Brice's friends and former husbands such as Polly Moran, George Cukor, Nick Arnstein and Billy Rose.

In her own words, Fanny Brice described her three marriages including her first marriage to Frank White:

> Now we're married, and the dinner is over, but I won't let him in my room.
>
> He's standing in front of the door, and I'm standing in front of the door. "Well, Frank," I say, "get a good night's sleep and I'll see you tomorrow."
>
> We're sleeping together, he says.
>
> Oh, no, we're not. You have to go somewhere else.
>
> Where? he asks me.
>
> I don't know where. You're a barber. You know those things, so good night.
>
> "I'm your husband," he says.
>
> "Now, Frank," I say, "it's been a hard day and tomorrow is a matinee, so go away."
>
> "Aren't you a virgin?" he wants to know.

> The only reason I'm a virgin is that nobody ever asked me.
>
> "Of course I'm a virgin," I say, "but you can't have anything to do with me until the show ends its run."[150]

Needless to say, the marriage did not last long.

Fanny next wed Nick Arnstein, famously portrayed in the film, *Funny Girl*. About Nick Fanny wrote, "Will Rogers was the only man I ever met who I would have sworn was true to his wife. Nick wasn't Will Rogers."[151]

Her last husband was Broadway producer Billy Rose. Rose commented about seeing Fanny perform: "I watched Fanny. She had it: the magic. It came from her eyes, from her hands, from her just being on the stage. She was one of the goose-flesh specialists, and you can't explain that quality, you have to see it. Watch Garland on a stage if you ever get the chance. She and Chevalier and Durante are the only three left."[152]

About her three marriages, Billy Rose recalls that Fanny told him, ". . . that she married Frank White, the barber, because he smelled so good; she married Nick Arnstein because he looked so good; and she married me because I thought so good."[153]

In her notes concerning her autobiography attempt, Fanny wrote: "And in what I've said for my book, I've said the truth. And if people will read about Fanny Brice they might remember that they thought she was very unfunny. They might open the book and throw it away and it can be a big flop, my book. But one thing it won't be: a lie."[154]

Later in 1953, Erskine Johnson wrote: "There was big movie excitement when Norman Katkov's 'The Fabulous Fanny' was published, but no deal to film Fanny Brice's life story has been set at any major studio. Fanny's heirs, it's said, never approved of the Katkov biography and want the movie about Fanny to be based on different material."[155] Presumably, "Fanny's heirs" refers to Fanny's daughter, Frances Brice and her husband, producer Ray Stark who later made

Funny Girl and *Funny Lady*, both featuring Barbara Streisand as Stark's mother-in-law.

Laurette – 1955

Another planned bio picture for Judy Garland, *Laurette,* focused on the career of renowned stage actress Laurette Taylor. Born Helen Loretta Cooney on April 1, 1883, she showed early talent for acting. To ensure her safety while on the road appearing in different plays, her mother had her wed twice-married Charles Taylor when he was thirty-six and she was sixteen. They both appeared in stage presentations – mainly melodramas. Nonetheless, she wanted to expand her range to real dramatic presentations and so compromised with her husband to do straight dramatic roles occasionally.

Her life was chronicled by her daughter, Marguerite Courtney, in a biography, *Laurette*, published in 1955.

Laurette established a method for rehearsing new plays by first getting the general sense of each scene, achieving a consistent character, and establishing a real relationship between her character and others. At the last minute, she would memorize all her actual lines.

Taylor eventually moved to New York to appear in Broadway productions after playing on the road mainly in the West for several years and appearing in several melodramatic plays that were popular with audiences at that time.

After divorcing Charles Taylor, she married playwright Hartley Manners who scripted *Peg O' My Heart*, the play for which she is best remembered. Laurette liked to sing. Manners would usually put a song in each of the plays he wrote for her.

The actress had a life-long struggle with her weight. Only five feet five, every summer she would take steps to shed the pounds she gained during the winter. Her routine included exercising, wearing heavy clothes to sweat off the fat, swimming, and watching other people eat fattening food while she would eat only diet food. Always concerned about her looks, Laurette preferred character roles even as a young actress which required wigs, costumes, and/or special make-up.

While best known for her appearances on the stage, Laurette Taylor did make a few silent features, most notably, *Peg O' My Heart* directed by King Vidor who showed her that acting techniques learned for the stage would not work on film.

Still married to Manners, Taylor fell in love with actor John Gilbert in 1924. She also began to drink more obsessively. Around the same time, Hartley Manners stopped writing and became interested in investing in the stock market. Eventually, she requested a divorce from Manners so she could marry Gilbert. When Hartley would not grant such, she ended her relationship with John Gilbert. Her drinking, however, did not end.

Subsequently, Hartley was diagnosed with cancer of the esophagus. Following his death, Laurette went into virtual seclusion away from the theater. While her late husband did provide for her in his will, the funds were less than adequate for her needs. With her continued drinking, she was deemed unreliable as a theater actress. However, in 1939, Ms. Taylor did make a comeback in a play titled *Outward Bound*. Her final heralded performance was in *The Glass Menagerie*. She passed away on December 7, 1946 at the age of sixty-three.

Soon after Laurette Taylor's biography was published, director George Cukor sought to adapt it for the big screen and wanted Judy Garland to star in the feature. His first attempt to make the picture was with MGM. A September 6, 1955 letter to Cukor from The Jaffe Agency indicated that Metro was not interested in the project with Garland. The letter stated, "Sol Siegel told me today that he had gotten a most emphatic, 'No' to Judy for 'Laurette' at Metro. As a matter of fact, 'No' to Judy for anything at Metro." Siegel apparently tried to persuade MGM management in both Los Angeles and New York that Garland would be perfect for the role, but the letter noted that "He was turned down coldly on both coasts, despite what, he thought were very persuasive arguments in favor of Judy. So that, obviously, takes care of the Lion, who will not roar again for Garland."[156]

A few days later on September 8, 1955, The Jaffe Agency sent Cukor another letter reporting that Mary Martin was interested in playing the role of Laurette Taylor. The name of another Judy – Judy Holiday, also was mentioned as a possibility for the role.

Flash forward to 1962, George Cukor was still pursuing the project. According to a letter from Cukor's agent, discussions were underway with United Artists about the film. Gene Allen would write the screenplay with Judy Garland once again as the star. United Artists was willing to put up $1 million for the picture with Judy receiving $75,000 for her part plus 15% of the profits. Garland was to film the picture after completing *I Could Go on Singing*. However, nothing came of this project.

The final word on the planned film appears to have come from Sam Jaffe himself in a letter to Cukor in 1968 stating that Elizabeth Taylor had been approached about starring as Laurette Taylor, but she expressed no interest in the part. The letter also asked what Cukor thought about Faye Dunaway for the role.

While no movie starring Judy Garland ever resulted chronicling the life and career of Laurette Taylor, at least one play was done based on her life.

In 1963, Mary Martin appeared in a Broadway production, *Jennie*, that started out as an account of Taylor's early life and career. Originally called *Blood and Thunder*, the musical was written by Arthur Schulman with music and lyrics by Arthur Schwartz and Howard Dietz. The original characters were to be Laurette Taylor, her first husband Charles, and Hartley Manners. By the time the musical premiered, the characters' names had been changed to Jennie Jerome, James O'Conner, and Christopher Lawrence Cromwell.

The stage presentation opens with Jennie and her husband James touring the West appearing in melodramas like *King of the White Slavers*. When James can't raise money to maintain his theater troupe, he and his wife decide to go their separate ways looking for work. Jennie travels to New York to live with her mother and loses touch with her husband.

In New York, Jennie meets playwright Christopher Cromwell, who gives her a role in his new production. Meanwhile, she receives a postcard from James who is performing in shows in Alaska. Christopher asks Jennie if she would like to marry him, but she says she still loves James. Just as Jennie is about to formally introduce Christopher to her family, O'Connor re-appears.

Jennie decides to accompany her husband to Seattle to open their own theater. What she finds when she arrives is a dilapidated church which they have to renovate to turn it into a performance venue.

Six months pass and the first play at the new theater is ready to open to a sold-out audience. Christopher turns up in Seattle and gives Jennie a new play he wrote for her. Her feelings for the playwright are rekindled.

On opening night of the new theater during a scene in the play, a fire accidentally breaks out destroying the building. Christopher helps the firemen extinguish the blaze. Later, he asks Jennie if she thinks that she made the right decision in reuniting with James. She responds that she can't leave him, but, in the end, she does. She departs Seattle with Christopher on the train.

The musical was not a hit. It premiered on October 17, 1963 and closed on December 28 of that year.

The Helen Morgan Story - 1956

In 1956, Judy reportedly had the inside track to star in a biopic about singer Helen Morgan, according to Erskine Johnson.[157]

Released by Warner Brothers in 1957, *The Helen Morgan Story,* starring Ann Blyth as the singer and Paul Newman as Larry Maddux, her on-again, off-again manager and lover, was a fictionalized biography of Morgan's career. Beginning in the 1920s in Chicago, Morgan became a dancer in a carnival sideshow managed by Maddux. He disbands the act but sleeps with Morgan before he leaves. Helen attempts to find jobs as a singer but is unsuccessful until she encounters Maddux again who pays a speakeasy proprietor to hire her. Subsequently, he persuades Morgan to travel to Canada with him to enter the Miss Canada contest.

Telling her the pageant is fixed so that she will win, she is awarded the title until one of the judges, Russell Wade (Richard Carlson) from New York City, checks into her background and finds she is not a Canadian resident.

Back in the United States, Helen meets Larry again after he is freed from jail having been convicted of smuggling Canadian liquor into the States. Morgan becomes an in-demand singer but begins drinking. Larry comes back into her life. He partners with Russell Wade to open a nightclub called the Helen Morgan Club featuring the singer. Flo Ziegfeld sees her act at the club and signs her to star as Julie Le Verne in the Broadway musical *Show Boat*. After learning that Wade has invested in the club, Morgan becomes distraught over the arrangement and tells Maddux that she is in love with the married Russell Wade.

Helen continues upping her quota of liquor and spending her money faster than she earns it. She learns from Russell's wife that Mrs. Wade won't grant Russell a divorce and that Helen should stop seeing him.

The Feds raid Helen's club and close the premises. Helen descends further into alcoholism. She reveals to Larry that she lost money in the stock market crash. Larry is involved in a shoot-out with a rival liquor smuggler and is seriously wounded. She goes to see him and calls an ambulance to take him to a hospital. After recovering, he is jailed.

Helen is noticeably inebriated in a subsequent performance falling off a piano as she tries to sing. Wade attempts to help her recover but is not successful. On the skids, she sinks deeper into alcoholism. Eventually, she is taken to a hospital to dry out. Larry visits her and encourages her to get back on her feet. He finally says he loves her. Helen is released from the hospital. Larry picks her up and proposes marriage, but Helen says it is too late. They go back to the abandoned Helen Morgan Club which is about to be demolished. As a surprise, a group of her friends are at the club welcoming her back. She sings one last song, "Can't Help Lovin' Dat Man of Mine."

Ann Blyth in a scene from The Helen Morgan Story. Reportedly, Helen Morgan sat on a piano to sing because she was so under the influence that she couldn't stand.

Despite not being married in the film, the real Helen Morgan married three times during her life and had a baby in 1926 which she gave up for adoption. She passed away at age forty-one from cirrhosis of the liver. Although Judy Garland was one of several actresses in contention for the lead in this film, apparently Jack Warner, given the issues with the making of *A Star Is Born*, wanted Garland's singing voice more than he wanted Judy herself for the movie. Helen Morgan had a light soprano singing voice as did Ann Blyth who got the part. However, Warner wanted a belting, Garland-type singer, and so Blyth's vocals were dubbed by singer Gogi Grant.

The Aimee Semple McPherson Story – 1966

Aimee Semple McPherson was an American Pentecostal evangelist born in 1890 who passed away in 1944. She was at the height of her fame in the 1920s and 1930s using radio and other forms of mass media in her evangelism.

McPherson arrived in Los Angeles in 1918. Her mother, Minnie Kennedy, rented the Philharmonic Auditorium for Aimee to preach her sermons. Later, she founded the Angelus Temple in Los Angeles which became the home of the Foursquare Church. McPherson raised funds to build the Temple which at one time had an enrollment of over 10,000. She also made national headlines several times most notably when she was kidnapped in 1926. McPherson contended that while on Ocean Park Beach in Santa Monica, a couple approached her wanting her to pray for a sick child. She was shoved into the couple's vehicle and a cloth, laced with a drug, was held against her nose from which she passed out. When the couple was away on errands, she escaped captivity.

Los Angeles authorities speculated that she had really run off with a former employee of her temple with whom she was supposedly having an affair. McPherson, her mother, and others were charged with criminal conspiracy, perjury, and obstruction of justice. However, the charges against them were dropped for lack of evidence.

At one point in Aimee's career after the kidnapping, officials at the Angelus Temple hired detectives to shadow her. They found no evidence of sexual affairs.

In 1966, numerous gossip columnists reported that Judy Garland would star in a feature film biography about Aimee Semple McPherson. A newspaper account from columnist Charles McHarry stated, "Judy Garland and MGM got an OK from the late Aimee Semple McPherson's estate to do her film biography."[158]

Beyond that notice, there is not much additional information that could be found about this project. However, as early as 1963, one of Judy's favorite directors, George Cukor, did consider making a feature about McPherson.

The names of the characters were changed so as not to entice a lawsuit over the planned biography. As indicated in a January 1963 letter to Cukor from his attorney:

> We strongly recommend that even though the story may be confined strictly within the bounds of true facts, a signed release from anybody who might be able to identify himself in the photoplay should be obtained. In this connection, also, Gene (Allen) should always keep in mind that the true facts have not been judicially determined. Consequently, the assumed facts on the basis of news reports and other public records may be highly controversial and may possibly lead to difficulty.[159]

In a treatment found among the Cukor papers at the Margaret Herrick Library, the characters for the movie included Theone Alexander Sutter, the "siren of evangelism;" Bessie Clayburg, Theone's mother; Elsa Sohrodee, Theone's secretary and companion; Ralph Ifverson, the Temple's architect and Theone's lover; and Frank "Butch" Gaston, a private investigator.

The single scene in the treatment concerns Theone's mother hiring Gaston to investigate her daughter and her affair with Ifverson. Mrs. Clayburgh instructs Gaston that she wants him to find out all there is about the architect. The mother goes on to remark, "Theone is such a fool when it comes to something like this . . . if you only knew how much like a child she is at times. . . When I think of all I've had to do for her. . . you'd think she would listen. . . but no . . . she just smiles."[160]

Subsequently, Gaston produces his report on Theone stating that he found three separate occasions when Theone was with Ifverson – twice in a hotel at the beach and once in a downtown hotel. Each time Theone registered under her own name, but Ifverson used a false name.

Whether based on the Gene Allen treatment and directed by George Cukor or else based on another work, *The Aimee Semple McPherson Story* would have been a major comeback for Judy in her film career if the movie had been produced.

Piaf – 1967

In 1962, J.P. Miller authored a script chronicling the life of French singer Edith Piaf. Garland was rumored to be in the running to play Piaf in her later years. In the booklet accompanying the Blu-Ray release of the restored version of *A Star Is Born*, John Fricke notes that George Cukor was planning a screen adaptation of the life of the French chanteuse starring Judy that would incorporate filmed sequences from Garland's concerts in which she would perform certain Piaf songs.[161]

Piaf, born Edith Gassion, was a street urchin who became a legendary, international singing star. The script opens in 1922 Normandy with a Dr. Descombes examining young Edith's eyes. The little girl cannot bear to see light at all. Madame Gassion, who is caring for Edith, prays that her sight will improve. Eventually, it does.

Edith's father begins caring for her. He is a street performer who enlists Edith as part of his act. However, after he physically abuses the now teenage singer, she leaves. A teen boy named P'tit Louis invites Edith to stay at his parents' house. She soon becomes pregnant and gives birth. Edith leaves P'tit Louis and hooks up with Albert, a legionnaire. P'tit races to see Edith telling her that their daughter is sick with a high fever. When he and Edith return to their home, the daughter has passed away. P'tit leaves her. Albert has shipped out to Morocco.

Louis LePlee, a cabaret manager, hires Edith to sing in his club. LePlee changes Edith's last name to Piaf, meaning the little sparrow. LePlee is subsequently murdered. When his club closes, Edith is out of work. She struggles to resurrect her career.

At the dawn of World War II, Edith becomes a success. During the war, she hides several French resistance fighters from the Nazis and provides false identification cards to prisoners so they can escape a German prison camp.

Piaf comes to the United States to entertain and falls in love with Marcel Cerdan, a prizefighter, but he is married with children. Tragedy strikes her life again as Marcel is killed in a plane crash. She performs "La Vie En Rose" at a memorial service for him but collapses on stage and subsequently gets drunk, continuing on the path of self-destruction.

Edith takes up with a new boyfriend but continues her binge drinking. She is severely injured in a car accident and is near death but miraculously recovers. She begs Saint Therese to help her resist alcohol and succeeds.

Piaf makes a comeback on stage at the Olympia Theater to thunderous applause.

The first of several subsequent biographical films about the life of Edith Piaf was not made until 1974. Produced in France, it was simply titled *Piaf*.

Chapter 9:

Other Dramatic Roles That Might Have Been

Before her appearance in a dramatic supporting role in *Judgement at Nuremberg*, Judy Garland's only non-musical drama was the 1945 MGM film, *The Clock* with Robert Walker. Directed by Judy's soon-to-be husband, Vincent Minnelli, the motion picture focused on Alice Mayberry meeting Corporal Joe Allen who has a forty-eight hour pass. They fall in love and marry before he returns to the military.

This chapter describes other dramatic roles for which Ms. Garland was considered in the 1950s and 1960s.

The Stubborn Wood – 1951-52

Actor/director Paul Henreid wanted to adapt *The Stubborn Wood* by Emily Harvin, published in 1948, for the big screen with Judy starring along with him. According to Louella Parsons' column, Henreid contacted the William Morris office to ask Judy Garland to play the female lead in the planned movie. Reportedly, Henreid offered Garland a generous portion of the profits and had ample financing for the project.[162]

The novel focuses on Monica Prystal who is married to architect Deemster Prystal and lives in fashionable Pintuna, a wealthy Southern California community. She had met her husband when she was nineteen and he was twenty-four. The couple has two sons.

One day, at a night club, Monica sees Deemster with his arms around her friend Alison Blanchard and another woman. His affairs with other women and his drinking continue to escalate. Monica is deeply in love with him and won't confront him about his extramarital affairs.

Monica consults a psychiatrist who advises her that Deemster "seems to have the illness while she exhibits the symptoms."

With Deemster's continuing womanizing, Monica suffers a miscarriage and becomes severely depressed. A doctor advises Deem to have his wife committed to a mental institution. The physician at the institution says to Monica that she is there where she'll bother no one and will be there a long time.

Monica attempts suicide by cutting her wrists and then tries to hang herself. Deem and Monica's mother visit and agree to move her to another institution. Initially, the new place appears to be as bad as the previous one. But, eventually, she is transferred to a cottage on the site which gives her more freedom. She continues to insist that she is not being given proper treatment for the injuries to her throat that resulted from the second suicide attempt.

After four months, she is required to do more work and receives less favors because Deemster owes more than $1000 on the bill.

Deem has her committed to a state mental hospital which is less expensive. Monica finds that it is more permissive than the prior institutions and her condition begins to improve. She seeks to be paroled, but her husband tells her that she belongs to the state.

Monica sends a letter to her brother to have him assume responsibility for her care instead of her husband. She is finally released and goes to live with her aunt. Monica consults an attorney who finds proof that Deem lied about his financial condition to have her committed to the state facility. Deem confesses to his wife that he never really loved her. He just thought that he did. Monica does reunite with her sons.

In his notes about developing a screenplay based on the novel, Henreid indicates that he would have eliminated one of the two suicide attempts but adds an attempted escape from the first institution. He also proposes to eliminate the second institution from the story and have Monica taken to the state hospital after having been a patient at the first asylum.

Henreid adds more detail about why Deem could not keep up with the payments to the private mental institution. The Deem character becomes quite extravagant with his money after Monica is institutionalized. He is out late every night dancing and drinking. His customers use other architects for projects that Deem would have otherwise gotten. After his income declines, he wants the state to take care of his wife.

The end of the film would have come after Monica implores Deem to end her parole so that she can be reunited with her children. After the conversation with his wife, Deem goes to a bar and gets drunk. Driving home, he is involved in an accident breaking both of his legs. Deem is hospitalized. None of his friends want to see him. A nurse suggests that he call his wife. Deem does not believe that she will visit because he has been so bad to her. But Monica, who has read about the accident in the papers, does appear to look after Deem having never ceased to love him.[163]

The film was never produced.

Three Faces of Eve – 1956

In 1956, producer-director Nunnally Johnson offered Ms. Garland the lead role in *Three Faces of Eve* which eventually went to Joanne Woodward.

The film concerned a timid wife and mother named Eve White who sees psychiatrist Dr. Luther after having severe headaches and blackouts. While with Dr. Luther, Eve reveals a more fun-loving personality, Eve Black. Eve is sent to a hospital for observation after her other personality Eve Black is found strangling Eve's daughter. After Eve White is released, her husband doesn't believe his wife has multiple personalities. Nevertheless, when Eve Black confronts the husband, he comes to realize that his wife does have split personalities. He ends up divorcing her.

Dr. Luther believes that Eve White and Eve Black are both incomplete personalities. Under hypnosis, another personality emerges named Jane. The doctor finds that when Eve's grandmother passed away, she was forced to kiss the body at the viewing. Evidently, the trauma from that event lead to the creation of the different personalities. After discovering this, Jane remembers her whole life and the Eve White and Eve Black personalities disappear.

When Hedda Hopper asked Johnson what Judy said about doing the film, he replied, "Well, she didn't say 'no.' I told her there were only three or four actresses in America of the right age who could play the role."[164]

Referring to Ms. Garland, Johnson remarked:

> Some of my friends said I should have been committed to an institution. But she is a great talent and it wasn't an expensive picture so there was some room for shenanigans. If it had been a three-and-a-half million dollar musical and I offered the part to Judy I would have really been crazy. But I was unable to fight the cobwebs that surround her so the whole thing collapsed. Getting to Judy was a little like trying to get through the Cleveland Browns' line. I don't think I'll go through that again.[165]

Sid Luft evidently felt the screenplay for *The Three Faces of Eve* was ". . . too close to home . . ." for his wife to take on the role.[166]

Butterfield 8 - 1960

According to Sid Luft, Garland was offered the starring role in *Butterfield 8* soon after the completion of *A Star Is Born*, "but she was not able to be so quickly back in front of the cameras."[167]

John O'Hara's *Butterfield 8* focused on the life and loves of model Gloria Wandrous (Elizabeth Taylor in the film) who uses an answering service called "Butterfield 8" to receive messages from her various male admirers. Gloria has been working her way from having affairs with male graduates of Amherst College to graduates of Yale. She doesn't consider herself a prostitute since she won't accept money from her various paramours. She lives with her mother and is friends with Steve Carpenter (Eddie Fisher), a composer.

Gloria's most recent affair has been with Weston Liggett (Laurence Harvey), a lawyer who is an executive at his wife Emily's (Dina Merrill) chemical company. He wants Gloria to be his mistress. Gloria believes she is liberated since she chooses her lovers and drops them when she wants to. She goes on an extended holiday with Weston. Getting to know him better, she falls in love. Weston decides to leave his wife and take a new position at a law firm.

When Emily returns to New York City after caring for her sick mother, she finds her mink coat, that Gloria had borrowed, missing from the Liggett's apartment. Weston goes looking for Gloria, desperate to find her to retrieve the mink. After Gloria receives a message from her answering service, she apologizes to Weston for taking the coat. He accuses her of stealing the fur and says that he is dropping her before she ends the relationship with him. His wife sees Weston return to their apartment in Gloria's car. He throws the mink at Gloria as he departs the vehicle. Gloria goes to Steve's apartment and admits to him that she takes gifts from men in exchange for sex. She tells Steve that when she was thirteen and, after her father had died, she had sex with an older acquaintance of the family and she enjoyed it.

Weston asks his wife for a divorce and wants to return to Gloria. Gloria closes her account at Butterfield 8, leaves her mother, and intends to travel to Boston to start a new life. Weston finds Gloria on her way to the Massachusetts city and asks her to marry him saying he really loves her. Nevertheless, Gloria refuses to marry him and leaves in her car. He follows her in his vehicle. Not seeing a construction sign, Gloria crashes her car in the construction area and dies.

Elizabeth Taylor won the Oscar for Best Performance by an Actress for her portrayal of Gloria Wandrous in this film.

A Handful of Dust – 1962

Based on the 1934 Evelyn Waugh novel, Judy Garland was to have a cameo role in this unmade feature which would have starred David Niven in the role of Tony Last, an Englishman who struggles to maintain Hetton Abbey, a castle he has inherited. He is married to Brenda, and they have a six-year-old son named John Andrew.

Reluctantly, Tony permits his bored wife to rent an apartment in London where she spends most weekdays and carries on an affair with a man named John Beaver. Nonetheless, to reduce his suspicions, she tells her husband that she wants to study economics in London. Tony has difficulty coping with his strong-willed wife who visits him on weekends bringing with her odd friends and strange characters. Believing that her husband also needs romantic diversions, she invites Jenny Abdul-Akbar to Hetton Abbey for the weekend. Tony is not impressed with Jenny, but his young son thinks she is fascinating.

The annual fox hunt is scheduled at Hetton with John Andrew, for the first time, riding his pony in the hunt. John Andrew rides home after the hunt along with a girl on an unruly horse. Along a highway, a motorcycle backfires, the girl's horse bumps into John Andrew's pony. The boy is tossed from his saddle, kicked by the horse, and dies.

Jock Menzies, Tony's friend, travels to London to inform Brenda of what happened. She initially believes that he came to inform her that an accident befell her lover, John Beaver, who is away. When he explains the situation, she is relieved that nothing happened to Beaver.

By letter, Brenda informs Tony of her affair, and a divorce is quickly arranged. Tony agrees to be the defendant in the divorce proceeding with Brenda as the plaintiff. To provide evidence of adultery, Tony hooks up with Milly, a prostitute recruited in a dance hall, and spends a bad weekend at Brighton with her and Winnie, Milly's eight-year-old daughter. Tony and Milly order breakfast in bed so that the servants can observe them and act as potential witnesses about their supposed affair. With the daughter in the hotel room, the evidence of supposed adultery is less than sufficient. Tony consoles himself at the hotel bar where he sees two private detectives that are surveilling him and invites them for a drink.

Brenda asks for four times the amount of alimony that Tony offered to settle the divorce. Tony would have to sell Hetton to pay that amount. He decides to leave England for six months. When he returns, he will see to a divorce settlement then.

Tony travels to the jungles of Brazil with an oddball explorer, Dr. Messinger. In a canoeing accident, Messinger drowns. Tony, racked with fever, is eventually found by natives whose chief is Mr. Todd. Todd nurses Tony back to health. The chief is the son of a native woman and a missionary. His father had left him a complete set of the works of Charles Dickens, but Todd cannot read. Tony begins reading the books to him.

Tony yearns to return to England. After taking some medicine offered by Todd, Tony sleeps and misses two men who have come to find him and Dr. Messinger. Todd gives the men Tony's watch, and they think that he has died. Brenda remarries, and Tony's estate passes to his cousins. He essentially becomes a prisoner in the jungle.

Before the novel was published, several chapters appeared in serialized fashion in *Harper's Bazaar*. One of the chapters presented a happier ending to the story with Tony returning to England and reuniting with Brenda.

Sam Marx and John Florea were to adapt the book for the screen and may have decided to use the happier ending for the script. The picture was to begin shooting in spring 1963 in England and Brazil with David Niven. John Huston was supposed to direct the picture with Peter Ustinov playing Mr. Todd, Peter Sellers appearing as Dr. Messinger, and Judy Garland as Milly.

Preparing for dinner with Tony, the Milly character is described in the book thusly, "She, in her best evening frock, backless and vermilion, her face newly done and her bleached curls brushed out, her feet in high red shoes, some bracelets on her wrists, a dab of scent behind the large sham pearls in her ears, shook off the cares of domesticity and was once more in uniform, reporting for duty, a legionary ordered for active service. . ."[168]

Producer Sam Marx abandoned the movie project in 1963 saying, "We are often forced to turn our backs on our fondest dreams." He continued, "It's a case where everyone loved it except the men we needed – the major-film distributors. Alexander Woollcott rated Waugh's book a modern classic, a commentary on English society comparable to 'Pygmalion' and 'Tom Jones.' So did John Huston, Michael Anderson, David Niven, Peter Sellers, Jennifer Jones, Peter Lawford, Judy Garland and – well, still others who wanted to participate in a movie of it."[169]

This Property Is Condemned – 1965

In early 1965, *Daily Variety* reported that Garland would likely be cast as Hazel Starr in the production of the film *This Property Is Condemned* based on a Tennessee Miller play.[170]

The story, starring Natalie Wood and Robert Redford, is told in flashbacks by Willie Starr, the younger sister of Natalie Wood's character. Willie's mother Hazel runs a boarding house near the railroad tracks in Dodson, Mississippi where a lot of employees of the railroad live. Alva Starr (Wood) is Hazel's attractive older daughter to whom all the men in town seem to be attracted. Owen Legate (Redford), arriving in town, stays at the boarding house. Alva is instantly drawn to him. Owen represents the railroad company and comes to Dodson to inform the railroad manager that the company will be cutting back its freight service and laying off employees since the local crops being transported on the train are not as productive as they used to be.

Hazel wants Alva to be "nice" to the male residents of the boarding house, particularly the older men, since the latter are good payers and long-time boarders. One of the residents, Mr. Johnson, wants to take Alva out for dinner but, she declines following her mother's instructions and instead, goes skinny-dipping with many of the men from the house. Subsequently, Alva finds out why Owen came to Dodson. After several men at the boarding house receive lay-off notices, Mrs. Starr is concerned about the future of her business. When the men who received the notices beat up Legate, Alva helps him back to the house.

Mama announces to Alva that the family will be moving to Memphis to start a new business thanks to a promised loan from Mr. Johnson. Alva wants to leave with Legate for New Orleans and not go with her mother and younger sister and Mr. Johnson who promises to put Alva up in an apartment of her own. Legate purchases a one-way ticket for Alva for New Orleans. However, after hearing Hazel talk on the telephone about the family leaving for Memphis, he argues with Alva saying that she is a peculiar little whore. After Legate departs alone, Alva marries her mother's boyfriend, J.J. (Charles Bronson). Upon waking the next morning, Alva leaves, stealing his money, and uses the ticket Legate bought to take the train to New Orleans.

In New Orleans, Alva eventually encounters Legate and moves into his apartment. When he receives a job offer to relocate to Chicago, he asks Alva to marry him. Hazel shows up at the Legate apartment. Alva fears her mother will tell Owen that she is already married. Alva's fears are realized. Alva runs out of the apartment and out of Owen's life. Flashing forward to the present, Willie explains that her sister died after contracting a lung infection and that her mother is still pursing business schemes outside Dodson.

Francis Ford Coppola, Fred Coe, and Edith Sommer are credited as the screen writers for this motion picture. Nonetheless, filming started without a complete script which underwent several re-writes. The actors would sometimes ad lib their own dialogue because the dialogue found in the script was unusable.

Harlow -1965

Initially, Judy Garland contracted to star as Mama Jean, Jean Harlow's mother, in this biopic of the 1930's Blonde Bombshell. Carol Lynley appeared as Jean Harlow. Garland was replaced by Ginger Rogers in the film.

William Sargent produced the picture using a process called "Electronovision" which involved videotaping the scenes and then transferring them to film. The movie was budgeted at $1.5 million and was to be taped like a TV series in one week. Given the ambitious shooting schedule, one wonders why Judy was hired to begin with, noting her unreliability on film sets. Rehearsals for the project were to begin March 22, 1965 with completion of the movie by April 6 and a release date of May 12. Mark Herron, Judy's companion at the time and later her husband, told reporters that he expected to be in the movie also, maybe playing one of Jean's lovers.[171]

The film did encounter several problems. One was that Joseph E. Levine was shooting a Harlow movie budgeted at $4 million at the same time with Carroll Baker in the lead. William Sargent originally signed actress Dorothy Provine to play Harlow in his film but subsequently hired Lynley. When Garland didn't show up on time for rehearsal, Sargent called her agent and demanded that she appear in ten minutes. When she didn't, he fired her and sought Eleanor Parker for the role of Mama Jean. After reading the script, Parker backed out, and Ginger Rogers was hired for the part.

TV personality and columnist Dorothy Kilgallen reported Garland's leaving the film as follows:

> The official reason given was a "commitment conflict," but anyone in the trade knows there's no such thing if you have a booking agent or a personal manager – a star's contract sometimes has more pages than the scenario, everything is spelled out, lawyers get into the act, and it's not likely that someone suddenly would say, "Oops! Sorry. We just noticed that Judy's supposed to be doing four weeks at the Olympia in Paris."
>
> Bill Sargent, president of the firm making the picture, alleges that "billing problems" were introduced by Judy's agent, Freddie Fields, when she wasn't present at the Desilu Gower studio in Hollywood one day while other members of the cast were rehearsing. But insiders loyal to Judy say she became "incensed and irate" because of a factor that made her feel she wasn't being treated as a pro.[172]

Evidently, Judy told the star of the film, Carol Lynley, "Honey, I'm not drunk, I'm not on drugs, and I'm telling you this is a piece of junk, and I'm getting out."[173]

The film begins with Marc Peters (Lloyd Bochner) discovering Harlow, after the actress had a bit part in a Laurel and Hardy comedy short. He asks a director to give her a screen test thinking she will be ideal for an upcoming film, *Hell's Angels*. Seeing actor William Mansfield (Efrem Zimbalist Jr.) on the set who doesn't have a high opinion of her acting talents, Harlow gives a poor performance. Nevertheless, she lands the part in the picture anyway when she takes off her bra and flings it at Marc.

Later, Mansfield visits Harlow to say he is against what she represents in films. She is more a celebrity than a real artist. Jean mainly appears in bathtub scenes. The actress eventually meets director Paul Bern with whom she falls in love. Harlow moves into a mansion with her mother, Mama Jean and stepfather, Marino Bello (Barry Sullivan), who are concerned that if she marries Bern, they won't have a home to live in. Bern's mistress warns Mama Jean about her daughter marrying Bern because he has never been physical with the mistress.. Mama Jean refuses to believe the mistress. Harlow marries Bern, but on their wedding night, he is unable to perform his husbandly duties. Harlow begins having affairs with other men. Depressed, Bern commits suicide.

L.B. Mayer visits the Harlow mansion after Bern's death wanting Jean to return to work. One can only imagine how Judy would have played the role of Mama Jean in this scene with Mayer portrayed by Jack Kruschen which echoes Garland's own interaction with Mayer before she was terminated from MGM.

> Mayer: Up to a point grief is to be respected. Beyond that, it becomes a luxury, even for great corporations, Mrs. Bello. If we don't start Jean's picture soon, we will suffer a substantial financial loss. People will be laid off – some lose their jobs permanently. I'm sure Jean wouldn't want that to happen.
>
> Mama Jean: I'll speak to her as soon as I can.
>
> Mayer: I've insisted on keeping Jean on the payroll all this time. But there's been criticism from my board of directors. They have a duty to the stockholders. So have I.[174]

As Mayer is about to leave, Mama Jean compliments him on the flowers delivered that morning to her daughter. Mayer replies, "They were from my Board of Directors."[175]

In the film, Harlow returns to movies, marries again, and then divorces. Harlow claims she has no money because her mother and stepfather spend her money faster than she earns it. Marie Dressler advises Jean to begin believing in herself and to throw her mother and stepfather out of her house. Harlow decides to leave the movies, sell her possessions, and take acting lessons.

When her mother writes saying that she is ill, Jean goes to her and finds Mama Jean living in the apartment where she resided before Jean became a star. Jean promises to go back to work to resume earning money for her mother.

William Mansfield re-enters Jean's life saying that he has been wrong about her and invites her to star in his next film. Jean begins to fall in love with him. While making their movie together, Jean begins to feel ill. Taken to her home, she passes away from uremic poisoning.

Harlow was Ginger Rogers final appearance in a motion picture.

Valley of the Dolls - 1967

Judy signed on for a supporting role in the movie version of Jacqueline Susann's book *Valley of the Dolls*. She was to play the role of Helen Lawson, a legendary Broadway star seemingly based on the career of Ethel Merman.

The motion picture chronicled the careers of three young women who become involved in the entertainment business. Anne Welles (Barbara Parkins) gains employment as a secretary at a theatrical agency; Jennifer North (Sharon Tate), a very attractive female, becomes more well-known for her beautiful body than for her acting talent; and Neely O'Hara (Patty Duke), a young singer and rising star, begins using drugs.

The O'Hara character had certain parallels to Judy's own career. Neely O'Hara is dismissed from a co-starring role in a Broadway musical starring Helen Lawson at Lawson's insistence thinking O'Hara will upstage her. After singing on a telethon, O'Hara has a screen test leading to a big role in a musical motion picture and a Grammy win. Along the way, she becomes hooked on pills (dolls) to pep her up and to help her sleep. Due to her drug dependency, she creates problems on the set of her next film by not showing up on time. Producers threaten to replace her with a younger actress. Her agent demands that she admit herself to a sanitarium to be rehabilitated. Later, after being released from the sanitarium, Neely and Helen encounter each other at a party. When Neely sees Helen leave the room, she follows her to the ladies' room where the two engage in a nasty confrontation with Neely ripping off Helen's wig revealing her gray hair. She tries to flush the wig down the toilet. Lawson leaves with a kerchief over her head.

At the end of March 1967, Judy Garland did wardrobe tests, make-up tests, and prerecorded the song "I'll Plant My Own Tree" written by Andre and Dory Previn which her character, Helen Lawson, sings as the showstopper in the fictional musical *Hit the Sky*, while the play is in tryouts in New Haven. Reportedly, Garland really wanted to sing "Get Off Looking Good" by Bobby Cole.[176] To be honest, "I'll Plant My Own Tree" did not include the greatest lyrics ever written by the Previn's, particularly as a supposed major number in a new Broadway-bound musical.

In addition to "I'll Plant My Own Tree," Judy was to perform other songs for the movie including the "Theme from Valley of the Dolls" which ultimately was sung by Dionne Warwick.[177]

Ms. Garland withdrew from the film on April 27, 1967. The studio, Twentieth Century Fox, indicated that she withdrew for "personal reasons." In reply, Garland said, "I have not withdrawn. How dare they say I've withdrawn? I was up at six this morning to go to work. I've done my work." She continued, "It's a shocking thing. Why? That's what I want to know, why?"[178]

However, in her biography of Judy Garland, Anne Edwards indicates that Judy wanted released from her contract after reading the script for the film which she had not done until the movie was about to get underway.[179] When the studio refused to grant the release, she refused to appear. The studio then fired her and replaced her in the role with Susan Hayward.

Other explanations for Ms. Garland's departure from the film project included Jacqueline Susann persuading Judy that she was not right for the part; Twentieth Century Fox not doing the rewrites demanded by

Judy for her part as well as for the Neely O'Hara character about the character's drug use; and how the director, Mark Robson, treated her on the set. Fox did pay the actress half of her $75,000 salary for her work on the film, of which, after expenses, Judy netted $10,000. She also got to keep a sequined pants suit made for her for the project.

Judy's fans wrote letters to the production company protesting her dismissal from the film. One fan in particular wrote to director Mark Robson pleading with him to reinstate her in the film.

In his reply, Robson wrote "At this stage it is too late to do anything further in the direction that you hoped for. We have already commited (sic) ourselves to Miss Susan Hayward who we expect will do a magnificent job in the role." Robson went on to write, "All of us, the cast, crew and executives, have the greatest respect for the contribution that Miss Garland has made to the entertainment world, and it is with regret on our part that things didn't work out."[180]

Judy Garland in 1967 after a quick trip to London.

Chapter 10:
The Final Movies That Were

After hiring Freddie Fields and David Beagelman as her talent agents, the two men attempted to resurrect Judy's movie career. The first motion picture project they lined up for her was the relatively small role in Stanley Kramer's *Judgment at Nuremberg*.

About her role as Frau Wellner in the film, a close associate of the actress indicated that, "Miss Garland worked hard for months to prepare for this. She's still a perfectionist. In New York she has been going down from 72nd street to Greenwich Village as often as three times a day to visit a German voice coach."[181] Garland was paid $50,000 for eight days' work on the project.

This was Garland's first on screen appearance in a feature film since *A Star Is Born*. Noting her screen comeback, Judy admitted that "It's exciting to be back. There is a feeling about working in pictures that you can't get in any other media. Actually, movies aren't my favorite working area but there is an excitement and a camaraderie in making pictures that is so good to get back to now and then. But I'd forgotten how hard we have to work." Further commenting about *Judgment at Nuremberg*, Garland remarked, "When Stanley Kramer offered me this part, I jumped at it because it's such a good part and because I was thrilled at the prospect of working with him. The fact that it was a nonmusical role didn't bother me; what interested me was that it was a solid dramatic role."[182]

According to Stanley Kramer, he was looking for an actress that ". . . had to have both a substantial dramatic quality and the ability to 'break' in front of the camera." He went on to say, "To me Judy Garland seems an obvious choice, but most people forget she was a tremendous dramatic actress. And the quality she possesses isn't growing on trees. Apart from that, I happen to think she is the world's greatest performer."[183]

In his autobiography, Kramer does admit that he agonized over the choice of Garland for the role writing that "... Judy's personal problems were well known in the industry, but the very disorders that made it difficult to work with her fitted perfectly with the role."[184]

He goes on to comment about the character she played,

> By the time she takes the stand in the war crimes trial against the judge who had once intimidated her, the unfortunate woman's life has already been destroyed and she is barely clinging to a semblance of sanity. Though Judy Garland may have been difficult for directors to handle, she had lost none of her skills as an actress, and they all were wonderfully evident in this role. One need say no more than to note that despite her fame, she was able to make herself eminently believable as an anonymous German hausfrau.[185]

Garland was nominated for Best Supporting Actress for her role in *Judgment at Nuremberg.* She lost the award to Rita Moreno who had appeared in *West Side Story*.

Gay Purr-ee- 1962

Judy Garland voiced a cat named Mewsette, a white Turkish Angora female feline, in this animated film. Mewsette lives in the south of France but yearns for the bright lights of Paris. She falls into the clutches of villainous Meowrice before being saved by Jaune Tom, an orange Taby. Set in 1890's France, the movie was released by Warner Brothers in December 1962.

The president of UPA Pictures, Henry Saperstein, signed Judy Garland, Robert Goulet, and Red Buttons for this animated project. Saperstein admitted that he got the inspiration for the movie from Walt Disney's *101 Dalmatians*. He indicated that the success of movies about dogs made nothing but money. "Then I found out there are more cats in this country and more cat owners than dogs and dog owners, and no one had ever made an entire picture about cats."[186]

Garland recorded the voice for Mewsette in Los Angeles during three weeks in November 1961. Gene Kelly was sought for the voice of Jaune Tom with Elvis Presley also being considered for that role which ended up being done by Robert Goulet. Producers hoped that Maurice Chevalier would narrate the story, but comedian Morey Amsterdam with a French accent got that part. Garland received $50,000 for her work on the film and 10% of the gross.

The story begins with Mewsette, living on a farm in Provence and in love with Jaune Tom whose sidekick, Robespierre (voiced by Red Buttons) is a domestic short-haired kitten. Upon hearing a conversation between her owner and the owner's sister, a Parisienne, talking about Paris, Mewsette is inspired by the tales of glamour and adventure in the City of Lights singing "Take My Hand, Paree." Rejecting the advances of Jaune Tom, who offers her a mouse he caught, Mewsette proclaims that she is not a "cat" but a "feline." She runs away by train to Paris where she encounters the devilish cat Meowrice (a Tuxedo cat voiced by Paul Frees) who says he will "sponsor" her. Meowrice, whose motto is "Evil is the root of all money," puts her under the care of his "sister" Madame Henretta Reubens-Chatte (a Persian cat voiced by Hermoine Gingold) who promises to turn Mewsette into "The Belle of Paris." Meanwhile, when Jaune Tom learns that Mewsette has left Provence, he and Robspierre follow her to the city.

Meowrice is grooming Mewsette to become a mail-order bride for a wealthy American cat living in Pittsburgh, Pennsylvania known as Mr. Henry Phtt. Madame Reubens-Chatte initially has trouble training Mewsette to refine her purr and her way of walking. Just as Mewsette is about to give up and return to Provence, Meowrice takes her on a tour of Paris including the Eiffel Tower and the "Mewlon Rouge." Refreshed, Mewsette returns to her studies with Madame Reubens-Chatte.

In Paris, Jaune Tom and Robspierre are waylaid by Meowrice's henchmen and barely escape drowning in the Paris sewer system. When mailing a letter to Mr. Phtt, Meowrice sees Jaune Tom's amazing skill at catching mice. Envisioning a money-making opportunity, Meowrice gets Jaune Tom and his sidekick drunk and sells them as mousers to a ship bound for Alaska. Robspierre attempts to cheer up a depressed Jaune Tom by telling him that problems can be broken down into manageable pieces and that the two of them will return to France. Jaune Tom has a vision of Mewsette singing "Little Drops of Rain."

After Mewsette completes her studies with the Madame, Meowrice commissions paintings of her done by such renowned artists as Claude Monet, Henri de Toulouse-Lautrec, Georges Seurat, Henri Rousseau, Amedeo Modigliani, Vincent van Gogh, Edgar Degas, Auguste Renoir, Paul Cezanne, Paul Gauguin, and, even though he didn't display his work until the 20th century, Pablo Picasso. Meowrice intends to send the paintings to Mr. Phtt. When Meowrice takes Mewsette to his place at Notre Dame, he reveals his plan to send her to America. After seeing a portrait of Phtt as a fat, old cat, Mewsette escapes from Meowrice. In the resulting chase, Mewsette, by chance, leads Meowrice and his cohorts to a bulldog who puts Meowrice out of commission for six weeks.

In the meantime, in Alaska, Jaune Tom goes after a mouse in the snow and ends up striking gold. Jaune Tom and Robespierre become wealthy and are able to return to Paris.

In Paris, Mewsette, disillusioned and singing "Paris Is a Lonely Town," roams the streets of the city stopping on a bridge thinking of leaping to her death. She is captured by Meowrice and his henchmen and taken to the railway station to be shipped to Pittsburgh. Jaune Tom and Robespierre arrive just in the nick of time. Jaune Tom struggles with Meowrice and ends up packing him in the shipping crate addressed to Mr. Phtt. Back together again, Mewsette, Jaune Tom and Robespierre enjoy the City of Lights ending with Mewsette and Jaune Tom singing a duet of "Mewsette."

As with most films, the original treatment for *Gay Purr-ee* differed from the final script. According to an outline found among the Abe and Charlotte Levitow papers at the Margaret Herrick Library, the producers initially thought of Richard Rodgers to write the songs for the movie until Judy Garland suggested Harold Arlen and E.Y. "Yip" Harburg. While Mewsette boards a train to Paris, Jaune Tom, in pursuit of Mewsette and who has never seen a train before, boards a train with Robspierre bound for Marseilles. The two then travel all over the world witnessing historical events. Their travels include Africa where they witness the Stanley-Livingston meeting; standing atop the Matterhorn as the first climbers arrive; walking through an earthquake in San Francisco, and eventually finding gold in Alaska.

Meanwhile, Mewsette meets Meowrice in Paris who charms her by showing the sites of Paris during the spring and summer and "never so much as touching a whisker on her pretty face." Having gained her confidence, Meowrice lures her to his luxurious studio-lair and reveals his true dishonorable intentions. She flees and finds refuge in the boudoir of Madame Henrietta Rubens-Chatte. Mewsette's respite at the Madame's place is short-lived, and she soon finds herself wandering the wintry streets of Paris looking for work and food. By modeling, she is able to occasionally pick up a small saucer of milk. She poses for the great artists depicted in the final film described above.

Jaune Tom and Robspierre, now wealthy from the gold find, arrive in Paris with Jaune Tom's heart set on finding Mewsette. Suddenly, he discovers the Picasso portrait of Mewsette and begins to hone in on her whereabouts. Depressed, Mewsette contemplates suicide by jumping off a bridge, but Meowrice's "catnappers" prevent her from diving into the water and take her to Meowrice's lair. Jaune Tom locates her there and battles Meowrice and the catnappers to save Mewsette. Victorious, Jaune Tom and Mewsette are together again touring Paris in the spring.

Some of the song titles for this early unproduced version of *Gay Purr-ee* included "Time Is on the Side of the Scoundrel" about Meowrice, "Enrietta" about Madame Henrietta Rubens-Chatte, "The Gargoyle Serenade" to be sung when Mewsette huddles in the cold under the gargoyles of Notre Dame, "Catnip Is Flat without Love" to have been sung while Robespierre is attempting to take Jaune Tom's mind off of finding Mewsette, and "The War Song" when Jaune Tom tangles with Meowrice to rescue Mewsette.

Evidently, sometime in April 1961, Judy phoned Harburg to discuss doing the songs for the movie. In reply to their conversation, Harburg wrote a letter to the singer stating in part, "What I find most touching is to see so many people expressing undiluted love for someone who has given them great joy. It makes me feel, in these times of dark hostility, that basically the world has a good foundation and that people would rather love than hate." He closes the letter by writing, "I would consider myself fully compensated and my life work richly rewarded because of your singing of Rainbow alone. It is a gift most writers are never lucky enough to know. Your voice, above all others, touches a song with immortality and carries in it the prayer and wonder of all mankind."[187]

On May 3, 1961, a meeting was held to discuss the story line with Arlen and Harburg together with Saperstein, Levitow, and Chuck Jones, who wrote the script. Harburg questioned the motivation for the story. The reply was that the film intended to be a good animated cartoon feature done at a reasonable price. Harburg suggested that a twist or surprise needed to be added to the plot. The producer and director apparently thought that having Mewsette become a model for famous painters such as Picasso was a sufficient surprise. The producer and director also stated that the picture relies on the artistry of animation – not the actors voicing the characters. Chuck Jones emphasized that the key to an animated feature is the story board – not necessarily the script. "As the story goes on the board in visual form, new ideas and directions always emerge."[188] Nonetheless, the story was revised as noted in the description of the actual film.

At the completion of her role in the animated film, Judy sent a telegram to Arlen and Harburg stating that "Recording Gay Paree is the most pleasure that I have had since the Wizard of Oz. The songs are so magnificent. Love, Judy."[189]

Upon its release on December 17, 1962, *Gay Purr-ee* received generally positive reviews, but the movie was not a box-office hit.

A Child Is Waiting – 1963

Between January 15, 1962 and April of that year, Judy Garland filmed a dramatic role in this movie produced by Stanley Kramer which co-starred

Burt Lancaster. Made at the Revue Studios in Los Angeles, the feature was released in January 1963.

Commenting to Sheilah Graham about Stanley Kramer asking her to star in *A Child Is Waiting*, Judy stated, "I adore Stanley Kramer. He called my manager, Freddie Fields. Said he had no doubts about me. It was an important picture, but he never questioned me about my so-called unreliability. He didn't question my weight – I was fatter before I started the picture."[190] She continued, "He treated me like an actress, and what it did for me! If Stanley ever wants me to play a leper on Molokai, I'll do it."

"A Child Is Waiting" initially premiered as an episode of *Studio One* on CBS, March 11, 1957 with actress Mary Fickett appearing as Jean Horst, a newly hired teacher at a home for mentally-challenged children. Twenty-five-year-old Horst had been a stenographer and sales clerk but was not a trained teacher. Desperate for help, the home's director, Dr. Clark (Pat Hingle), hires her for $30 a week plus room and board. He warns her about becoming emotionally involved with any of the children. Nevertheless, almost by accident, Jean grows very fond of one young boy, Reuben Widdicombe (Miko Oscard), whose mother, Mary, played by Marian Seldes, has not visited her son for over two years. Jean observes how Dr. Clark communicates with the children and begins to disapprove of his methods when he asks an unresponsive Reuben to leave the room. Despite the doctor's denial of her request to write to Reuben's mother about visiting him, she sends a letter anyway stating that Reuben is ill. Mary Widdicombe and her husband visit the facility. Mrs. Widdicombe informs Jean that she cannot really take care of her son, that he really needs to be with children like himself. Mary leaves without seeing Reuben. The next day, Jean informs Dr. Clark that she is resigning saying that she cares for the children too much. The doctor replies that loving the children is not enough. Love without understanding and some kind of objectivity doesn't help. He tells her that she should focus on what the children can do and not on what they can't do. Jean decides to stay. Subsequently, she receives an invitation to visit

Mrs. Widdicombe who wants Jean to become Reuben's permanent teacher and guardian. Jean doesn't think that will really help Reuben. He remains at the facility waiting every Wednesday afternoon for his mother to visit.

The script for the film adhered closely to that of the television program. The name of the character played by Judy Garland changed to Jean Hansen instead of Jean Horst, and the character's prior occupation was that of a woman who had studied to be a concert pianist but dropped out of Julliard and now thinks that working with mentally-challenged children will bring meaning to her life. In the movie, Reuben's parents are divorced.

As in the television version, Jean, despite being forbidden by Dr. Clark, sends a letter to Reuben's mother stating that her son is ill and asking her to visit him. After seeing his mother leave the school without visiting him, Reuben runs away. The police find Reuben, and Dr. Clark takes him back to the school. When Jean offers to quit her job over the situation she created, Dr. Clark shows her a hospital ward for mentally disturbed adults who had not attended a school like his when they were younger. The doctor does this in order to demonstrate the importance of what Jean is doing with the children.

The Garland character prepares a Thanksgiving show featuring the children at the facility. Reuben's father arrives wanting to take his son to a private school. When he hears Reuben recite a poem during the show, he becomes aware of his son's need to achieve something for himself. At the end of the film, Reuben has a chance to visit with his father.

About her role in *A Child Is Waiting*, Judy related the story of meeting a mentally-challenged young girl who had helped her get well while at a hospital in Boston in 1949 after a nervous breakdown. Judy began visiting a children's hospital next to the one where she was a patient. She met a six-year-old girl who had been mistreated by her family and refused to talk. "I stopped by every day to talk to her especially. For some reason, I was smart enough to know I shouldn't ask her any questions."

Judy continued:

> After eleven weeks, I was well enough to go back to Hollywood, and my manager came to get me. I went to the children to say goodbye. . . My own little special friend was waiting for me, with flowers she had crumpled and torn in her nervousness. I sat down with her and told her I had to go home because I was well now, and I told her how much I would miss her. She began to cry. Then, for the first time in months, she spoke: "Don't go, don't go away!" She began to scream, and people ran over to us, astonished. . . Then she talked and talked and talked to me. She told me some of the things that were troubling her. I made her promise to tell these things to the doctors and nurses after I had gone, and told her they would do everything to help her.[191]

Stanley Kramer asked John Cassavetes to direct *A Child Is Waiting*. According to Ray Carney's book, *Cassavetes on Cassavetes*, the filming was not without its problems. As Carney writes:

> The notoriously insecure Judy Garland threw fits of temperament and argued with him about his direction. The fights were serious enough that at least once Cassavetes and Garland actually had to be separated by crew members. Meanwhile, Lancaster took Garland's side against Cassavetes about his direction. The result was a directional nightmare: Cassavetes' two stars formed an alliance against him, consoling each other off-camera and openly defying Cassavetes' direction on the set, appealing to Kramer or an assistant director when they disagreed with Cassavetes' direction.[192]

Carney went on to indicate that the director asked Burt Lancaster to verbally attack Garland in the scene where Lancaster's character finds that, contrary to his instructions, Jean Hansen has invited Reuben's mother to visit him. According to Lancaster, "'John really wanted me to be angry, to rip into it, to tear her to pieces, to tell her she's a fucking idiot.' When Lancaster resisted, giving the reason that it would be out of character for Dr. Clark to behave this brutally to one of his teachers, Cassavetes forced him to play the scene his way anyway; but Kramer did not allow it to be included in the final edit."[193]

In the end, Stanley Kramer re-edited the film to makes its depiction of mentally-disabled children more sentimental than Cassavetes had wanted. With a $2 million budget, the movie made only $925,000 at the box office.

I Could Go on Singing - 1963

In October 1961, the news media reported that Ms. Garland signed a contract to star in what was then titled, *The Lonely Stage*, based on a story by Robert Dozier. Filming was to begin in spring 1962 in England under the direction of Ronald Neame. The producers for United Artists were Lawrence Truman and Stuart Millar who hoped to sign either Laurence Olivier or Peter Sellers as Garland's co-star. In the end, Dirk Bogarde was hired for the role.

As with *A Child Is Waiting*, *I Could Go on Singing* was based on a *Studio One* episode written by Robert Dozier that aired on CBS on February 24, 1958 and titled "The Lonely Stage." Mary Astor, who had been featured with Judy in *Meet Me in St. Louis*, appeared as Harriet Brand, a legendary stage actress who is in a play previewing in Boston. The Brand character has a history of missing performances at times and going on drinking benders.

She appears at the theater twenty minutes before her next performance apparently drunk. George (Jack Klugman), her director calls her out for this, but she says she is only acting drunk. Or, as the director says, maybe she is really drunk but acting sober. Harriet has been waiting in front of the theater building for some friends to show up. They never appear, but she thinks they may have been in the audience during the performance and will come back stage after the show. Lennie Brynes (MacDonald Carey), his wife Beth, and twenty-year-old son Matt (Darryl Hickman) do appear backstage after the play to meet the actress. Even though Matt had met Harriet ten years earlier, he barely remembers her.

The actress wants the Brynes' to attend a late supper with her at a restaurant. Matt reveals that he is being drafted into the military in a week and wants to see his girlfriend instead of going to supper. His father talks him into bringing his girlfriend to the restaurant. After Matt departs to pick up his girl, Lennie and Beth warn Harriet not to divulge that Harriet is Matt's mother.

At supper, Matt says that he is adopted and doesn't know his real parents whom he has been told are both dead. Harriet, who is drinking a lot of champagne, questions him about his biological parents. Matt becomes frustrated and leaves with Sally, his girlfriend. Harriet informs Lennie that for twenty years, she's been a star, has several awards, but hasn't anyone who loves her. She wants Matt to know that she is his real mother and that, if Lennie doesn't tell him, she will.

The next morning, at the Brynes', Matt asks his father why Harriet was questioning him so much about his real parents. Lennie then goes to see Harriet who explains that she wants to tell Matt herself that she is his mother. Lennie takes Harriet back to his home so they both can tell Matt the truth. Alone with Matt, Harriet indicates that she is his biological mother. Upon hearing this, he calls for his adoptive parents to come into the room. Lennie confirms that Harriet is indeed telling the truth. Matt replies saying that he doesn't want Harriet for a mother and leaves the room.

Harriet departs the house. Lennie then confides to Matt that he is his real father. Matt asks for the car keys and leaves. He shows up at the theater where he gives Harriet violets as he did ten years earlier and says that he should start getting to know her better.

The Garland version of "The Lonely Stage" focused on a singer instead of a theater actress with the main character having had an affair with a British doctor which resulted in her giving birth to a son who was adopted by the father and his wife at the time.

Judy played Jenny Bowman, a legendary concert singer touring the world. During a concert series in London, Bowman visits with David Donne (Bogarde), a recently widowed surgeon who has a young son named Matt. Matt has been told that he was adopted when, in actuality, Matt is Jenny's son with David. She had given Matt up for adoption by David and his wife. David takes Jenny to Matt's boarding school to meet him with the promise that it would be there only meeting while she is performing in London. Jenny invites David and Matt to her concert. David is called out of the country and so is not able to attend. Jenny decides to spend more time with the boy exploring London while his father is away. When David finds out that Matt has been with Jenny and not attending boarding school, he becomes furious. Returning to London, David and Jenny argue with Matt overhearing that Jenny is his mother. Jenny wants Matt to accompany her on her concert tour. Matt rejects Jenny's offer, but the two agree to see each other sometime in the future.

Reacting to Matt's decision not to accompany her, Jenny spends a night on the town drinking and ends up twisting her ankle. David comes to treat her. During a pivotal scene, Jenny says she is quitting performing. David responds that he loves her and that she must go on with her career. He agrees to be with her at the concert that night. Seeing that she is performing as her old self, he leaves midway through her first song.

Dirk Bogarde, who played opposite Garland in the film, described how Judy offered him the role by phoning the actor at 5:00 am London time. She asked if he had ever heard of a script called "The Lonely Stage," to which he replied "No." Judy responded that the script stinks but thinks it is a good idea. She went on to summarize the plot, "This big, big Star goes to London to do a concert at the Palladium and finds the man who got away . . . It's about me; I guess someone has read my lyrics." Bogarde suggested that she get a new writer for the script. Judy then asked if Dirk would do the film with her. He responded that, of course, he would but thought the producers actually wanted an American actor for the role.[194]

Judy in a scene from I Could Go on Singing.

Mayo Simon was hired to rewrite the script for *I Could Go on Singing* deemphasizing the love story aspect and tailoring it more to Garland's personality. He was asked to attend a Judy Garland concert in New Jersey to capture her speech patterns, her wit, her charm, and her connection with audiences. After the script was completed, Simon flew to London to do further rewrites if the situation warranted. Simon was fired by Garland after a few weeks working on the film. The producers suggested that they will pretend to hire a new writer but keep Simon working on the rewrites. As Simon described, "I'm secretly rewriting my rewrite of the original writer's script, adding more of Judy's wit and charm."[195]

Garland also tried to fire director Ronald Neame saying that he didn't understand her. The crew said that if Neame goes, they'll leave also. Neame stayed with the movie until it was completed.

Simon writes, "Occasionally, I sneak into the studio to talk over the next day's shooting with the director. Neame shows me some of the uncut dailies from the film. I marvel at Judy's screen presence, even in the out-takes. What a good actress she is. When she works, she works hard."[196]

Arlen and Harburg, who wrote the theme song for the film, were also asked to do another number for Judy to sing with the following requirements: that it would be directed to winning over her son who is viewing Garland from the wings and isn't aware that her character is his mother; it would supply background for a spin around London for the Bowman character and her son; it would induce leap-frogging on Westminster Bridge in the sunlight; it would be used as a reprise for the end of the movie to accommodate a sad situation of heartbreak and loss of her son and her lover; and that it must be ready by February 23, 1962.

Harburg replied to the letter from Saul Chaplin by writing:

> "Good troopers that we are, Harold and I immediately went to work, hired an IBM Computor (sic) Machine and fed into it all the data proposed to accommodate the given situation. With nuclear lightening, molecular rapidity, and electronic transistors, we received the following answer after a short wait of 48 hours: 'Don't waste your time. Have Arlen set music to 23rd psalm.'"[197]

Arlen and Harburg did come up with a song that they hoped would meet the requirements. "Such Unusual Weather" was submitted to Saul Chaplin in February 1962 but was rejected for the motion picture. The number, originally written for the Abbott and Costello motion picture, *Rio Rita,* was a charming little song about two unusual people who have feelings for one another on an unusual day.

Producer of the film, Lawrence Turman, indicated that he thought some of the lyrics for the title song, "I Could Go on Singing," were "clunky." He wrote, "I could go on singing 'til the cows come home!' 'Til the cows come home. . . that's romantic? Not to me, but the highly credentialed music mavin Saul Chaplin . . . convinced us the lyrics were fine, and I was too intimidated to disagree."[198]

To be fair, lyricist Yip Harburg did suggest some alternative lyrics for "I Could Go on Singing" to replace "'Til the cows come home." These included, "'til the house caves in," "'til the rafters ring," and "'til the brass and the strings take me over the rainbow on wings of a song."[199] Garland stuck with the original lyrics.

Judy's co-star in *I Could Go on Singing*, Dirk Bogarde describes what it was like filming their last big scene together in the clinic where she is being treated for her ankle injury:

> My final day was our big scene. We started together rehearsing in her dressing room at eight-thirty. No one came near us. She had wanted to play it sitting down, not to move; I wrote it so that she had sprained an ankle and was carted, drunk, to St George's Hospital. She sat in a chair, I knelt at her feet. We rehearsed for six hours, with half an hour for a sandwich. . . At four-thirty we went on the floor and shot the entire scene just once. It lasted eight minutes and was one of the most perfect moments of supreme screen-acting I have ever witnessed. I shall never see its like again. She never put a foot wrong, not an effect was missed, the overlaps, the stumbling, the range, above all the brilliance of her range. The range was amazing; from black farce right through to black tragedy, a cadenza of pain and suffering, of bald, unvarnished truth. It had taken us three days to write; she passed every line as I set it down, "warts," she said, "and all"; it took six hours to rehearse, eight minutes to shoot, and when it was over one of the crew walking across the stage was stopped by one of his fellows.
>
> "What," said the man, "happened on your stage today?"
>
> "A miracle," said Bob.[200]

The scene in the hospital went as follows:

> Jenny: Have you come to take me home?
>
> David: No, I've come to take you to the theater.
>
> Jenny: Oh, no, you haven't. I'm not going back there again – not going back there ever, ever, ever again.
>
> David: *They* are waiting.

Jenny: I don't care if *they're* fasting. Give them their money back and tell them to come back next fall.

David: Jenny, it's a sellout.

Jenny: I'm always a sellout.

David: You promised.

Jenny: The hell with them. I can't be spread so thin, I'm just one person. I don't want to be rolled out like pastry so that everyone has a nice big bite. I'm just me. I belong to me. I can do whatever I damn well please and no one can ask any questions.

David: You know the last is not true.

Jenny: I'm not going to do it anymore and that's final. It's just not worth all the deaths I have to die.

David: You have a show to do. You're going to do it and I'm going to see that you do.

Jenny: You think you can make me sing? You think George can make me sing, or Ida? You can get me there, but can you make me sing? I sing for myself. I sing what I want to, whenever I want to – just for me. I sing for my own pleasure. I'll do whatever I damn well want. You understand that?

David: I understand that. Just hang on to that. But just hang on for a minute.

Jenny: I've hung on to every bit of rubbish in life there is and thrown away the good bits. Can you tell me why I do that?

Before the scene ends, David says that he loves Jenny.

Saul Chaplin, who supervised the music for the picture, described the filming of the foregoing scene as follows:

. . . Judy, who had had a couple of drinks before the scene started and was a little high, was so brilliant that Ronnie (Neame) just let the camera roll, and the entire seven-minute scene was shot in

> one take. We all watched in wonder as she improvised lines, wept, laughed, and seemed to be bearing her soul. We were all feeling the same thing: She wasn't playing a character. She was playing herself.
>
> After it was over, there was a hushed silence. Then Ronnie whispered, "Cut." This was followed by loud cheers and bravos from all of us. We all had the rare privilege of watching a consummate artist practicing her craft.[201]

During the filming of the movie, Judy overdosed. The producers were told by the actress' psychiatrist that she could work for only a total of ten more days on the project. She owed the producers sixteen more days. The producers and director told Simon to shorten the script but add continuity so that the story still makes sense.

Judy completed the picture in July. She recorded most of the songs for the film near the end of production. As Mayo Simon states, "Finally, Judy sings. It's brilliant. Full of emotion. Endlessly moving. Super professional. And so we have a picture. Will it be any good? We're way beyond that. We have a picture. The film gets respectable reviews, though modest box office returns."[202]

I Could Go on Singing was Judy Garland's final silver screen appearance.

Appendix:

Judy's Broadway Roles that Might Have Been

Although Ms. Garland performed several of her concerts at Broadway's Palace Theater, she never stared in a character-driven Broadway musical comedy or drama. Presented here on some plays for which newspapers or other sources reported the legendary singer may have been considered.

Judy Garland in concert.

Private Confusion – 1940-41

The New York Times published a brief article on August 19, 1940 indicating that Sidney Hirsch, a general manager for producers, sought to become a producer himself and intended to offer two new plays on Broadway in the fall of 1940. For one of the new plays titled *Private Confusion*, Hirsch considered Judy Garland for the lead. If he had been able to get Judy for *Private Confusion*, it would have been her first appearance on Broadway as an actress.

Not known is if MGM subsequently sought to purchase the screen rights to this play, but Fox was successful in obtaining the rights and attempted, without success, to turn the play into a movie.

Private Confusion, by Austin Parker and Hardie Albright, concerned the confusing relationships among a brother, sister, and their best friend. The three main characters are Benita Crosby, eighteen-year-old female who is the sister of Rick Crosby, her handsome brother. Their best friend is Jimmy Graham. All three are tight-knit and live together on a large estate bequeathed to the Crosby siblings by their parents who have passed away. The siblings along with Jimmy are into cruising by boat to various locales.

The story line focuses on Benita Crosby, a tomboy, who is attracted to her brother Rick. To eliminate any suggestions of incest, Rick turns out to have been adopted as was Benita and so they are really not biological siblings. Rick ends up marrying another girl; and Benita falls in love with Jimmy Graham.

If the play had made it to Broadway and Judy was interested in the role, she would have played Benita Crosby.

Miss Liberty – 1948

"And the big news of the moment on Broadway is the report – and apparently it's more than just a rumor, too – that Judy Garland will be the star of 'Miss Liberty,' the musical Irving Berlin and Robert E. Sherwood have in the works at the moment," so wrote columnist Harold V. Cohen in December 1948.[203]

Miss Liberty concerned a news reporter at the *New York Herald* named Horace Miller whose assignment is to find the woman who served as the model for the Statue of Liberty done by Frederic Auguste Bartholdi.

The plot involves Horace Miller traveling to the sculptor's studio in Paris where he sees a photo of Monique DuPont and believes that she is the model for the iconic statue. Monique and her mother accompany Miller back to New York City, where she becomes a celebrity. However, a rival publisher, Joseph Pulitzer, discovers that it was Bartholdi's mother who was the real model for the Statue of Liberty. He exposes Monique as a fraud. She faces deportation back to Europe until Pulitzer, feeling sympathy for her, takes steps to keep her in America. Miller breaks up with his girlfriend to begin a relationship with Monique.

The musical opened in 1949 with actress Allyn Ann McLerie as Monique. While not one of Berlin's big hits, the composer still thought the play should be turned into a film. On August 7, 1951, he wrote Arthur Freed at MGM: "I sent you a copy of 'Miss Liberty' yesterday and this note is to again tell you that, in my opinion, you should give this property a lot of consideration. The fact that it wasn't an 'Annie Get Your Gun' or even a so-called great big hit shouldn't disturb you. That works in your favor because it makes it a very cheap property." Berlin went on to write: "As I told you on the phone, if that French girl in 'An American In Paris' is a hit, she should be fine for the part."[204]

Notice that there is no mention of Judy Garland for the role of Monique. The "French girl in 'An American in Paris'" was, of course, Leslie Caron

Three years later, in 1954, Robert E. Sherwood wrote Martin Jurow at the William Morris Agency still attempting to interest Hollywood in a motion picture adaptation of the musical. In the letter, he admitted two shortcomings in the book for the play. He indicated that the character of Monique was so diluted that the character seemed "positively anemic" and that he attempted to represent Joseph Pulitzer and James Gordon Bennett, the publisher of the *New York Herald*, as historical figures. Sherwood indicated that he should have made them fictitious characters so that the parts could be played completely for comedy.[205]

Nonetheless, *Miss Liberty* never became a motion picture.

Careless Love - 1950

A report from 1950 indicated that Judy Garland had been given a script for a potential Broadway musical titled *Careless Love*, an updated retelling of the Frankie and Johnny love affair immortalized in the ballad of the same name. Johnny was Frankie's man but "he done her wrong" when he got involved with another woman named Nellie Bly. When Frankie discovers the affair, she retrieves Johnny's gun and shoots him. Frankie is arrested for the crime.

The report stated that Judy would have liked her then-husband Vincente Minnelli to take a leave of absence from MGM to direct her in the Broadway play [206]- a musical version of "Frankie and Johnny" written by H. L. Fishel with music by George Lessner and lyrics by Edward Eager.

The production never happened.

Pygmalion – 1952

Hungarian film maker, Gabriel Pascal, made a film version of the George Bernard Shaw classic play, *Pygmalion*. Pascal held the rights to the story and planned to turn it into a musical well before Lerner and Lowe adapted the Shaw work for *My Fair Lady*.

The characters of Professor Henry Higgins and Eliza Doolittle were the focus of *Pygmalion*. On a bet, Higgins, a professor of phonetics, turns a poor Cockney flower girl, Eliza Doolittle, into a member of high society after teaching her to speak properly.

On May 9, 1952, Sheilah Graham wrote, "If Gabriel Pascal were gabby, he would tell you about the Theater Guild project for a musical 'Pygmalion' to star Judy Garland. Which explains his recent lunch with Sid Luft . . ."[207]

Fanny – 1952

Based on three motion pictures, *Fanny*, *Marius*, and *Cesar*, by Marcel Pagnol, the musical *Fanny* opened on Broadway in 1954 with Florence Henderson in the title role. Fanny is a young unwed mother whose long-time love, Marius, has left for sea before she knew she was pregnant with his child. She marries an older man, Panisse, who keeps the baby's background a secret. After a year at sea, Marius returns, but his father forbids him from seeing Fanny and his son. Twelve more years pass. Fanny's son runs away to follow Marius to sea, but Marius returns his son to Fanny. Panisse, who is heartbroken over the situation and is dying, insists, as his last wish, that Fanny and Marius finally be together.

After Garland was a big success with her Palace concerts in 1951, Broadway producers considered her for roles in various musicals. Harold Arlen and E.Y. Harburg were originally to write the score for *Fanny* with Frances Goodrich and Albert Hackett, who had done the screenplay for *Easter Parade*, writing the book.

Husband and wife team Hackett and Goodrich began writing the story line for the musical in 1951 with David Merrick as the producer. According to Frances Goodrich's notes on the project, she and her husband along with Merrick went to see Judy at the Palace on February 3, 1951. Goodrich and her spouse, as well as Merrick, all agreed that Judy would be wonderful for the role of Fanny. "We went backstage afterwards to see her, but did not get a chance to talk privately to her. Told her we were working on something that we thought would interest her."[208]

In the version of the script written by Goodrich and Hackett, Fanny is eighteen years of age. By the time the musical premiered in 1954, Judy Garland was thirty-two and so may have been a little too old to play the character.

Unknown is if there was any subsequent follow-up with Garland about the project. The Hackett's also attempted to enlist Harold Arlen and E.Y. Harburg in doing the music and lyrics for the play. In June, 1952, the couple urged Merrick to sign contracts with Arlen and Harburg, but the producer resisted saying, "What would happen. . . if Harburg wrote two songs and then died. We urged him to put it in the contract that Harburg couldn't die til he had completed the score. Merrick didn't laugh."[209]

In any event, after working on the book for *Fanny* and doing five versions of the script, Goodrich and Hackett wanted out of the contract they signed with Merrick stating that the producer had not contracted with a composer or a lyricist. The dispute was submitted to arbitration with the Hackett's being able to keep their retainer for the project as well as earning up to $20,000 from the profits for the work.

The Goodrich/Hackett version of the story line generally follows the one that premiered on Broadway with a few exceptions. In the version written by the Hackett's, Marius first returns from sea after an absence of two years – not one. Also, Fanny's son doesn't run away to be with his father at sea. Instead, Marius returns after twelve to fourteen years abroad. Panisse has died. Fanny then informs her son as to who is his real father. In the final scene, Marius finally meets his son.

Harold Rome ended up doing the music and lyrics with S. N. Behrman and Joshua Logan writing the story line. Logan also co-produced the work with David Merrick. The musical opened in 1954 and ran for 888 performances.

Notably, in 1954, Janis Paige, then starring in the Broadway production of *Pajama Game*, encountered Garland in New York City and told Judy that she should try a live Broadway show and ". . . experience the thrills which go with it at every performance. 'Not for me,' said Judy. 'I wouldn't be any good in a stage show because I never sing the same song twice in the same way.'"[210]

Hold Back the Dawn – 1961

In early 1961, Mary Martin thought of appearing in a musical version of *Hold Back the Dawn* based on the 1941 picture that starred Olivia De Haviland and Charles Boyer.[211] Shortly thereafter, Judy Garland was considering this proposed Broadway play.[212] French actor Yves Montand was thinking of playing the male lead in the play which would have had lyrics written by Dorothy Fields for unpublished Jerome Kern music discovered after Kern's death. The musical would have premiered in fall 1961.

The 1941 film concerned a Romanian gigolo, Georges Iscovescu (Boyer), living in Mexico who marries school teacher, Emmy Brown (De Haviland), to gain entry into the United States.

According to a summary of the book for the proposed musical, Georges Iscovescu had been a dancer and entertainer in Europe and arrived in Mexico contemplating immigrating to the United States to become involved in show business. He finds that he has a very long wait to enter this country given the quotas on immigrants from his home country. Georges is working in the bar at the hotel in which he is staying having hocked his valuables to live in the small Mexican border town. He is having an affair with a Mexican dancer named Anita whom he wants to partner with when they get to the United States.

Each weekend, when American tourists come to the village, Georges searches for a woman to marry. He dons his best clothes and takes his gold jewelry out of hock to impress the visitors.

One weekend, a tourist named Emmy Brown misses the bus to return to the States. Georges finds ways to keep her in the border town longer as he attempts to woe her. He is successful and they marry. On their honeymoon in Mexico, he begins to develop real feelings for her. Although he wants to, as does Emmy, Georges finds excuses not to consummate the marriage.

Discovering that Georges is really falling in love with Emmy, Anita reveals to her the whole sordid truth about him. In addition, an official interrogates Emmy in Georges' presence. Emmy defends him telling the official that she knows all about his past and that she asked him to marry her. Georges is overwhelmed at Emmy's defense of him, but Emmy leaves and runs off to the border gate and hitch-hikes back to her home.

When she arrives home, she finds Georges sitting there. He has given everything to prove himself to her. An Immigration Official arrives to send Georges back to Mexico.

Time passes. Georges is back at the Mexican hotel when another bus from the United States arrives. On it is Emmy who sits quietly at a table near Georges who eventually notices her. She declares that she has always wanted to live in Mexico. According to an Immigration Official, the law requires a full month from the date of marriage before Georges can legally enter the States provided that he does nothing foolish like trying to crash the border gate in the meantime. Georges replies that he would never do anything so imprudent as a love song swells and the couple toasts each other.

Songs thought to have been included in the musical were "Introduce Me" to be sung by Georges and "Azusa" to be performed by Emmy, the role in which Judy Garland expressed interest. The latter was about Emmy's home town in California. Emmy would also perform "April Fooled Me" and "What Do I Know about You."

In addition, there would have been duets between Georges and Emmy such as "Once There Were Two of Us" written by Ira Gershwin and Jerome Kern.

The Unsinkable Molly Brown – 1961

Judy wanted to star in *The Unsinkable Molly Brown* musical on the London stage as a possible prelude to doing the film version. *Molly Brown* was an account of the life of Margaret Brown and her wealthy husband. Brown was among the survivors of the sinking of the Titanic.

Speaking to reporter Stephen Franklin of *The Ottawa Citizen*, Ms. Garland said, "I'm supposed to do a Broadway show, which will be a new experience for me. I have a choice of four shows, all musicals, with very good books and good scores."[213] One of the possibilities was the London production of *The Unsinkable Molly Brown.*

Garland later remarked to Hedda Hopper about doing the movie version of *The Unsinkable Molly Brown*, ". . . I doubt Metro would give it to me. They decided some years ago that I was washed up and apparently haven't changed their opinion."[214] Debbie Reynolds played Molly Brown in the film.

The Owl and the Pussycat – 1964

Written by veteran sitcom scribe, Bill Manhoff, who had done teleplays for shows like *The Odd Couple*, *All in the Family*, and *Room 222*, *The Owl and the Pussycat* featured characters, Doris and Felix. Each believes they are something that they really aren't. Doris is a prostitute but wants everyone to think that she is really an actress. Felix is a bookstore clerk who wants everyone to believe that he is a writer even though he has never published anything. The two meet and fall in love, but their refusal to look at themselves honestly prevents them from finding happiness with each other. They can see each other's weaknesses but not their own.

Hedda Hopper reported that "Judy Garland says she will do 'The Owl and the Pussycat,' a straight drama without songs on the stage in London and New York. It will be backed by 'Hamlet' financier Alexander Cohen, with Ray Stark producing."[215]

The role of Doris, the pussycat, was ultimately played by actress Diana Sands although, in addition to Judy, Kim Stanley, Glynis Johns, Shelly Winters, and Eva Marie Saint also expressed interest in the role. Alan Alda appeared as Felix, the owl. Barbara Streisand and George Segal portrayed these two characters in the movie version of the Broadway play.

Mame – 1968

With music and lyrics by Jerry Herman, *Mame* was the musical adaptation of the Patrick Dennis' 1955 novel, *Auntie Mame*. The musical focused on the life of Mamie Dennis who takes custody of her ten-year-old nephew after his father dies.

In January 1968, Judy Garland met with Jerry Herman and others to discuss taking over from Angela Lansbury the title role in the musical. Lansbury was due to leave the show in the spring. Judy sang the entire score of *Mame* for those present. According to Herman, when Judy expressed interest in the role, "I just about lost my mind. I was the craziest, most ardent Judy Garland fan of all time… She sang, and it was a religious experience to me."[216]

The financial backers of the show agreed that Judy would have first call on the movie version of the musical but didn't believe she would be a reliable candidate to take over the role on Broadway. Herman eventually agreed although as he remarked, "Even a bad performance from Judy Garland would be an event. Just to have Judy Garland in this show for one night would be magical – historical."[217]

Endnotes

[1]John Fricke, *Judy: A Legendary Film Career*, Philadelphia: Running Press, 2010, 209.

[2]Quoted in Joe Morella and Edward Z. Epstein, *Judy: The Films and Career of Judy Garland*, New York: Cadillac Publishing Co., Inc., 1969, 30-31, 33, 35, and 38.

[3]Joe Hyams, "Calculated Risk in Hiring Judy," *The Boston Globe*, September 20, 1956.

[4]Doug McClelland, "Arthur Freed, Mr. Musical," *Record World*, March 23, 1968, 30.

[5]Danny Miller, "Child Star Cora Sue Collins Talks Garbo, Garland, and the Day Jean Harlow Came to Her Birthday Party," www.cinephiled.com, April 19, 2015, retrieved September 20, 2021.

[6]David Dahl and Barry Kehoe, *Young Judy: The Incomparable Judy Garland*, Frogmore, St Albans, Herts: Mayflower Books Ltd, 1977, 206.

[7]Ibid., 202.

[8]Ralph Wilk, "A Little from 'Lots,'" *Film Daily*, September 24, 1935.

[9]Louella O. Parsons, "Gossip of Movieland," *Courier-Post*, September 5, 1935.

[10]Lloyd Pantages, "Pantages Covers Hollywood," *Pittsburgh Sun-Telegraph*, January 15, 1936.

[11]Nacio Herb Brown and Arthur Freed, *Yours and Mine*, MPAA/PCA Records, Margaret Herrick Library.

[12]Quoted in Joe Morella and Edward Z. Epstein, *Judy: The Films and Career of Judy Garland*, 36.

[13]Edwin Schallert, "Directors Get Unusual Contracts; Franklin Guides 'Sea of Grass,'" *The Los Angeles Times*, February 25, 1937.

[14] "'Valiant' Goes as Metro Epic," Variety, March 3, 1937.

[15] Edward Schallert, "RKO Arranges World Release of English Film Starring Walbrook," The Los Angeles Times, April 1, 1937.

[16] Louella O. Parsons, "Metro Takes Life Story of Sergeant York," Pittsburgh Post-Gazette, February 13, 1937.

[17] "Selznick to Film 'Sarah Bernhardt'," Brooklyn Eagle, November 30, 1946.

[18] Sheilah Graham, "In Hollywood Today," The Indianapolis Star, January 7, 1947.

[19] Louella O. Parsons, "Kate Hepburn's 'Stage Door' to Be Trailed by Comedy, 'Bringing Up Baby.'" The Courier, May 27, 1937.

[20] Florence Fisher Parry, "I Dare Say – The Crazy Quilt," The Pittsburgh Press, June 7, 1937.

[21] Louella O. Parsons, "Frederic March Gets Jean Lafette Role for 'Buccaneer,'" The Morning Post, (Camden, New Jersey), April 13, 1937.

[22] Frank Scully, "Scully's Scrapbook," Variety, May 16, 1951.

[23] "M-G-M Selects Judy Garland To Star In "Wonder Child," The Miami News, January 28, 1938.

[24] Edwin Schallert, "Smilin' Through' Planned as Musical," The Los Angeles Times, March 10, 1938.

[25] Kaspar Monahan, "The Show Shops," The Pittsburgh Press, February 28, 1938.

[26] Story line from Catherine Chisholm Cushing, Topsy and Eva: A Comedy with Music, Unpublished Typescript with Revisions, 1923.

[27] Louella O. Parsons, "Topsy, Little Eva and Old Uncle Tom Are Coming Back," The Gazette, January 28, 1944.

[28] Louella O. Parsons, "Mickey to Travel to Europe in Style," The Philadelphia Inquirer, June 7, 1939.

[29] Edwin Schallert, "Janitor to Be Hero in Metro's "Valedictory'," The Los Angeles Times, June 24, 1939.

[30]*Edwin Schallert, "Judy Garland Likely for 'Susan and God,'" The Los Angeles Times, October 5, 1939.*

[31]*Hayden R. Palmer, "From the Front Row," Lansing State Journal, August 7, 1940.*

[32]*Douglas W. Churchill, "Screen News Here and In Hollywood," The New York Times, December 14, 1940.*

[33]*Story line from Daniel Fuchs, "Strange Things Happen in Brooklyn," Collier's, February 1, 1941.*

[34]*Edwin Schallert, "Metro Gets 'Cimarron' as Subject for Tracy," The Los Angeles Times, February 21, 1941.*

[35]*Story line excerpts from Oscar Hammerstein, "Very Warm for May," Oscar Hammerstein Collection, Library of Congress, July 22, 1941.*

[36]*Christian Nieland, "Show Me a Hero and I'll Write You a Tragedy," Kingsport Times-News, March 12, 1977.*

[37]*F. Scott Fitzgerald, Letter to Edwin Knopf, F. Scott Fitzgerald Papers, Princeton University Library Special Collections, October 26, 1938.*

[38]*Ibid.*

[39]*F. Scott Fitzgerald, Possible General Line For – "The Captured Shadow," F. Scott Fitzgerald Papers, Princeton University Library Special Collections, undated.*

[40]*Louella Parsons, "Youth Has Its Fling," Star Tribune, September 26, 1938.*

[41]*Story line from Agnes Christine Johnston, "High School: Short Structure Outline," Agnes Johnston/Frank Dazey Collection, Margaret Herrick Library, August 6, 1938.*

[42]*Louella O. Parsons, The San Francisco Examiner, November 17, 1939.*

[43]*John Monks and Fred Finklehoffe, "Dear Old Broadway" Synopsis, Arthur Freed papers, Cinematic Arts Library, University of Southern California, March 16, 1940.*

[44]*Virginia Wright, "Cinematters," Daily News (Los Angeles, California), January 1, 1940.*

[45]*Quoted in Hugh Fordin, MGM's Greatest Musicals: The Arthur Freed Unit, New York: Da Capo Press, 1996, 31.*

[46]*Quoted in Hugh Fordin, 40.*

[47]*Ibid., 41.*

[48]*Edwin Schallert, "Historical Romance Again to Star Crawford," The Los Angeles Times, September 23, 1940.*

[49]*Monroe Lathrop, "'King' Rooney May Be Himself in Unique Biography," St. Louis Globe-Democrat, October 13, 1940.*

[50]*"Hollywood Star-Lites," The Marion Times-Standard (Marion, Alabama), March 20, 1941.*

[51]*John Scott, "New Stage Spectacle Announced for Mason," The Los Angeles Times, February 13, 1934.*

[52]*Dorothy Kilgallen, "Wedding Bells Soon Ringing Out for Glamour Girl," Detroit Free Press, August 8, 1941.*

[53]*Thomas F. Brady, "Bergman Sought for Lead in Film," The New York Times, May 15, 1950.*

[54]*"Garland, Grayson to Battle for Song Honors," The Los Angeles Times, May 31, 1941.*

[55]*Edwin Schallert, "Garland, Grayson Will Play Musical Sisters," The Los Angeles Times, March 11, 1942.*

[56]*"News of the Screen," The New York Times, April 20, 1943.*

[57]*"Produce Films in French Here," The Gazette, May 4, 1944.*

[58]*Hedda Hopper, "Hedda's Hollywood," The Herald-News, February 18, 1944.*

[59]*Arthur Freed, Letter to Oscar Hammerstein, 2nd, Oscar Hammerstein Collection, Library of Congress, October 14, 1943.*

[60]*Louella O. Parsons, "In Hollywood," Pittsburgh Sun-Telegraph, January 5, 1944.*

[61]*Louella O. Parsons, "In Hollywood," Pittsburgh Sun-Telegraph, September 27, 1944.*

[62]*Hedda Hopper, "Looking at Hollywood," The Los Angeles Times, December 14, 1945.*

[63]*Danton Walker, "Broadway," The Philadelphia Inquirer, April 3, 1946.*

[64]*"Freed Talks with R & H on New 'Show Boat,'" Variety, June 14, 1949.*

[65]*"Hollywood Inside," Variety, June 30, 1950.*

[66]*Thomas F. Brady, "Warners to Film Communist Story," The New York Times, August 8, 1950.*

[67]*Betrothal Dinner Menu, Arthur Freed Papers, Cinematic Arts Library, University of Southern California, March 1, 1945.*

[68]*Sheilah Graham, "In Hollywood," Chattanooga Daily Times, October 10, 1940.*

[69]*Hedda Hopper, "Sub Capture by Bomber Will Be Clipped into Film," The Minneapolis Star, September 22, 1941.*

[70]*Louella O. Parsons, "In Hollywood," Pittsburgh Sun-Telegraph, August 11, 1942.*

[71]*Melville Baker and Jack Kirkland, Gaby Deslys, Arthur Freed Papers, Cinematic Arts Library, University of Southern California, 12.*

[72]*Hugh Fordin, MGM's Greatest Musicals, 555.*

[73]*Paul Denis, "New Play on Broadway," The Billboard, February 27, 1943.*

[74]*Arthur Freed, Memorandum to Judy Garland, Arthur Freed Papers, Cinematic Arts Library, University of Southern California, February 25, 1943.*

[75]*Mary Leighton, "Templeton Set for Movie; Has Score Written Already," The Cincinnati Enquirer, November 3, 1944.*

[76]*Virginia Safford, "Virginia Safford," The Minneapolis Star, February 17, 1947.*

[77]*"Four Cast for 'Cabbages and Kings,'" Variety, October 9, 1946.*

[78]*Sheilah Graham, "Hollywood Today," The Times-Tribune (Scranton, Pennsylvania), June 21, 1945.*

[79]*Sheilah Graham, "News, Views and Gossip," Dayton Daily News, July 29, 1945.*

[80]*E. V. Darling, "On the Side," The San Francisco Examiner, January 22, 1949.*

[81]*Hedda Hopper, "Looking at Hollywood," The Los Angeles Times, January 30, 1946.*

[82]*Paul Green, "Forever Notes to Arthur Freed," Arthur Freed Papers, Cinematic Arts Library, University of Southern California, December 12, 1945.*

[83]*Miriam Stuart and Robert McElaine, Letter to Voldemar Vetluguin, Arthur Freed Papers, Cinematic Arts Library, University of Southern California, September 30, 1946.*

[84]*Hedda Hopper, "Hedda Hopper in Hollywood," The Miami News, January 19, 1947.*

[85]*Summary of story line from Sally Benson, Pride and Prejudice, Arthur Freed Papers, Cinematic Arts Library, University of Southern California, April 22, 1947.*

[86]*Sidney Sheldon, Pride and Prejudice, Arthur Freed Papers, Cinematic Arts Library, University of Southern California, August 29, 1947.*

[87]*Sheilah Graham, "Hollywood Today," Honolulu Star-Bulletin, April 29, 1947.*

[88]*Alan K. Rode, Michael Curtiz: A Life in Film, Lexington, Kentucky: The University Press of Kentucky, 2017, 413.*

[89]*Sheilah Graham, "Now It's Mrs. Larry Parkes Getting Break in Pictures," The Indianapolis Star, May 23, 1947.*

[90]*Story line from J. Hartley Manners, Peg O' My Heart script, 1918.*

[91]*Judy Garland, Note to Arthur Freed, Arthur Freed Papers, Cinematic Arts Library, University of Southern California, undated.*

[92]*Brent Phillips, Charles Walters: The Director Who Made Hollywood Dance, Lexington, Kentucky: The University Press of Kentucky, 2014, 115.*

[93]*Sheilah Graham, "Judy Garland Eyed for Role," The Spokesman-Review, September 22, 1950.*

[94]*Louella O. Parsons, "Judy Garland to Star in 'Anchors Aweigh'," The Philadelphia Inquirer, Oct 24, 1942.*

[95] *"Judy Preps Dance Chore with Astaire," The Miami News, September 5, 1943.*

[96] *Hedda Hopper, "Looking at Hollywood," Harrisburg Telegraph, September 22, 1945.*

[97] *Frances A. Clear, Synopsis of Irving Brecher Script dated July 24, 1944, Turner/MGM Collection, Margaret Herrick Library, February 27, 1946.*

[98] *Judy Garland, Thank-you note, Arthur Freed Papers, Cinematic Arts Library, University of Southern California, undated.*

[99] *Earl J. Hess and Pratibha A. Dabholkar, Gene Kelly: The Making of a Creative Legend, Lawrence, Kansas: University Press of Kansas, 2020, 217.*

[100] *George Wells, Take Me Out to the Ball Game Screenplay, George Wells Collection, American Heritage Center, University of Wyoming, October 10, 1946 – February 14, 1947, 13.*

[101] *Ibid., 16.*

[102] *Erskine Johnson, Los Angeles Daily News, February 10, 1947.*

[103] *A. H. Weiler, "Random Notes on the Film Scene, The New York Times, August 1, 1948.*

[104] *Hedda Hopper, "Judy and Gene Dance Together Again in 'Lovely to Look At'," The Salt Lake Tribune, November 20, 1948.*

[105] *Hugh Boswell, Inter-Office Communications, Arthur Freed Papers, Cinematic Arts Library, University of Southern California, June 22, June 30, July 6, July 8, July 9, July 10, and July 12, 1948.*

[106] *Quoted in Hugh Fordin, 246.*

[107] *Stephen M. Silverman, Dancing on the Ceiling: Stanley Donen and His Movies, New York: Alfred A. Knopf, 1996, 181.*

[108] *Edwin Schallert, "Finlay Currie Signs Term Deal; Judy Garland 'Brigadoon' Possibility," The Los Angeles Times, November 29, 1951.*

[109] *Doug McClelland, "Arthur Freed," March 23, 1968, 67.*

[110] *"Let's See the Girls," The Brooklyn Daily Eagle, December 12, 1950.*

[111] *"Wald-Krasna," Variety, January 10, 1951.*

[112]*Louella Parsons, "In Hollywood," Deseret News, May 23, 1951.*

[113]*Edwin Schallert, "Mayer 'Wagon' Purchase Stirs Garland Rumors; 'Boccaccio Loves' Shapes," The Los Angeles Times, February 6, 1952.*

[114]*Sid Luft, Judy and I: My Life with Judy Garland, Chicago: Chicago Review Press, 2017, 283.*

[115]*Erskine Johnson, "Jane Wyman Favors Early Date for Wedding Despite Protest," Fremont Tribune, March 28, 1952.*

[116]*Hedda Hopper, "Judy Garland Sought for Runyon Film," The Salt Lake Tribune, February 18, 1952.*

[117]*Louella O. Parsons, "Louella's Movie-Go-Round," Albuquerque Journal, September 29, 1950.*

[118]*"Fred Finklehoffe, Judy Garland Talk Upcoming Picture," Variety, August 24, 1951.*

[119]*Louella O. Parsons, "Big Plans for Judy," Pittsburgh Sun-Telegraph, October 4, 1954.*

[120]*Sid Luft Strikes Back at Trade 'Propaganda' Against His Wife; Garland Has Many Film Bids," Variety, November 28, 1956.*

[121]*Sheilah Graham, "Skelton Doing Diary on Tots," The Spokesman-Review, October 17, 1950.*

[122]*"Sid Luft Strikes Back at Trade 'Propaganda' Against His Wife," November 28, 1956.*

[123]*Sid Luft, Judy and I, 332.*

[124]*Walter Winchell, "On Broadway," The Bangor Daily News, March 24, 1956.*

[125]*Mike Connolly, "Hollywood Is Remakeville," The Desert Sun, August 6, 1957.*

[126]*Hedda Hopper, "Susan Makes Musical," The Miami News, August 31, 1957.*

[127]*Emily Belser, "Judy Garland Won't Quit," February 26, 1955.*

[128]*Dorothy Kilgallen, "Ingrid's Husband Seeks Stage Production Team," Arizona Republic, May 8, 1961.*

[129]*Joe Hyams, "Wilder Is Getting Wild with 'Irma,'" Star Tribune, November 1, 1962.*

[130]*Mike Connolly, "Notes from Hollywood and Television," Pasadena Independent, January 9, 1962.*

[131]*Mike Connolly, "Gypsy Violins Break Spell for Natalie," Star Tribune, March 24, 1962.*

[132]*The story line excerpts in this section are from Betty Smith and George Abbott, A Tree Grows in Brooklyn, New York: Harper and Brothers, Publishers, 1951.*

[133]*"MGM 'Say It' Early; Irv Berlin's 75th Birthday Celebrated 12 Days in Advance," Variety, May 1, 1963.*

[134]*When contacted by this author, George Chakiris didn't recall this project, Message from George Chakiris, September 11, 2021.*

[135]*Mike Connolly, "In Hollywood," Pittsburgh Post-Gazette, March 10, 1964.*

[136]*Jack Lait, Jr. "Hollywood," The Brooklyn Daily Eagle, April 25, 1951.*

[137]*Hedda Hopper, "Clifton Webb Will Star in 'Elopement'," The Los Angeles Times, February 21, 1951.*

[138]*Allida Allen, Famous Synopsis, Paramount Pictures scripts, Margaret Herrick Library, December 7, 1950.*

[139]*Sheilah Graham, "Hollywood Today," The Tacoma News Tribune, October 9, 1955.*

[140]*"Judy Garland Spurns Movies to Tour with Own Revue," The Montgomery Advertiser, July 17, 1955.*

[141]*Darryl F. Zanuck, June 16, 1955 memorandum, Darryl F. Zanuck Papers, Margaret Herrick Library.*

[142]*Darryl F. Zanuck, June 29, 1955 Western Union Cablegram, Darryl F. Zanuck Papers, Margaret Herrick Library.*

[143]*Louella O. Parsons, "Hollywood," The Cincinnati Enquirer, October 12, 1956.*

[144]*"Judy Garland Jumps into 'Sea' for MGM, and onto UA 'Stage' for Millar-Turman," Variety, June 9, 1961.*

[145]*Louis Berg, "Irrestible, Irrepressible Judy," The Des Moines Register, November 25, 1956.*

[146]*Sophie Tucker in collaboration with Dorothy Giles, Some of These Days, New York: Doubleday, Doran and Company, Inc., 1945, 33.*

[147]*Ibid., 133.*

[148]*"Broadway Melody of '38 Stars Taylor and Powell," Valley Morning Star, August 22, 1937.*

[149]*Lyn Connelly, "A Peek at the Stars," The Bingham Bulletin, April 24, 1953.*

[150]*Norman Katkov, The Fabulous Fanny: The Story of Fanny Brice, New York: Alfred A. Knopf, 1953, 55-56.*

[151]*Ibid., 188.*

[152]*Ibid., 202.*

[153]*Ibid., 215.*

[154]*Ibid., 337.*

[155]*Erskine Johnson, "In Hollywood," Visalia Times-Delta, October 26, 1953.*

[156]*Mary Baker to George Cukor, The Jaffe Agency, George Cukor Papers, Margaret Herrick Library, September 6, 1955.*

[157]*Erskine Johnson, "Writer Lists His Picks for Movie Oscar Awards for '55," The Sacramento Bee, March 12, 1956.*

[158]*Charles McHarry, "On the Town," New York Daily News, August 22, 1966.*

[159]*Earl Wright, "Letter to George Cukor," Gene Allen Papers, Margaret Herrick Library, January 21, 1963.*

[160]*Gene Allen, "Aimee," George Cukor Papers, Margaret Herrick Library, January 1, 1963.*

[161]*John Fricke, A Star Is Born, Warner Brothers Entertainment, 2010, 33.*

[162]*Louella O. Parsons, "Judy Garland Paged for Stubborn Wood Lead," The San Francisco Examiner, February 7, 1952.*

[163] *Paul Henreid, "Outline for a Screenplay Based on Emily Harvin's Novel, 'The Stubborn Wood,'" Paul Henreid Collection, Margaret Herrick Library.*

[164] *Hedda Hopper, "Hedda Hopper in Hollywood," The Salt Lake Tribune, August 4, 1956.*

[165] *Joe Hyams, "Calculated Risk in Hiring Judy," The Boston Globe, September 20, 1956.*

[166] *Sid Luft, Judy and I, 300.*

[167] *Ibid.*

[168] *Evelyn Waugh, A Handful of Dust, New York: Little, Brown and Company, 1934, 167.*

[169] *Phillip K. Scheuer, "Waugh Bites Dust for Cowboy in Italy," The Los Angeles Times, December 19, 1963.*

[170] *Army Archerd, "Just for Variety," Daily Variety, January 6, 1965.*

[171] *Herb Kelly, "Judy Garland Will Play Harlow's Mother in Movie," The Miami News, March 13, 1965.*

[172] *Dorothy Kilgallen, "The Voice of Broadway," The News Journal, March 30, 1965.*

[173] *Quoted in Scott Schechter, Judy Garland: The Day-by-Day Chronicle of a Legend, London: Taylor Trade Publishing, 2006, 298.*

[174] *Karl Tunberg, Harlow, First Draft Script, undated, 91.*

[175] *Ibid., 92.*

[176] *Schechter, Judy Garland, 325.*

[177] *"'Valley of Dolls' Offers Judy Garland New Songs," The Daily Record, March 21, 1967.*

[178] *"Judy Garland, Studio Hassle." The Salina Journal, April 30, 1967.*

[179] *Anne Edwards, Judy Garland: A Biography, London: Taylor Trade Publishing, 1974, 235.*

[180] *Mark Robson, Letter to John Cancellieri, May 16, 1967, Mark Robson Papers, Theater Arts Library, University of California at Los Angeles.*

[181] *Vern Alves quoted in The Ottawa Citizen, June 3, 1961.*

[182] *"Judy Garland Is Happy Doing a Movie Again," Pittsburgh Post-Gazette, July 11, 1961.*

[183] *Stephen Franklin, "Judy Garland: A Star Is Reborn," The Vancouver Sun, June 3, 1961.*

[184] *Stanley Kramer with Thomas M. Coffey, A Mad, Mad, Mad, Mad World: A Life in Hollywood, New York: Harcourt Brace & Company, 1997, 182.*

[185] *Ibid., 182-183.*

[186] *Vernon Scott, "Voices of Judy Garland, Red Buttons and Robert Goulet Will Co-Star in New Movie," The Daily News, June 19, 1962.*

[187] *E.Y. Harburg, Personal Correspondence to Judy Garland, E.Y. Harburg Collection, Yale Music Library Special Collections, April 25, 1961.*

[188] *Chuck Jones Comments on Meeting with Arlen and Harburg, Abe and Charlotte Levitow Papers, Margaret Herrick Library, May 3, 1961.*

[189] *Judy Garland, Telegram to Arlen and Harburg, E.Y. Harburg Collection, Yale Music Library Special Collections, November 17, 1961.*

[190] *Sheilah Graham, "Everything Looks Good to Judy Garland Today," Express and News, March 4, 1962.*

[191] *Quoted in Jack Hamilton, "Judy," Look, April 10, 1962 in Randy L. Schmidt, Judy Garland on Judy Garland: Interviews and Encounters, Chicago Review Press: 2014, 287-288.*

[192] *Ray Carney, Cassavetes on Cassavetes, New York: Farrar, Straus and Giroux, 2001, 120.*

[193] *Ibid., 120-121.*

[194] *Dirk Bogarde, Snakes & Ladders, London: Orion Books, 1978, 211.*

[195] *Mayo Simon, "The Agony and Ecstasy of Working with Judy Garland," Stuff, co.nz, October 11, 2019, retrieved July 2, 2021.*

[196] *Ibid.*

[197]*E.Y. Harburg, Letter to Saul Chaplin, E.Y. Harburg Collection, Yale Music Special Collections, February 10, 1962.*

[198]*Lawrence Turman, So You Want to Be a Producer, New York: Three Rivers Press, 2005, 124.*

[199]*E.Y, Harburg, Alternative "I Could Go on Singing" refrains, E.Y. Harburg Collection, Yale Music Special Collections, undated.*

[200]*Bogarde, Snakes & Ladders, 219-220.*

[201]*Saul Chaplin, The Golden Age of Movie Musicals, Norman and London: University of Oklahoma Press: 1994, 206.*

[202]*Simon, "The Agony and Ecstasy"*

[203]*Harold V. Cohen, "The Drama Desk," Pittsburgh Post-Gazette, December 7, 1948.*

[204]*Irving Berlin, Letter to Arthur Freed, Arthur Freed Papers, Cinematic Arts Library, University of Southern California, August 7, 1951.*

[205]*Robert E. Sherwood, Letter to Martin Jurow, Arthur Freed Papers, Cinematic Arts Library, University of Southern California, May 13, 1954.*

[206]*Louella O. Parsons, "Alan Ladd Would Step Out of Gangster Roles to Star in 'Quantrill's Raiders'," Fort Worth Star-Telegram, September 27, 1950.*

[207]*Sheilah Graham, "Theater Guild Play for Judy," The Tampa Times, May 9, 1952.*

[208]*Frances Goodrich, Chronology of Work on Fanny, Frances Goodrich and Albert Hackett Papers, Wisconsin Historical Society, 1952.*

[209]*Ibid.*

[210]*John Chapman, "Curtain Going Up!," Daily News, December 5, 1954.*

[211]*Mike Connolly, "Mary Martin Studies Boyer Show Remake," Pasadena Independent, January 31, 1961.*

[212]*Hedda Hopper, "Hollywood," New York Daily News, March 6, 1961.*

[213]*Stephen Franklin, "Judy Garland: A Star Is Reborn," The Ottawa Citizen, January 3, 1961.*

[214]*Hedda Hopper, "Looking at Hollywood," The Bangor Daily News, November 7, 1962.*

[215]*Hedda Hopper, "Judy Garland to Do Non-Musical Drama," The Los Angeles Times, April 24, 1964.*

[216]*Jeremy Scott Bluestein, "Mame Fact #5:'Multitudes of Mame-ies," I willregretthislater.com, September 11, 2017, retrieved October 28, 2021.*

[217]*Ibid.*

Index

www.ingramcontent.com/pod-product-compliance
Ingram Content Group UK Ltd.
Pitfield, Milton Keynes, MK11 3LW, UK
UKHW021905190726
13853UKWH00002B/528

9 798887 710860